D1321601

Modern Business
Administration

Modern Business Administration

Robert C. Appleby
B.Sc. Econ.(London), A.C.I.S., A.M.B.I.M.

Head of Department of Business Studies
Worcester Technical College

Pitman

PITMAN PUBLISHING LIMITED
39 Parker Street, London WC2B 5PB

Associated Companies
Copp Clark Ltd, Toronto
Fearon-Pitman Publishers Inc, Belmont, California
Pitman Publishing Co. SA (Pty) Ltd, Johannesburg
Pitman Publishing New Zealand Ltd, Wellington
Pitman Publishing Pty Ltd, Melbourne

© R. C. Appleby 1969, 1972, 1976

First published in Great Britain 1969
Revised and Reprinted 1972, Second Edition 1976,
Reprinted 1977

All rights reserved. No part of this publication may be
reproduced, stored in a retrieval system, or transmitted,
in any form or by any means, electronic, mechanical,
photocopying, recording and/or otherwise without the prior
written permission of the publishers. This book may not be
lent, resold, hired out or otherwise disposed of by way of
trade in any form of binding or cover other than that in
which it is published without the prior consent of the
publishers. This book is sold subject to the Standard
Conditions of Sale of Net Books and may not be resold in
the UK below the net price.

Reproduced and printed by photolithography and bound in
Great Britain at The Pitman Press, Bath

ISBN 0 273 00433 6

Preface to First Edition

The subject of management and administration is so vast that one book alone cannot be sufficient to impart more than an outline of the subject. An outline, though, is all this book attempts to present. This book should be regarded as a key, explaining succinctly the important aspects of management.

Management is a process which is constantly changing as the results of continuous research are made available and incorporated in management knowledge.

This book is written particularly for students preparing for examinations. There are review questions at the end of each section; and at the end of each chapter, questions of a more involved nature are asked in order to test the ability of students to apply their knowledge.

Students preparing for professional examinations, including the Institute of Cost and Management Accountants, the Association of Certified Accountants, the Chartered Institute of Secretaries, Institute of Works Managers, the Institute of Marketing, as well as those taking courses leading to the Diploma in Management Studies, Higher National Certificate and Diploma Examinations, will all find the book particularly valuable. In addition it will serve as a sound introduction to degree courses.

The treatment is brief, simple, factual and practical; unimportant words have been omitted and the latest ideas and techniques have been incorporated. The book should provide a firm basis for the subject and point the way to further specialist reading, which is indicated in the bibliographies at the end of each chapter. If readers are encouraged and stimulated to read further, then this in itself is a satisfactory result.

R. C. Appleby

Preface to Second Edition

The response to the publication of the first edition has been most encouraging. Since the first edition was written in 1968, numerous changes have occurred in management and administration.

The first edition omitted many important areas and it is hoped that most of these have now been included. To keep the book a reasonable size, some aspects have been omitted. There is a great problem in deciding what to leave out in an introductory book.

Behavioural aspects, the systems approach to management and organization, worker participation, goals and goal conflicts, the management of change, are all introduced. The requirements of new examination syllabuses from 1976, e.g. Institute of Bankers (Stages 2 and 3), have been noted.

The way the book is set out is again conventional, although the need to adopt a completely 'systems approach' was strong. The conflict of ideas of what are the elements of management, and what should or should not come under any one heading will still be present. Such classifications are unnecessary when a systems approach is adopted.

The bibliography has been extended and brought up to date and it is hoped that this will encourage readers to select areas of interest and examine them in more depth. It is only in this way that a more complete understanding can be obtained.

March, 1976

Acknowledgements

The author wishes to express his sincere appreciation to all those colleagues at Worcester Technical College and the West Bromwich College of Commerce and Technology who made valuable suggestions in the writing of this book, in particular—B. Parry, D.M.S., Dip. I.A., F.I.P.M., A.M.B.I.M., M.I.S.M.

Thanks are also due to Mrs R. Oakes, Mrs C. M. Greenwood and Mrs B. D. Mealand for their help in the typing of the manuscript.

Other acknowledgements are owed to the staff in the library at Worcester Technical College and the Tutor Librarian Mrs H. M. Jones, M.Sc., Dip.Ed., A.L.A., for their assistance, also—Urwick Orr and Partners Ltd, for the diagrams of 'Management by Objectives', Figure 4, and 'Improving Management Performance', Figure 30.

The British Productivity Council for Figure 14 which was reproduced with their permission; from the National Productivity Year Conference Papers.

The British Broadcasting Corporation, for Figure 19, which was reproduced with their permission from Mathematics in Action (B.B.C. T.V. for Schools) Summer, 1966.

English Electric Computers Ltd (now part of International Computers Ltd), for the details of their system regarding vehicle routing and fleet planning.

P. F. Drucker, for quotations on pages 8 and 29 from *The Practice of Management* (William Heinemann Ltd).

E. F. L. Brech, for quotations on pages 4, 6 and 55 from *The Principles and Practice of Management* (Longmans, Green Co. Ltd).

Sir W. Brown, for quotation on page 51 from *Exploration in Management* (Heinemann Educational Books Ltd).

The Institute of Cost and Management Accountants, the Chartered Association of Certified and Corporate Accountants, and the Chartered Institute of Secretaries, for permission to use recent examination questions.

Scott Bader Co. Ltd, for permission to use extracts from their Objectives and Code of Practice (parts of their memorandum).

J. Argenti, for the definition of Corporate Planning, *Corporate Planning*, G. Allen and Unwin, 1968.

E. F. L. Brech, *Managing for Revival*, Management Publications Ltd, 1972.

H. I. Ansoff, *Corporate Strategy*, Penguin, 1968.

D. M. Gregor, *Human Side of Enterprise*.

Manpower Society, Checklist on Manpower Costs.

Ceramics Industry Training Board, 'Management Training Techniques Table'.

H. Buckner, *Business Planning*, Methods of Training Managers Diagram Business Books.

Contents

Part Two   Management in Action

Part One
Management Principles

1 Nature of Management

There have been many attempts to describe the contents of the 'job' of management. It has been considered to be a separate activity from the technical functions of production, marketing and finance. Various economists, for example Alfred Marshall, separated it from the other factors of production (land, labour and capital). Another economist, J. A. Schumpeter, agreed with the idea that management was a separate entity, being concerned with innovation as well as administration.

In recent years, writers on management have recognized that management deals with a number of variables that are dependent upon each other. These variables will surely increase as companies grow more complex and it will then become more difficult to trace the side effects of a change in dealing with a specific area of management responsibility.

There are many problems to be solved. Some people try to solve them by considering changes in the *structure* of organizations and the locations of authority and responsibility. Others hope to do it by improving the quality of decisions by new *technological* ideas and the use of modern methods of data processing. Yet another group expects to solve the same problems by concentrating on *human relations*. The vital point to be considered is that the structural, technological and human aspects *cannot be separated* as they all interact. For example, if a firm changes from a functional to a product grouping, problems of interpersonal relations occur. This may in turn affect the techniques of control (i.e. new financial systems may be needed). A knowledge of the above facts should enable a manager to understand that it may not be easy to find a simple answer to a problem but, by acknowledging this fact and wisely using available knowledge, answers can be much more accurate and effective.

This chapter deals with the elements of management, planning, organization, direction and control. Other chapters deal with other activities, including marketing, production, personnel and office organization, and a final chapter on developments. The plan of a book which covers diverse areas could vary widely, but the above arrangement is considered to be suitable and helpful for readers who are approaching the subject for the first time.

A. PROBLEMS OF TERMINOLOGY

The first step in any subject should be to understand the basic terms used, and in many arts and sciences this presents no real problem. In business administration, terms are not precisely defined and some are regarded as interchangeable.

The dictionary definition (*Concise Oxford*) of Administration is, 'management,' one word being substituted for another. An Administrator is a 'manager'; 'one capable of organizing.' Many writers adopt this simple approach and regard the words as interchangeable. This surely should not be allowed to remain the position and indeed cannot in a body of knowledge which people wish to call a science. A precise analysis of theory is possible only when terms are specifically defined.

The words management and administration are defined by writers in accordance with their own needs and purposes. Many other terms used have been in popular use for long periods and have a variety of meanings. A word in country X with *apparently* the same meaning in country Y, may have a different *emphasis* owing to the differences in the history of the country's institutions (e.g. president, *président*).

A few of the terms which have varying meanings will be considered here, others will be introduced in the text.

1. Administration and management

Administration is often used to refer to the activities of the higher level of the management group who determine major aims and policies. This can be called the broader use of the term which is often used in government departments (e.g. the Civil Service). It is also used in the narrower sense, of controlling the day to day running of an enterprise.

The distinction between administration and management is more clearly apparent in Public Corporations (e.g. the nationalized Electricity Industry). The government lays down broad policies which must be carried out by the various Electricity Boards, who have to work out detailed policies and procedures. The Boards are in effect administering, and each Area or District has managers who control certain areas and they see that the policies as laid down by the administrators are carried out.

An administrator can also be a manager; this occurs when he is concerned with implementing policy in his dealings with employees to whom responsibilities have been delegated.

The present writer prefers to regard administration as the determination of major aims and policies, but recognizes that some authorities consider that the term management is gaining ground as the general descriptive label.

Brech defines *administration* as:

That part of the management process concerned with the institution and carrying out of procedures by which the programme is laid down and communicated, and the progress of activities is regulated and checked against targets and plans.

Management has even more meanings than administration. The writer prefers to regard it as the carrying out of operations designed to accomplish aims and effectuate the policies (which of course are determined by the administration).

Management can mean:

(*a*) A *process* by which scarce resources are combined to achieve given ends. This describes an activity which can be better described by the word *managing*.

(*b*) The *management* referring to those people carrying out the activity. This should really be the *managers*.

(*c*) The body of knowledge about the *activity of managing*, regarded here as a special field of study, i.e. a *profession*.

Of these three, the first is preferable, management referring to the *process* of management.

A useful approach is to consider management to be a process whereby a suitable environment is created for effort to be organized to accomplish desired goals.

Brech defines *management* as:

. . . a social process entailing responsibility for the effective and economical planning and regulation of the operations of an enterprise, in fulfilment of a given purpose or task, such responsibility involving:

(*a*) judgement and decision in determining plans, and the development of data procedures to assist control of performance and progress against plans; and

(*b*) the guidance, integration, motivation and supervision of the personnel composing the enterprise and carrying out its operations.

It can be seen from the above that the process as a whole is called management—administration being part of it. It may well be that this usage will be officially accepted, but until then the student is advised to define the terms in the manner he intends to use them.

The words *top management*, usually refer to management above departmental level and is loosely applied to the directors.

The term *executive* is correctly used when referring to a person who carries out policy. The phrase 'top executive' is used, especially in the U.S.A., for people of a high status, who in fact do no *executive* work at all, as they spend their time formulating policy. (They are of course responsible for executive action done under their jurisdiction.) Where words are associated with status rather than function, precision is impossible.

2. Organization

There is really no doubt about the present meaning of organization. Its purpose is to create an arrangement of positions and responsibilities through and by means of which an enterprise can carry out its work.

Brech's definition is:

... the framework of the management process as formed by the definition of:

(*a*) the responsibilities by means of which the activities of the enterprise are dispersed among the (managerial, supervisory and specialist) personnel employed in its service;

(*b*) the formal interrelations established among the personnel by virtue of such responsibilities.

It should be noted that organization should not be regarded as rigid as the term 'framework' implies. Organization structure must be constantly reviewed and note taken of informal relationships which develop.

B. SCIENCE OR ART ?

A great deal of discussion has centred around the question as to whether management is an art or a science. A brief comment is all that need be given on this matter.

The development of any science needs a conceptual framework of theory and principle. Principles of management have existed for a long time, but an acceptable framework to encompass was needed. A large debt is due to the many writers and researchers who have contributed a great deal to existing principles and accepted practices. It is in the formulation of principles that the science of management can be developed. A management principle distils and organizes knowledge that has been built up through experience and analysis. Management is far from being an exact science at present but, by understanding and applying accepted principles, the quality of management practice can be greatly improved. It is most probable that management will never become wholly an exact science as personal judgement will always be needed to supplement available knowledge; therefore, as a practice, management will always be an art.

In the natural sciences, a theoretical principle is deduced from particular facts which are applicable to a defined group or class and is expressed by a statement that a certain happening *always* occurs if certain conditions are present. Management principles are not fundamental truths, they are *conditional* statements qualified by adverbs, e.g. usually, normally.

It is worthwhile looking briefly at the nature of the two methods of reasoning, deductive and inductive.

The *deductive* method—reasons from the general to the particular, i.e. from the attributes of a *class* it will deduce the attributes of an *individual member* of that class. The following example of deductive reasoning illustrates that if certain facts are admitted as true, then such a thing must be true about the particular case in question, for if it were not so, it would be inconsistent with the fact already admitted as true.

It does mean that premises should be carefully tested before any inference is made from them.

1st premise—All men are mortal
2nd premise—Wilson is a man
Deduction from these premises—Wilson is mortal.

If the deduction is made from false premises the conclusions are worthless—for example:

All good sailors have beards
Robinson is a good sailor
Therefore he has a beard.

The *inductive* method is the opposite of the deductive.

It starts by *collecting facts* relating to a given point, these facts emerging from observations. Then a statement or *premise* is proposed which is true of all cases observed. For example if, by observation, a number of men— Wilson, Robinson, Smith, Brown—are discovered to be mortal, we can have confidence in this premise, if a sufficient number of cases have been examined under a variety of circumstances, to see if any conflicting case was noted. A generalization is then built up, or reasoned, regarding the cases in the light of the observed characteristic, e.g. each of the cases examined was a man and therefore all men are mortal. This generalization is no more than a *hypothesis*, the product of inductive thinking, which must now be proved. When the hypothesis is *tested* and no conflicting case found, then a *law* is formulated and this is used to control the present or to predict the future.

Scientific method can be applied to management, for example: The method of inductive thinking can be applied to policy making where work is measurable.

Observation, leads to objective examination of present practices; *analysis*, in breaking them down and studying them; *classification*, means comparing them with basic principles and the resultant hypothesis will be an improved new method or practice. A trial run or test will be critically examined and only then accepted and a law formulated.

It can be applied in the management of people, by studying the human factor and observing principles of human relations. This is an important area especially in relation to motivation and co-ordination.

It can also be applied to the manager himself, in developing a scientific attitude of mind towards his problems and the making of his decisions.

C. MANAGEMENT—A PROFESSION?

In recent years there has been further consideration as to whether management can be regarded as a profession. The conflicting arguments can be considered only if a profession is defined. The following main points seem relevant in the discussion:

(*a*) There must exist a body of principles, skills and techniques and specialized knowledge.

(*b*) There must be formal methods of acquiring training and experience.

(*c*) An organization should be established which forms ethical codes for the guidance and conduct of members.

If the above standards are considered, then management cannot really be called a profession. There are no licences for managers or accepted code of ethics, but there are tendencies towards professionalization and these will undoubtedly increase. Mary Parker Follett regarded a profession as connoting a foundation of science and *a motive of service*.

P. F. Drucker does not agree that it is desirable for management to be a profession. He states: 'management is a practice, rather than a science or profession, though containing elements of both.' He feels that economic performance and achievement are the proper aims of management and that a manager's primary responsibility is to manage a business. He should not therefore devote time to objectives such as professionalism which lie *outside* the enterprise.

The solution may lie in a balanced approach. At present there are trends towards professionalism, seen in the development of skills and techniques, more formal training facilities and the greater use of management *consultants* and specialized associations.

There have been recently, in a number of countries, attempts to specify codes of conduct for managers.

In 1974 The British Institute of Management put forward such a code for individual members of that institute; in addition there were guides to good practice, and a disciplinary structure. Only a few of the points can be mentioned here.

The Institute stressed that a manager has to balance his obligations to the undertaking which employs him, with the community at large, with other employees, suppliers, consumers and his own conscience. The Institute believes that because of the growing professionalism of managers there is need for such a code of conduct, brief details are noted below:

to act loyally and honestly in carrying out the policy of the organization and not undermine its image or reputation;

accept responsibility for his own work and his subordinates;

not abuse his authority for personal gain;

not to injure or attempt to injure, the professional reputation prospects or business of others;

always comply strictly with the law and operate within the spirit of the law;

order his conduct so as to uphold the dignity, standing and reputation of the Institute.

Other points refer to—dealing honestly with the public, to promoting the increase in competence, and the standing of, the profession of management, and recognizing that the organization has obligations to owners, employees, suppliers, customers, users and the general public.

Guides to good practice include:

establishing objectives for himself and subordinates which do not conflict with the organization's overall objectives;

respect confidentiality of information and not use it for personal gain;

make full disclosure of any personal interest to his employer.

Other points refer to helping and training subordinates, ensuring their safety and well being, honouring contracts to customers and suppliers, ensuring correct information is produced and not to tolerate any corrupt practices and finally to set up a disciplinary structure to implement the code.

D. MANAGEMENT—A UNIVERSAL PROCESS?

It was previously noted that a suitable environment is desirable in order to apply the principles of management effectively. Environments differ, and it has to be considered whether management problems vary with the environment and whether management skills can be effectively transferred. A point worth further thought is that in privately-owned and capitalistic enterprises, which have reasonable freedom from government control and influence, managers are free to make the basic decisions necessary for profitable operations and where the risk of wrong decisions is accepted by owners and management. The profit motive and free competition is the system now largely in operation and this book is based upon these assumptions. It can be realized that, where government influence increases, managers are less free to make decisions and many principles may be affected.

If one agrees that management is a universal process, i.e. a fundamental process with universal characteristics and principles, it appears that management skills are transferable, and a manager can successfully apply his knowledge and skill in a wide variety of industries. It implies general principles are at work and that detailed specialist work in the various businesses can later be absorbed. It then appears to follow that all types of organizations can benefit from such universality, even non-profit-making concerns.

P. F. Drucker holds the opposite view. He considers that management skill and experience, as such, cannot be applied to the running of different institutions, as the main objective of business is profit, consistent with its security, and stability. This differs from a non-business organization, whose officers do not have the responsibility for producing goods and services or maintaining wealth-producing resources.

Ernest Dale is another who does not agree with this idea of universality —if one considers this to be a theory of universal principles applicable in every field. He does not believe any one person could be a good administrator in academic, business, military or religious concerns, as the underlying philosophy in each constitution is so varied in nature and it is not possible for *one person* to know so much.

It appears to the writer that all resources needed by organizations are scarce and even non-business organizations must allocate men, materials and equipment, time and money to varying needs and aims. This can be done only by managers using their skill and knowledge and to this extent it seems that management skills are transferable.

E. DEVELOPMENT OF MANAGEMENT THOUGHT

Management is an applied technique and is closely related to many allied fields, e.g. economics. Disciplines devoted to studying people, e.g. psychology, sociology and political science have grown and generated an expansion of management knowledge.

The development of management thought can, for convenience, be considered to comprise four main periods—early influences, scientific management movement, human relations movement, modern influences, e.g. revisionist movement.

There are many writers on management subjects and a great volume of interesting material is being published. While many of the ideas may be valid for the particular survey, it does not mean that the idea can be used or introduced in *any* organization.

There are many reasons for this, e.g. the statistical base may be suspect, the organization studied, the nationality, etc., may produce different results in a different environment. So findings in one area or country may not necessarily be valid for other areas or countries. Points to consider are:

(*a*) The *age of those* in the survey—older persons have different ideas, e.g. on job security.

(*b*) The *age of the survey*—many important writings, e.g. Fayol, were written many years ago, are they therefore still relevant today?

(*c*) Changes in the *law* since the date of the original research may affect conclusions drawn, e.g. attitudes and practices changed after the 1971 Industrial Relations Act and the 1975 Employee Protection Act.

(*d*) Work done in *one country* may not be the same as in another country with different characteristics.

(*e*) Surveys based upon *women* may not produce the same results as if based on men.

Other points to note before deciding to introduce new ideas into an organization are: was the period in question a boom or slump, was it a large manufacturing company or a small service company; would Hertzberg's work on accountants and engineers apply equally to other professional areas?

1. Early influences

Ancient records in China and Greece indicate the importance of organization and administration, but do not give much insight into the principles of management. Outstanding scholars have referred to management activities in the running of city states and empires.

The administration of the Roman Empire was a complex job. The Romans effectively used many basic management ideas, e.g. scalar principle and delegation of authority.

In addition, many important principles may be traced to military organizations. An interesting book by Anthony Jay, *Management and Machiavelli*, makes analogies between the way one ruler, Machiavelli, effectively governed his empire and how modern boards of directors rule theirs. Machiavelli considered the use of supporting armies to rule outlying territories, and decided that too much reliance on them could cause problems as any internal dispute they may have would affect the strength of the ruler himself. How similar this appears today to associate companies, which have their own internal disputes and delivery crises, but which are beyond the control of the main company. Machiavelli therefore advocated few, if any, of such armies and would no doubt today encourage firms to make as much as they can themselves.

In a much later period, Charles Babbage (1792–1871), who was a professor of mathematics at Cambridge University, recognized that science and mathematics could be applied to the operation of factories and also that more detailed cost measurements were needed. He also developed a calculating machine, but lack of suitable materials made it difficult for him to make many refinements.

2. Scientific management

In the years after 1900 conventional management practices were found to be inadequate to meet demands from the changing economic, social and technological environment. A few pioneers examined causes of inefficiency and experimented to try and find more efficient methods and procedures for control. From these basic experiments a system of management thought developed which came to be known as scientific management.

The method was to investigate every operating problem and try to determine the 'best way' to solve the problems, using scientific methods of research. The concept involved a way of *thinking* about management.

F. W. Taylor (1856–1917)

F. W. Taylor was one of the principal people to be associated with this movement. He was from a middle-class background and worked his way to a high position in an American steel firm; most of his work was involved in experiments to find the 'best method' of doing jobs.

In 1911, he published his book *Principles of Scientific Management*. He spoke on the subject in the U.S.A. in 1911 at a conference and stressed that there were mistaken tendencies in uninformed people to grasp at some of the new techniques and then expect these techniques to solve management problems. He warned them against confusing techniques with aims. This comment is surely very relevant today, when many more new techniques are being introduced, e.g. linear programming. The student of management should consider whether some people are not *again* confusing techniques with aims at the present time.

The following principles were suggested by him to guide management:

(*a*) Each worker should have a large, clearly-defined, daily task.

(*b*) Standard conditions are needed, to ensure the task is more easily accomplished.

(*c*) High payment to be made for successful completion of tasks. Workers should suffer loss when they failed to meet the standards laid down.

Taylor listed 'new duties' for management. These were:

(*a*) The development of a true science.

(*b*) The scientific selection, education and development of workmen.

(*c*) Friendly, close co-operation, between management and workers.

A brief summary of the factors he emphasized would cover the need for time and motion study, effective control over performance by the use of the 'exception principle' (see p. 118), the definition of responsibility and effective selection and training of personnel.

Taylor's work may be overestimated, but he codified and clearly stated practices which had been developing in many well-run factories. He and his contemporaries Gantt, Gilbreth and Emerson stressed the 'engineering approach' and a brief look at their contribution to the subject will now be made.

H. L. Gantt (1861–1919)

He worked with Taylor for a time and improved upon Taylor's ideas. He believed management was responsible for creating a favourable environment to obtain worker co-operation. Some of his main contributions were:

(a) The setting up of a *well-measured task* for a worker, thus giving him a goal to achieve—this made the worker interested in attaining the goal.

(b) He believed management had a *responsibility to train workers*.

(c) He advocated proper *methods of planning and control*. This is perhaps his most well-known contribution. He used graphical recording systems, machine and man record charts. His charts showed relationships between 'events' in a production programme and he recognized that total programme goals should be regarded as a series of interrelated plans that people can understand and follow.

F. Gilbreth (1868–1924)

He started work as an apprentice bricklayer and later managed his own business. He became very interested in the 'best way' of doing a job. This involved doing the job in the most comfortable position, in the fewest motions.

In operating his system of *motion study*, he identified seventeen basic elements in job motions, and any motion can be broken down into all or some of these basic elements. He created a flow process chart, which facilitates the study of complete operations and not just a single task. (See p. 317.)

H. Emerson (1853–1931)

He wrote two important books on the subject of efficiency and emphasized the importance of correct organization to achieve higher productivity. He advocated the now popular 'line and staff' organization (see p. 70), and set out his 'principles of efficiency' which are:

(a) A clearly-defined ideal.

(b) Common sense.

(c) Competent counsel.

(d) Discipline.

(*e*) A fair deal.
(*f*) Reliable, immediate, adequate and permanent records.
(*g*) Standardized conditions and operations.
(*h*) Standards and schedules.
(*i*) Written standard practice instructions.
(*j*) Reward for efficiency.
(*k*) Dispatching.

3. Human relations movement

Since Taylor, much of the emphasis on scientific management has centred on the worker, and his relationship to the company, his job, and his fellow workers. Advances in the sciences of man, and his behaviour as an individual and in groups, e.g. psychology, sociology, etc., have revealed a number of factors which helped business and industrial problems.

Industrial psychology emerged as a specific field about 1913. It was concerned with problems of fatigue and monotony and efficiency in work; also in the design of equipment, lighting and other working conditions. It later dealt with problems of selecting and training employees and developed techniques of psychological testing and measurement. Industrial psychology emphasized the study of large and small groups in industry. The basis of the human relations movement was the integration of various disciplines, i.e. industrial psychology and sociology, applied anthropology and social psychology, and was concerned with the human problems which management encountered.

In 1941 the publication of the results of the psychological experiments of Elton Mayo at the Hawthorne (Illinois) plant of the Western Electric Company was a notable landmark. It revolutionized management thinking by focusing attention on the *components of job and work satisfaction* on the part of employees.

These *Hawthorne Experiments* (as they are referred to) were divided into three phases.

(*a*) *Test room studies*

These were to assess the effect of *single* variables upon employee performance. A group of women were segregated and variations made in the intensity of illumination, in temperature, hours of work and rest periods, and their performance was noted. The results were surprising, as output rose, even though some changes were made which made working conditions poorer.

The reasons considered were that the more important factors were not incentives or working conditions, but the high *esprit de corps* that had developed in the *group* and the more *personal interest* shown by the supervisor and higher management. So, in themselves, conditions of work, lighting, hours, rest periods, etc., could not be viewed as affecting people's work—people subject to the conditions develop attitudes and interpretations which are important factors.

(b) *Interviewing studies*

This first study led to an interest in the *attitudes* of the plant population towards their jobs, working conditions, and supervision, and a *morale survey*, comprising over 21,000 interviews was taken. It was not, though, easy to find out objectively the cause of an individual's dissatisfaction.

(c) *Observational studies*

These studies were made to study the normal *group working*. It was found the group developed 'norms' of conduct, output and relations with others *outside* the department. It became obvious that to each individual in the group the relations with his fellows were important in his motivation and the study showed the importance of *informal organization* in worker motivation.

To summarize it was obvious a worker was not motivated solely by money. The superior's rôle was important for morale and productivity. Group spirit and teamwork were vital to accomplish organizational goals and worker satisfaction. Since then, it can be seen how the studies contributed to the growth of personnel management and human relations and pointed the way to the need to study in detail the 'informal group.'

4. Modern influences

W. Bennis has used the term 'revisionist' to describe a current group of researchers in the field of organizational and administrative theory. They are dissatisfied with the validity of the concepts of both scientific management and the human relations movement. They do not think either is sufficiently 'scientific' to develop really valid principles. They use modern research techniques (especially mathematics and computers) to explain behaviour and it is possible that they will encourage a more thorough integration of the various disciplines which are concerned with human beings at work in industrial society. The systems approach to management and organization is an important influence today (see p. 21).

5. Other pioneers

Taylor, Gilbreth and Mayo were concerned mainly with techniques that might be used by management on the workers. Emerson considered the subject from the viewpoint of higher management and the direction of the business as a whole, but was still closely involved with techniques. None of them really attempted to deal with management as a *specific function* and it was not until the publication of the work of Henri Fayol that this was done.

Henri Fayol (1841–1925)

He was a qualified mining engineer and managing director of a large French company. A year after the death of Taylor he published *General and Industrial Management*. Neither Taylor nor Mayo was concerned much with the problems of top management. Fayol, unlike Taylor, started in management and attempted to develop a science of administration for management. He believed that there was a universal science of management applicable to 'commerce, industry, politics, religion, war or philanthropy.' He was one of the first practising managers to draw up a list of management principles.

Fayol thought principles would be useful to all types of managers, but he did not consider that a manager needs anything more than a knowledge of management principles in order to manage successfully. At higher levels he said managers depended less upon technical knowledge of what they were managing and more on a knowledge of administration. In the next section on Elements of Management, his ideas will be further discussed.

Mary Parker Follett (1868–1933)

Born in America, she spent five years at university there and one year in England at Cambridge University. She was greatly interested in social work and had a gift for relating individual experience to general principles. She concentrated not on methods or systems, but on realities of human behaviour (i.e. what makes people behave as they do).

She contributed on the psychological implications of authority, leadership and control, and stated four 'principles of co-ordination.' Her ideas will be discussed in more detail in later sections, especially her concept of the 'law of the situation.'

F. ELEMENTS OF MANAGEMENT

Whichever way one defines management, a biased approach is of no service to anyone. Too much emphasis on one element does not help to make the subject any easier to understand.

We have seen that the economic system is a complex of activities and these must form the background of management. The goods and services consumers need must be supplied and the means by which they can purchase these must be provided. Management's rôle must therefore be to promote this in the most efficient manner, by combining factors of production and distribution and directing the efforts of the people concerned to the given purpose.

No matter what type of enterprise (e.g. highly centralized government departments or nationalized industries, or commercial concerns) the progress of management is fundamentally the same. Enterprises need plans, direction and control and these will not function without effective organization.

These elements, planning, directing, controlling and organizing, are often called 'Functions' by some other writers; the use of this word in this book will be confined to the specialist departmental groupings, e.g. production, marketing, finance, etc. (See next section on Organization for more discussion on this aspect.)

Emphasis on these elements will vary according to the size of the enterprise. Although external environmental conditions affect management policy, these cannot be changed. Internal environmental conditions can be moulded to enable the objectives to be attained and this, the provision of a suitable environment, is part of the job of management. A manager must first of all plan the work for his subordinates, organize them effectively, seeing that they are selected and trained wisely, direct their work and measure results. Later, the ideas of wider responsibility for management, e.g. responsibility to society, which appears to widen management activity, will be considered.

Fayol's classification can be used as a starting point. He listed six spheres of activity—Technical, Commercial, Financial, Security, Accounting, Managerial. It is the last of these, i.e. Managerial, of which he wrote, 'to manage is to forecast and to plan, to organize, to command, to co-ordinate and to control.'

1. Planning

This referred to forecasting future circumstances and requirements, deciding objectives, making long- and short-term plans, determining policies to be followed and the standards to be set.

2. Organizing

This activity was concerned with dividing work and allocating it among groups and persons and determining their responsibilities and relations and the extent of their delegation.

3. Co-ordinating

Co-ordinating involved seeing that all groups and persons work efficiently and economically, in harmony, towards the common objective.

4. Command

This was the exercise of centralized authority and leadership.

5. Control

This activity involved checking to see that plans have been carried out and attending to any deviations.

Modern writers largely accept this classification. Brech sees organization as a function of planning and motivation and leadership is preferred to command. No real point appears in attempting to justify unduly the various classifications of the elements of management, as they are really very closely related. For the purpose of analysis the following classification has been adopted.

1. Planning

This includes the forecasting and selecting of objectives with the policies, programmes and procedures for achieving them. It involves making choices, i.e. decision-making.

2. Organizing

This involves determining and noting activities needed to achieve objectives of the undertaking; grouping these and assigning such groups of activities to managers, ensuring effective delegation of authority to enable activities to be carried out and providing co-ordination of authority relationships.

N.B. Staffing involves manning positions needed in the organization structure, this needs a definition of man requirements for each job, appraising and selecting candidates, training and developing them. Some writers consider this a *separate* element of management and, in practice, much of this work is delegated to a Personnel Manager; but it must be remembered that ultimately top management is responsible for staffing.

3. Direction

This involves guiding and supervising subordinates. These subordinates must be orientated into the undertaking's ways, guided towards improved performance and motivated to work effectively towards enterprise goals.

4. Control

Performance should be measured and deviations from plans corrected or accounted for. It is preferable that someone should be responsible for variations as control of people ensures the control of materials.

N.B. Co-ordination is considered by many authorities as a separate element of management. Others regard it as the *essence* of management; the reasoning here is that one needs to achieve harmony of effort to accomplish the desired goal and this is itself the purpose of management, and each of the managerial elements can be considered to be an exercise in co-ordination.

It should be noted that an efficient organization can help towards creating effective co-ordination.

We should note that there are dangers in simplifying and classifying the elements of management as there is a wide range of managerial tasks that do not lend themselves to simple classification. Another danger in attempting to be specific about elements, is that each element appears to have equal prominence and emphasis. At each level of management the emphasis changes on the various elements. In other organizations, it can be quite different, e.g. 50 per cent of time spent may be on control, and in other organizations only 20 per cent. The importance of the elements cannot be assessed by the time spent on them.

G. A MANAGEMENT SYSTEM

Many activities in an organization were treated in a purely descriptive fashion before N. Weiner published his book on *Cybernetics* in 1948 which allowed the activities of management to be examined analytically. He stressed the inter-disciplinary approach. Other writers tried to classify various systems—biological, physical and social—and a new *systems theory* evolved.

Thinking about management with a knowledge of the systems approach can help us to postulate conceptually ideas underlying management theory for the first time. Systems theory tries to synthesize ideas common to several disciplines.

A system is an organized combination of parts which form a complex entity, with inter-relationships or interactions between the parts and between the system and the environment. Examples of a system are: the school system, or the telephone system or the solar system.

It was not until about the early 1960s that a change in management thought began which reflected the impact of systems thoughts, but it was slow to start and it was not until the 1970s that ideas of general systems appeared in formal management theory. Basic systems thinking is becoming more firmly established and is waiting to be further developed.

A management system implies the *cutting across* of traditional boundaries of responsibility of departments. Distinct demarcation lines between purchasing, manufacturing, engineering, marketing, etc., may become less distinct as departmental interactions are known, and a revision of organization may become essential. This is essential in viewing the management process as a system. Russell L. Ackoff in the *General Systems Yearbook* (Vol. 5 1960, p. 6) commented, 'We must stop acting as though nature were organised into disciplines.'

Recent applications of this approach have presented complex systems in the form of *models* for ease of manipulation, to simulate a portion of reality. Others have tried to model the life of cities or tried to solve problems of society with the new tools available. The main problem is that these systems (e.g. cities) are only products of those systems which interact with other more complex systems, which are more difficult to model. A city's problems for example derive from its relation to its environment.

A system may be said to comprise the following elements, which are termed *sub-systems*:

(*a*) A *sensing* system or mechanism, to find out the situation and what is going on.

(*b*) An *information coding* or processing system, to ensure that data are in usable form.

(*c*) *Physical processing* system, requiring two-way communication and feedback of results.

(*d*) *Regulating and control* system, based upon actual output and measurement of deviations.

(*e*) *Information storage and retrieval* system.

(*f*) A *goal-getting or policy-making* system.

Computers have been used for simpler tasks, e.g. record keeping and clerical work, while more important issues were neglected. Even though modern computers have greatly improved in speed and capabilities there is still the danger of generating large quantities of meaningless data.

New ideas are postulated by the systems approach:

(*a*) Management is achieved largely by the instrumentality of a system of *operating relationships* that have been built up in advance.

(*b*) Systems not people are the real managers.

(*c*) Functions of management, whatever they are deemed to entail (e.g. plan direct control, etc.), do not contribute to any understanding of management according to systems thinkers.

The organization is seen as a system and by ignoring the restrictive traditional views of management structure, we can then open our minds to conceptualize the reality of the whole to improve relationships. For example, a person's actions in an organization reflect his understanding of the organizational world around him. The more he is made aware of the realities of his environment, he sees the consequences of his actions differently and new insights lead to new types of action.

General systems theory provides valuable insights into the structure

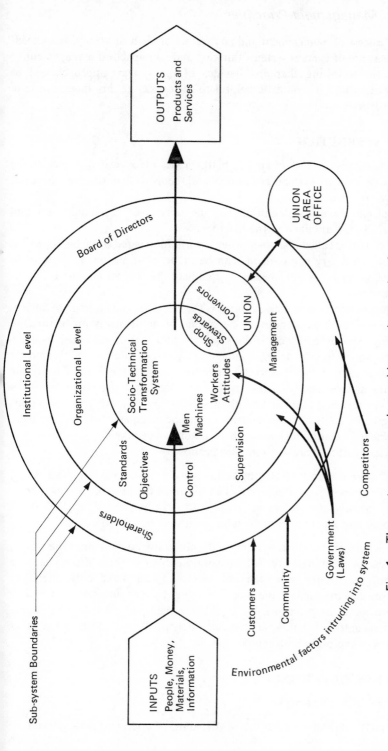

Fig. 1. The systems approach provides an integrative framework for modern organization theory and management practice.

and process of management and any serious student of management needs to be aware of general systems thinking and its impact on management.

In the following chapters the idea of the systems approach will be illustrated, and it would be helpful to introduce, at this stage, the term cybernetics.

H. CYBERNETICS

Cybernetics is a branch of applied mathematics and is related to operational research. Control systems are studied and theories of control are developed in precise terms.

Norman Weiner's definition is: 'the science of communication and control in the animal and the machine.'

A system is called *open-loop* when information is fed out from a process so that necessary comparisons can be made by a person. If the loop is *closed*, a person is not needed to complete the control circuit; it is self-correcting.

The essence of cybernetic control is the effort to reach a stage of *homeostasis* (i.e. a stable condition) by means of adjustments made through feeding back into the controlling system information obtained from its interaction with outside environments. A good example is the thermostat which is sensitive to temperature changes and automatically adjusts the heating mechanism. *Feedback* involves passing information from one point in a system back to an earlier point with a view to modifying behaviour. Cybernetic control is dependent upon the adequacy of feeding back reliable information to a point where action can be taken.

Systems can be divided into two groups:

(*a*) *Deterministic;* where the behaviour can be completely determined, e.g. we know what will happen when we touch the keys of a typewriter.

(*b*) *Probabilistic;* where behaviour can only be guessed, e.g. the result of tossing of a coin is unpredictable, as it may be a head or a tail.

In a very probabilistic system we do not know how the machine works, because of its complexity. All we can do is treat it like a '*black box.*' We cannot see inside the system, or box, and can make only intelligent guesses and manipulate the box, obtaining, by trial and error, some way of predicting its reactions. We could, for example, institute a sales promotion campaign, but we cannot accurately predict its effect, as the situation is of the probabilistic type.

REVIEW QUESTIONS

Nature of Management

(1) Distinguish between the words administration and management.

(2) Is management an art or a science?

(3) To what extent can management be regarded as a profession?

(4) What is meant by 'scientific management'?

(5) What did the following persons contribute to management thought—
F. W. Taylor; H. L. Gantt; F. Gilbreth; H. Emerson; H. Fayol; Mary
Parker Follett?

(6) Why is so much attention paid to the 'Hawthorne Experiments'?

(7) Is there any point in considering the elements of which management
is composed?

(8) What is meant by 'a management system'?

(9) Explain the term 'cybernetics.'

BIBLIOGRAPHY

Nature of Management

Ackoff, R., *The Systems Age* (Wiley, 1974).

Barnard, C. I., *The Functions of the Executive* (Cambridge, Mass., Harvard
University Press, 1938). Chapters 15–17.

Brech, E. F. L., *The Principles and Practice of Management* (London,
Longmans, Green & Co., 2nd edition, 1963). Pp. 1016–38, and Part 5,
Chapter 2.

Drucker, P. F., *The Practice of Management* (London, Heinemann, 1961).
Conclusion.

Fayol, H., *General and Industrial Management* (London, Pitman, 1949).
Chapters 1–9.

Follett, M. P., *Dynamic Administration, collected papers*, ed. H. C.
Metcalf and L. Urwick (London, Pitman, 1941).

Kempner, T. (ed.), *A Handbook of Management* (London, Weidenfeld
and Nicolson, 1971).

Stewart, R., *The Reality of Management* (London, Heinemann, 1963).
Chapters 6 and 8.

(For Review problems see p. 142.)

2   Planning

Planning involves selecting enterprise objectives and department goals and then finding ways of achieving them. Plans depend upon the existence of alternatives and then decisions have to be made regarding *what* to do, how to do it and by *whom* it is to be done. A plan is a pre-determined course of action which helps to provide purpose and direction for members of an enterprise. The planning process can be aided by working in an environment which is conducive to it. This is important, as plans develop from the lower levels of administration whose reaction and responses may change and help to form plans.

The most important way management can contribute to growth is by systematic planning. Probabilities are forecast and programmes developed to take advantage of them. Constant attention must be given to changing circumstances and many revisions of plans may be needed. Economists use the terms *ex ante* and *ex post* for this approach, that is, revision is continually made of the *basic assumptions* on which the plans were based, as circumstances change and thus new plans have to be developed.

A.   FORECASTING

Economic forecasting is basic to planning. Forecasting precedes the preparation of a budget and is concerned with probable events. The future is uncertain and numerous techniques have been evolved to try and limit the amount of uncertainty. (See section on control.) Probability theory is one statistical method used widely. A newer development is *econometric* forecasting. This is done through the construction of mathematical models in which various factors of the economy are given mathematical values and their effect upon each other ascertained through the solution of equations. The level of a country's economy is of course a vital factor upon which a company's sales and revenue plans are based.

Such a forecast enables a *premise* to be made from which plans can be developed and enables the right objectives to be selected. It is in effect a special tool of planning and Fayol considered it so important as to state it was the *essence* of management. He used the word *prévoyance*, or foresight, and referred to plans as syntheses of forecasts and recommended annual forecasts and ten-yearly projections, which were revised every five years or less, depending upon trends.

Sales forecasts are affected by many factors which include trends relating to the general economy, political, international, industrial trends, the strength of competitors and manufacturing cost trends.

Forecasts make management think ahead and give a singleness of purpose to planning by concentrating attention on the future.

Items affecting forecasts

1. Political stability.
2. Population trends.
3. Price levels.
4. Government controls and fiscal policy.
5. Employment, productivity and national income.
6. Technical environment—some areas have shown great changes, e.g. computers and the impact of the speed of developments must be especially noted.

A simple cycle of business activity can be seen in Fig. 2. This figure shows that production is distributed via an intermediary to customers. A

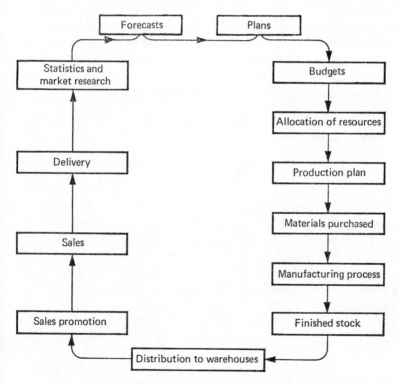

Fig. 2. Simple cycle of business activity.

more accurate cycle would be more involved and refinements will be mentioned in later chapters.

Forecasts of sales are used to determine the scale of activity needed to satisfy the expected market and to indicate the necessary financial resources. Such forecasts are a necessary preliminary to the construction of budgets which can be used to set targets to achieve the objectives which become effective when they are set out in policies.

The sales forecast, which shows the number of units to be sold and the price expected, will enable the budget of revenue to be calculated. Then the budgeted production costs for this level of sales, plus expected administration costs, can be deducted from expected revenue to give a budgeted profit figure, which will then show the amounts available for appropriation. Budgets for total resources needed to finance the level of expected production can be drawn up.

Other chapters will show the place of the other activities in more detail, i.e. Production, Sales, Distribution and how control is effected over the entire cycle of business activity.

B. OBJECTIVES

Objectives are goals; they are aims which management and administration wish organizations to achieve. They are related to the future and are an essential part of the planning process. The determination of objectives is the responsibility of top management and has a great influence on policy, organization, personnel, leadership and control.

1. Nature of objectives

Authorities differ as to the exact nature of objectives for business enterprises. Perhaps the better approach is to consider first what is the objective of our economic system. This is, broadly, to provide goods and services to customers. Industrial and commercial concerns, which comprise the greater part of the economic system, must therefore have the same objective. The objects clause, which is part of the Memorandum of Association of a limited company, invariably states the objective is to manufacture a commodity or provide a service. Nationalized industries have the predominant objective of providing an efficient and economical service to customers.

The following extract from the Memorandum and Articles of Association of the Scott Bader Co. Ltd, shows a wider definition of goals and objectives.

Company Objectives
The basic purpose of the company is to render the best possible service

as a corporate body to our fellow men. Towards this end we strive particularly:

(1) To develop the strengths of the company, its efficiency and means of production.

(2) To provide economic security to members and to relieve them of material anxiety or striving for personal advancement at the cost of others.

(3) To produce goods not only beneficial to customers of the company at a fair price and as high a quality as possible, but also for the peaceful purposes and general good of mankind.

(4) To conduct research and provide technical education mainly in synthetic resins and their applications in the paint, plastics and allied industries.

(5) To contribute towards the general welfare of society, internationally, nationally and in the company's immediate neighbourhood.

A newer approach to the consideration of objectives is the 'stakeholder' theory which suggests that a firm has responsibility to maintain an equitable and working balance among the claims of the interested groups, i.e. stockholders, employees, customers, suppliers, vendors and the public.

The theory maintains that the objectives of the firm should be derived by balancing the *conflicting claims* of the various 'stakeholders.' The firm has a responsibility to all these and must structure its objectives to give each a measure of satisfaction. In this context the ideas of Maslow seem relevant, that is, that managers have a hierarchy of goals or motives, and once managers have achieved one goal, e.g. x per cent profits, then they will turn to satisfy other goals, e.g. improved working conditions for employees.

Another related approach to the 'stakeholder' theory is suggested by Cyert and March who state, 'organisations do not have objectives, only people have objectives.' They suggest a firm's objectives are in reality a consensus of objectives of the participants which have been *negotiated.* (A good discussion on their ideas is in *Management and the Social Sciences* by Tom Lupton (chapter 4).)

They suggest that in large firms the task of decision-making is distributed throughout the firm, and that companies have five main goals: sales, production, inventory, market-share and profit.

These are target areas for managers who are aiming to achieve their particular goal. Managers therefore *bargain* among themselves and eventually this 'conflict' will be resolved by compromise and the goals achieved by the organization may only then be *satisfactory*. This theory may be said to bring into the decision-making process, social as well as economic variables.

The position of 'profits' must now be considered (there are many definitions of profit). Profitability is, to many people, the main objective of a business. They stress that, if a concern had no profits, a business could not exist for very long, and therefore consider profits to be the main objective.

The real answer may be to recognize that the supply of a particular commodity is the *object* of a trading concern, but the *motive* is profit, which is also used as a criterion of success.

Profits, as *an* objective, or as a motive, are becoming increasingly qualified by questions of public importance. It will be seen later in this chapter that business is deemed to have a *social responsibility*.

A brief consideration of the recent views of other writers in Britain and America may throw more light on this disagreement of the real object of a business.

Brech refers to the overall objectives as prosperity, growth and the continued life of the business. Some firms may have as their main object the provision of the finest car in the world. Others may consider it to be giving the public a service which provides the maximum value for money. Again, *satisfactory*, rather than maximum, profits may be the object, and prosperity may be measured by the annual profit which gives a satisfactory return on capital employed.

Professor Galbraith has stated that, in the U.S.A., businesses are now more interested in growth and stability, rather than profit making. Growth can be measured by the actual turnover increase, or an increase in the share of the market, and this appears to be an important objective and in this connexion a lower return may be accepted now if future prospects appear good. *Continued life* of a business is related to growth and stability and this will suffer a great deal if no provision is made for innovation, research and development and management succession.

It is important to realize that objectives may change in *emphasis* over a period of time. At certain periods one or another objective may be dominant. For example, at present the objective may be to stimulate sales to attain maximum profit; later it may be to maintain a satisfactory profit, while selling a better quality product or giving better quality service to customers.

2. General and specific objectives

Objectives can be general or specific and may range in time from months to years, they may apply to the whole company or to units or persons. General objectives are determined by the Board of Directors who approve other objectives.

It is preferable for objectives to be specific and expressed in quantitative terms. The first question to be answered is, what is the *nature* of the present business? This as we saw previously may change, but it must be understood in order that adaptation to changing customer needs be possible. For example, a firm selling typewriters and accounting machines can expand with technology and move on to punched cards and computers. If it decides it is in the 'information processing' business, rather than the 'office machine' business, then expansion will be easier.

Specific objectives usually have time limits, e.g. to open a new spare-parts section in six months' time; or it could be to diversify in certain fields in order to avoid relying on the fortunes of a single market or industry. It can be mentioned here that the big problem in such a venture is whether staff of the right calibre are available effectively to operate these *newer* types of business.

The ideal is for a company to formulate specific objectives and develop policies, within the framework of general objectives, which together result in co-ordinated, and controlled, decision-making. Careful planning of objectives helps management to give members a sense of direction and purpose—this is essential to achieve effective results.

To be able to survive, a firm must earn sufficient profits to sell services or products, of a certain quality, at a competitive price. Drucker stresses that survival depends upon the ability to cover the costs of staying in business. These costs include providing for replacement and obsolescence and market risk and uncertainty. But it is rare to see survival stated as an objective.

Drucker considers objectives are important in every area where performance and results directly affect the survival and prosperity of a business. These 'key areas' must be carefully selected and he distinguishes them by considering:

in what areas would excellence really have an extraordinary impact on the economic results of our business, to the point where it might transform the economic performance of the entire business? . . . in what areas would poor performance threaten to damage economic performance greatly, or at least significantly?

Knowledge of these 'key areas' should enable management to:

organize and plan the whole range of business phenomena in a small number of general statements; to test these statements in actual experience; to predict behaviour; to appraise the soundness of decisions when they are still being made; and to enable practising business men to analyse their own experiences and, as a result, improve their importance.

He then goes on to mention eight specific areas in which objectives have to be set, in terms of performance and results. These are—market standing; innovation; productivity; physical and financial resources; profitability; manager performance and development; worker performance and attitude and public responsibility.

It must be stressed that whatever areas are deemed important, it is preferable that any standards desired should be capable of being expressed in quantitative terms (e.g. number of items to be produced monthly).

It is also important to note that if the *organization structure* is not well designed, managers will find it difficult to achieve really high performance.

3. Some advantages of objectives

(*a*) They embody basic ideas and theories concerning what the enterprise is trying to accomplish.

(*b*) They provide a basis for directing and guiding the enterprise and provide targets which enable efforts to be observed and aided.

(*c*) They help to motivate people and they provide a sense of unity to the various groups in the organization, as an individual unit's contribution can be seen to be integrated with total enterprise goals.

C. POLICIES

In the administration of business one of the most important tasks is to formulate policy; the work of planning and the determination of company objectives become effective when expressed in policy form.

A policy is a guide to the action or decisions of people. Policies are directives, issued from a higher authority, and provide a continuous framework for the conduct of individuals in a business—they are in effect a type of planning. Policies are expressions of a company's official attitude towards types of behaviour within which it will permit, or desire, employees to act. They express the means by which the company's agreed objectives are to be achieved and usually take the form of statements, telling members how they should act in specific circumstances. Policies reflect management thinking on basic matters and inform those interested in the activities of the company about the company's intentions regarding them.

1. Formulation of policy

Policy formulation may begin at any level of management and may flow upwards or downwards along the levels of organization. Policy usually is formed by:

(*a*) The Board of Directors and senior management, who determine the main policies.

(*b*) Being passed up the chain of command until someone takes responsibility for making a decision.

(*c*) External influences, e.g. government legislation, may force a policy change.

Policy formulated by executives is usually on broad lines and subordinates have scope in applying it. Any policy should be as specific as possible.

2. Specific policies

It is not always easy to be specific; words must be carefully chosen and policies must be basically sound and well administered. It may be difficult to state policies that will cover all eventualities, and this therefore may tend to limit the range of the policies and therefore be unduly restrictive.

Advantages of specific policies

(*a*) They are easy to refer to and absorb.
(*b*) Misunderstandings are fewer.
(*c*) New employees can easily be made aware of them in their induction.
(*d*) They are a good exercise for management who must have thought about them seriously before writing them down.

Media for communicating policy, i.e. manuals, letters, conferences, etc., will be discussed later in this chapter under Communications.

Policies should be *flexible* and allow executives discretion in their application. They are more likely to be accepted if they are applied consistently and fairly.

3. Implied policies

If too much is implied in policies it can be dangerous. For example, if a firm does not employ union labour, it may be implied that this is the policy of the company and this could cause the company to suffer loss at a future date. Or, if all promotions were made in the past from within a firm, this would appear to be implied company policy. There would be great concern, therefore, if a new appointment were made from outside, as a 'change of policy' would be assumed.

4. Examples of policy

Policies regarding functional areas will be shown in more detail in the following chapters, but a brief indication will be given now of some of the major types of policy.

(*a*) *Product policy*

A product policy involves deciding upon the products to make and depends upon many factors, particularly upon market conditions. Such a policy in turn generates other policies, e.g. Marketing, Finance and Research.

(b) Production policy

This sort of policy deals with, for example: what proportions of plant should be devoted to flow or job or batch production? What items to make or to buy, and what use should be made of by-products?

(c) Market policy

This policy involves determining distribution channels, pricing structure of products, volume and type of advertising, credit policy, method of sub-dividing territory and remuneration of salesmen.

(d) Purchasing policy

A purchasing policy involves what firms to buy from and to what extent, and what are alternative sources of supply.

(e) Personnel policy

This policy involves methods of training, education, pension schemes, incentive plans, management succession and development, benefits, union relations.

All other functions need policies, but the above will serve to indicate the necessity for clear-cut policies in all sections of an enterprise.

Rules and procedures are often confused with policies.

Rules are more specific than policies and they usually entail penalties for misuse. Policy establishes a guiding framework for rules. Policies are broader than rules and are usually stated in more general language.

Procedures reflect policy and provide a standard method by which work is performed and provide a *check* when events do not occur. They are subordinate to policy and are a useful aid to training.

D. PRINCIPLES AND PROBLEMS OF PLANNING

1. Principles

(a) Plans should be based upon a clearly-defined objective and should conform with policy, making use of all available information.

(b) They should be precise, practicable and simple to understand and operate.

(c) They should take account of the existing organization and provide for control, so performance can be checked with established standards.

(d) They should be flexible and balanced. Flexibility will ensure that if circumstances necessitate change, this can be effected without disrupting the plan.

2. Problems

(a) Time-span

The greater the time-span, the greater the number of mistakes. *Present conditions* are dominant in the planner's mind when he initiates a plan and these may be overstressed. For example, a new building for a computer based upon present ideas (i.e. for use by the finance function only) may be found to be too small; if, in fact, all functions make use of the computer, a larger computer building may be needed.

Variable factors are of course easier to estimate in short periods of time, e.g. consumer tastes and technology.

(b) Human errors

The ability to see *all* the alternatives in a situation in order to evaluate their effect is essential.

(c) Unforeseen events and lack of communication

Many events are obviously unforeseen, but planning can be aided by wide consultation with workers to enable them to understand the nature of obstacles and the reasons why management is taking a certain course of action to overcome them.

E. CORPORATE PLANNING

Terminology in the area of planning can be confusing, as numerous terms are used with similar meanings, e.g. long-range planning, corporate planning, business forecasting and business strategy.

Corporate planning is one of the newer terms to denote a line of approach or a style of management, an attitude of mind, which uses a systematic and integrated approach to all aspects of a firm's activities.

The idea is to treat the company as a corporate whole, rather than a collection of departments, and on a long-term basis, rather than a short-term.

The company is studied within its environment, past, present and future, and with a precise definition of objectives.

A well-known writer on the subject, John Argenti, defines corporate planning as:

A systematic and disciplined study designed to help identify the objective of any organisation or corporate body, determine an appropriate

target, decide upon suitable constraints and devise a practical plan by which the objective may be achieved.
(*Corporate Planning*, 1968, G. Allen & Unwin Ltd.)

This approach is similar to management by objectives (M.B.O., see p. 36). The most interesting and important features of the M.B.O. approach is the emphasis on the *joint* establishment of objectives between manager and superior.

The approach taken in this book is that corporate planning involves more than long-range planning and adopts a more systematic and integrated approach to all the firm's activities.

In this approach, the economy of the country, the position of the company in its markets and the corporate structure is analysed.

The *whole of the industry* of which the company is part should be examined, noting the nature of the supply and demand factors, possible future trends and new opportunities, threats or problems. A *comparison* should be made of the company's performance as compared with its competitors. *Trends* in economic and political areas should be noted, e.g. government controls on mergers, economic groupings of countries (European Economic Community). Certain key factors should then be identified which appear likely to improve the company's position.

The final assessment would cover specific areas and their problems and opportunities. A brief summary follows:

Research and Development—need for new products and product improvements.

Personnel—need to ensure staff available of desired quantity and quality.

Sales and Marketing—relevance of sales policies; share of market, suitability of quality, design and price of products, marketing mix.

Production—to ensure production capacity adequate and other facilities and costs of production are acceptable.

From the above analysis the possibility of reorganization, mergers, diversification, etc., can be considered.

The essential need is for the plans from various areas of a business to be *integrated*, so that functional plans are interlinked to form an overall company plan.

A corporate plan though is more than just an interlinking of functional plans, it can be considered as a systems approach to achieve the aims of the firm over a period of time. Ansoff states this clearly in *Corporate Strategy* (pp. 18–19):

A very important feature of the overall business decision process becomes accentuated in the strategic problem. This is the fact that a large majority of decisions must be made within the framework of a limited total resource. Regardless of how large or small the firm, strategic decisions deal with a choice of resource commitments among alternatives; emphasis on current business will preclude diversification, over-emphasis on diversification will lead to neglect of present products. The object is to produce a resource allocation pattern which will offer the best potential for meeting the firm's objectives.

An interesting account of the various strategies which can be adopted and classifications of opportunities and risks is given in *Managing for Results* by P. F. Drucker (chapters 12 and 13).

He points out two important strategies which have to be decided:

(*a*) One is to decide what *opportunities* or wants the company wishes to pursue and what *risks* it is willing and able to accept.

(*b*) The other is to decide on the scope and structure and the right balance between, specialization, diversification and integration.

His classification of opportunities (additive, complementary and break-through) and of risks, are interesting and practical guides to help the formulation of strategies.

A *capability profile* of company strengths and weaknesses can be drawn up; one method is by a points scale related to a desired level of performance.

One large company found out for the first time in such an analysis that 75 per cent of its profits came from one product and this market was slowly declining. Many other important factors can come from such an analysis, e.g. under-utilization of financial assets.

A final point regarding this aspect is mentioned by Ansoff (chapter 5, *Corporate Planning*), where he considers that the measurement of 'synergy' is similar to what is frequently called 'evaluation of strengths and weaknesses.'

In synergy, *joint* effects are measured between two product markets; in strength and weakness evaluation, the firm's competences are rated relative to some desired performance level.

Synergy is concerned with the desired characteristics of fit between the firm and its new product-market entries. In business literature it is frequently described as the $2 + 2 = 5$ effect, to denote that the firm seeks a product-market posture with a combined performance that is greater than the sum of its parts.

If a company adds to its existing activities, the extent to which the new activity makes use of existing resources will determine the extent of the synergy. If, for example, the return on investment of the company as a whole, is just the return on the existing activities plus that of the new activities—there is no synergy ($2 + 2 = 4$). But where the new activity *makes use of* existing resources, the return for the company as a whole will be *greater than* the average of the new and existing activities $(2 + 2 = 5)$.

Plans range from those of a broad scope concerned with a long time span, which are the concern of top executives, to short-run, day to day operating plans which are the concern of managers at lower levels in the organization.

It is useful to visualize plans in the form of a hierarchy as it gives a more complete picture of the need for inter-relation of all plans.

The number of firms which plan for long periods is slowly increasing. As technology changes quickly there is a need for greater emphasis on co-ordination and the need for more specific objectives. One industry, which has greatly increased in a few years, is the electronic industry.

As the amount of innovation increases in a given period, the time available for new product *exploitation* diminishes. But it still takes the same time to develop and test new products; money has still to be spent on promotion and selling activities and, as the life span of a product falls, profitability will be reduced.

Long-range planning enables management to anticipate difficulties and take steps to eliminate them before they arise and can help to bring about a more unified approach to the various factors in a problem. Plans, though, must clearly state which manager is accountable and for what results, i.e. it must be management by specific objectives.

The length of plans varies from industry to industry. The more fortunate can plan a few years ahead, e.g. the motor-car industry. Others may plan only six months ahead, e.g. the fashion industry. Often, different aspects of the plan will cover different periods of time, e.g. money needed on loan can be planned a year ahead, whereas plans for a new car cover at least four years ahead. The L.R.P. will of course contain the short-range plan (S.R.P.) which for convenience will be assumed to cover one year. Freedom to change the S.R.P. is limited and may be broken down into monthly commitments, major variances being closely noted. It is imperative to note that assumptions made in L.R.P. must be specified and any change in them examined carefully. (Consider Fig. 3, p. 37, showing the Long-range Profit Gap.)

F. MANAGEMENT BY OBJECTIVES

This system must not be considered to be 'just another management technique' and given little consideration. It can be considered to be a new approach to practical management. In essence it embraces a clear-cut strategic plan and its translation into departmental and *personal* goals, which are reviewed when results are obtained.

This approach has been developed by J. W. Humble and the following points show the idea in outline:

(1) The *desired results* (objectives) set by management are clarified and defined.

(2) *Performance standards* are set, which must of course not conflict with the main objectives of the business.

(3) The *organization structure* must be provided, within which the manager has the maximum freedom and flexibility to perform.

(4) *Control information* must be supplied at suitable times so the manager can take corrective action quickly.

(5) *Appraisal performance* by identifying areas where a manager needs help, and providing him with guidance.

(6) *Motivating* employees, by relating results achieved to rewards and promotion opportunities.

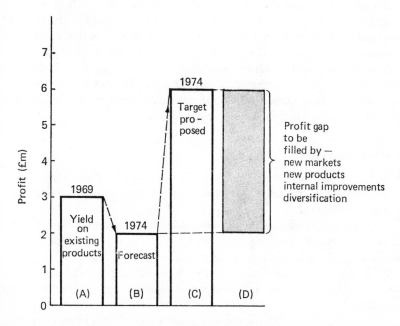

Fig. 3.   Long-range profit gap. (A) If the company continues as it is, the profit in five years will be £2 m. (B) The proposed target in five years' time is £6 m. (C) and this can only be obtained by a marked change in the factors shown beside the 'Profit Gap' (D).

Other points to note are that each functional objective and target is tied to the *overall* objectives. It may mean reorganization is needed as quite often many organization schemes are either very elementary and leave our vital functions, or so complicated that they are very difficult to understand. (The next chapter will discuss Organization.)

Another important point is that *new techniques are no better than the people who use them* and proper attention must therefore be given to the training and development of management at all levels. Also, advanced methods of performance appraisal are needed to identify areas where managers need help and guidance.

Figure 4 attempts to show the relationship between the Long Range Plan and the Annual Profit Plan and how the manager's standards and priorities can be integrated and put into perspective. Further consideration of this approach will be made in the chapter on Personnel Management.

G. DECISION-MAKING

1. Definition

A decision is a choice whereby a person forms a conclusion about a situation. This represents a course of behaviour about what must or what must not be done. It is the point at which plans, policies and objectives are translated into concrete actions. Planning leads to decisions guided by company policy and objectives and implies the *selection from alternative* objectives, policies, procedures and programmes. The purpose of decision-making is to direct human behaviour towards a future goal. If there were no alternatives, there would be no need for a decision.

2. Types of decisions

A brief comment on some of the ways decisions can be distinguished is all that is needed at this stage. Drucker distinguishes between 'tactical' and 'strategic' decisions.

Strategy can be defined as the behaviour of management in trying to achieve success for company goals in an environment of competition. It is based upon the action, or possible action, of others. Strategies are solely calculated to implement plans and objectives, bearing in mind all manner of uncertainties, so that an advantageous position is attained over an opponent.

'*Tactical*' decisions are routine and usually contain few alternatives and relate to the economic use of resources.

'*Strategic*' decisions are made by management and involve 'either finding out what the situation is, or changing it; either finding out what the resources are, or what they should be.' These include decisions upon basic objectives and may affect productivity, organization or operation of the business.

Other classifications include a division between *organizational* and *personal* decisions:

(*a*) *Organizational* decisions are those made in the rôle of an official of the company and reflect company policy.

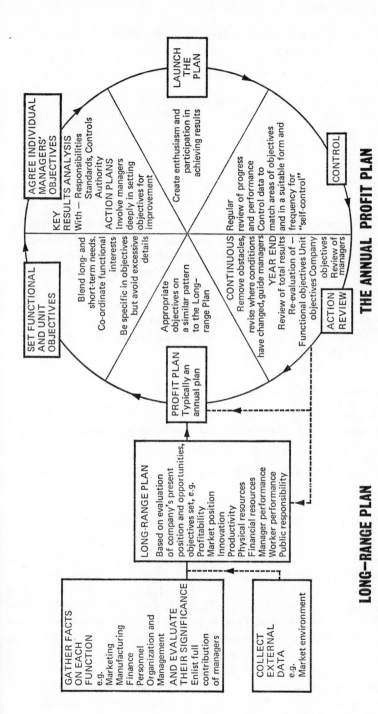

Fig. 4. Management by objectives. (Reproduced by permission of Urwick, Orr and Partners Ltd.)

(*b*) *Personal* decisions refer to those made by a manager as an individual and cannot be delegated.

Another classification is between *basic* and *routine* decisions:

(*a*) *Basic* decisions are long-range in scope, e.g. location of factory in a Development Area, or deciding what product to make. Wrong decisions on these matters can be costly.

(*b*) *Routine* decisions are those which are made repetitively and need little thought.

A final, similar, classification by H. A. Simon distinguishes between *programmed* and *unprogrammed* decisions:

(*a*) *Programmed* decisions are those which are routine and repetitive and have procedures set up to deal with them. Risks involved are not high and they therefore can be more easily delegated. Assessment can often be made in quantitative terms and can therefore more easily be *programmed* into a computer.

(*b*) *Unprogrammed* decisions are new and non-repetitive, where risks involved are high and they cannot easily be assessed in quantitative terms. There are many courses of action possible and decisions made will mean a greater expenditure of resources.

3. The process of decision-making

A little earlier on in the chapter, it was stated that knowledge of objectives and policies is needed before decisions can be taken. Such decisions may be said to consist of the following steps:

(*a*) Define the problem to be solved.
(*b*) Find alternative solutions.
(*c*) Analyse and compare these alternatives.
(*d*) Select the plan to be followed noting relevant factors.
(*e*) Make the decision effective—by taking action to put the decision into effect.

Decision-making really involves removing doubt. It involves having an objective to achieve and the tests of whether that objective is being achieved or not form the control criteria. Decisions involve the future and involve choice, therefore they can be wrong. The point to consider is, who makes decisions in a firm, and what are the criteria in delegating some decisions to subordinates? These questions can be answered by finding out those decisions where the chances of being wrong are high and the cost of correction is large; these can then be *reserved for top management*. Lower ranks would be allowed to decide where there was more certainty of being correct and the cost of correction is low.

One important point to consider is that no course should be taken that would create the need for a *new* decision after a short period of time.

Research into how decisions are made has greatly increased in recent years; the results show that decision behaviour is very complex and variable.

Many decisions are made by managers from a certain number of factors they have considered. The reality of the situation is that there may be in fact many more factors unknown to them, that they should have considered.

Analysis of alternatives and their possible consequences can be assisted by techniques, particularly by mathematical models and the use of probability theory (e.g. decision tree, see p. 42).

A premise is made, e.g. if A then B (see p. 44). Factual premises can be observed and measured and any value judgements involved must be recognized in any decision.

Once a decision is made it needs to be accepted by staff, who must first of all have the decision *communicated* to them and then they must be *motivated* to implement the decision.

A few of the *rules* used today in making decisions are:

(1) *Minimax Rule*—this is said to guarantee a minimum gain, or avoidance of maximum loss. This is often used when risks are high, or when a possible loss could be serious. If a stock controller observed this rule, he could hold too much stock which may be uneconomic, but he cannot be criticized for being out of stock.

(2) *Maximax Rule*—is the opposite of the above, where the aim is the highest possible value of an outcome regardless of risks involved.

(3) *The Average Rule*—is simply mid-way between the other two rules.

It should be noted that, whatever decision criteria are chosen, decisions are affected by:

(*a*) the importance of the decision;
(*b*) characteristics of the organization;
(*c*) the personality of the decision maker;
(*d*) his state of mind when making the decision.

It may be useful to look at decisions in terms of systems theory. Any choice that induces *flow*, or changes in the flow rate, is a decision. Rates are where the action *is*, i.e. what takes place between levels in a system. An example of this is when a person withdraws money from a bank; the level of money in the bank has been reduced—thus the action (decision) has caused a change from the previous state.

Another example is that if an accountant decides to stop credit to a customer (this action changes the flow rate), this is a decision in systems terminology. This can be further considered. If the flow rate continues (i.e. of credit) it can be said that a decision has been made to *let it continue*.

Decisions result from a comparison of actual with standard. Some decisions are made without being influenced by man. For example, if the temperature outside a person's body changes, then, without any effort by man, his body temperature changes. The aim of the human system is to maintain standards; therefore any decision taken aims to effect changes in flow rates *to move existing states* in the desired direction.

4. Techniques used in decision-making

There is a current emphasis on quantitative analysis. Various disciplines have contributed to research and the development of applications of mathematical techniques for certain types of organizational decisions.

It is important to realize that *by themselves techniques can do nothing*; the significance of their contribution depends essentially on the management attitude behind them, or underlying their application.

New developments in management science abound, Fig. 5 shows many of them. They are essentially 'tools of management,' i.e. instruments to be used by a skilful manager to *aid his judgement*, they are *not substitutes for management*.

Planning and control are closely interrelated and these new techniques will be discussed in more detail after the other elements of management, organization and direction have been considered.

Decision trees

By means of a diagram a number of future chance events which may affect a decision can be shown. A set of values is arrived at for predicted outcomes of each possible decision. The highest value indicates the course most likely to produce the greatest return.

This is a procedure for ensuring that alternatives are considered at every stage of an operation, as they may otherwise have been overlooked.

The tree is usually horizontal and the base of the tree is the *present* decision point (usually shown as a square); it is here where alternative courses of action present themselves. Branches begin at the *first chance event* (shown as a circle); each chance event produces two or more possible effects, some of which may lead to other chance events and subsequent decision points. The values of the tree are based upon research which provides *probabilities* that certain chance events will occur, showing predicted payout or cash-flow estimates for each possible outcome as affected by possible chance events.

The statistical probability is based upon knowledge and experience. Subjective probabilities can range from complete certainty (probability

Specialist Skills

General management, Economics, Statistics, Accounting, Mathematics, Computing, Psychology, Engineering, Physiology, Work study, Personnel, Educational methods.

Techniques

Corporate planning—Decision theory—Game theory—Company models—Costing systems—Management by exception—Organization and methods—Systems analysis—Computers for data processing, forecasting, production control, scientific calculations—Critical path method—PERT—PERT/cost—Branching networks—Resource allocation—Exponential smoothing—Moving averages—Market research—Time series analysis—Box Jenkins—Value analysis—Marginal costing—Contribution analysis—Breakeven charts—Linear programming—Simulation Monte Carlo—Queuing theory—Statistical quality control—Mathematical programming—Method study—Incentive schemes—Productivity bargaining—Programmed learning—Business games—Job description—Job evaluation—Merit rating—Salary progression curves—Time span of discretion—Manpower planning—Intelligence, personality and aptitude tests—Quality protection—Statistical stock control—Economic batch ordering quantities—Brainstorming—Variable factor programming—Group capacity assessment.

Problems Solved?

Objectives Achieved?

The above skills and techniques are available to modern management, but the factor to be stressed is, that *a business cannot solve its problems merely by buying a technique or a system*. The comment by L. F. Urwick is very relevant. "Every business is a living organism, with its own traditions, its own climate of opinion, its own special make-up. Every situation is different. And every kind of system has to be custom-built to the individual business."

Fig. 5.

of 1.0) through situations giving an even chance (0.5) to completely impossible situations (probability of 0.0).

It is basically a simple graphic method for analysing potential outcomes of a complex decision. It provides a way of showing the interplay among present decisions, chance events and possible future decisions, so enabling the manager to evaluate the various opportunities available at a given decision point.

More precise figures can be obtained, by *discounting* values assigned to *future* stages of the tree.

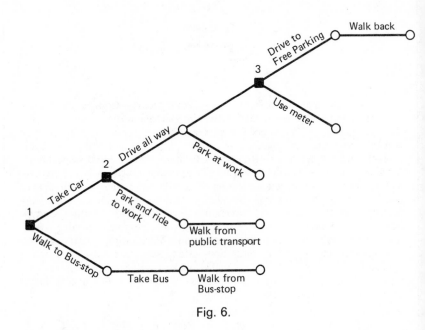

Fig. 6.

1st decision—to take car or bus.
2nd decision—to drive all the way, or stop and use public transport.
3rd decision—to use meter or drive to free parking area.

Each action can be given a financial or convenience value. Problems are more easily defined, risks, costs and opportunities quantified by the use of decision trees (Figs. 6 and 7).

In Fig. 7, A and B are chance events affecting the decision either to continue with regional distribution or have national distribution of a product. Assume national distribution is considered and research has shown that if there is a large national demand it will be £5.0m. and the probability of this is 70 per cent (i.e. 0.7). There is a 30 per cent chance demand will be limited, this may realize £0.5m.

Assume regional distribution is considered—and national demand is large—firm could realize £3m.

Assume regional distribution is considered—if national demand is limited—firm could realize £2m.

Payout amounts are then multiplied by the figure for probability, e.g.

$$0.7 \times £5 = £3.5m.$$

Each two amounts from the same 'branch,' i.e. national or regional, are added together and the amounts compared—the highest result is to be taken and this is to *expand nationally*.

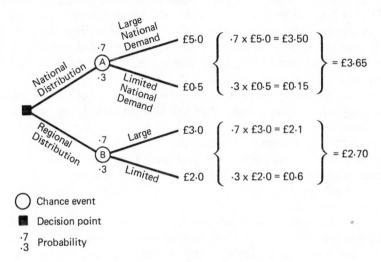

Fig. 7.

A French mathematician, René Thom, used a branch of mathematics to prove a theorem which would be useful in studying the behaviour of human activity systems. This is that *gradual* changes in control can cause *sudden catastrophic* changes in *behaviour*, and if these changes could be predicted, this would be very beneficial. Nature is itself full of discontinuities; for example, a gradual rise in the temperature of water eventually causes a marked change, it boils. In economics, after controls are steadily relaxed after an economic 'squeeze,' a sudden inflation explosion may occur. The protagonists of this *catastrophe theory* hope that it may provide a mathematical theory that can handle *discontinuities* as the calculus cannot, and become a useful tool in the study of the behaviour observed in human activity systems.

5. Social responsibilities of management

This topic is frequently discussed and it would take many pages to deal with it adequately. The following brief points may serve to illustrate what is meant by the term.

Managers have a responsibility to their shareholders—this is accepted. Do they have a responsibility to others, particularly the community as a whole?

(*a*) *A firm cannot exist in isolation* from the society in which it has its being. A firm provides goods and services for the community and uses raw material and labour and also makes use of other facilities of civilization, e.g. laws, which protect the company. No management can ignore the environment in which it operates and the success of firms may depend to a large extent on their public image. The attitude of the firm to their employees forms part of this image. Throughout history management has been influenced by social concepts.

(*b*) The *attitude of management to labour* is at the core of the social responsibility of management. Workers have become better protected, e.g. collective bargaining has given more security to workers, and the recent Staff Status schemes and the Redundancy Payments Act, 1963, are for the benefit of the workers. Management must give a lead in these matters and the government periodically 'exhorts' industry to do things which would aid the country socially; for example, the location of firms in development areas.

(*c*) *Economic and social responsibilities may clash*, for example, when a Nationalized Industry (e.g. Electricity) is asked to give distant farmers electricity; it may be socially desirable, but may not be economic, as the Industry has to make a certain percentage return on capital as laid down in the Government White Paper, *Financial Obligations of Nationalized Industries—a Re-appraisal*, 1967.

(*d*) *Subscribers of capital*, e.g. shareholders and debenture holders, have allowed their money to be used, and the firm is responsible to them, as they are entitled to a fair reward for the use of capital and the risk involved. If such obligations are not honoured, future capital would be harder to obtain and unemployment may result.

(*e*) *Consumers* have a right not to be exploited by a firm which depends upon the community in many ways. The question then arises—should a firm *share* its prosperity with its customers, e.g. by lowering prices, because of reduced costs of mass production and increases in sales? Recent legislation, e.g. on resale price maintenance and monopolies, has shown that the government adopts the attitude that companies must act in the public interest. Management therefore cannot avoid the fact that its responsibility for industrial and commercial direction is mainly its responsibility to society.

Other social issues managers face and upon which they have to decide policies are:

(*a*) Marketing policies—should they avoid manufacturing products detrimental to health, e.g. cigarettes, weapons.

(*b*) Policies that imply social costs—e.g. pollution of rivers, the firm reduce their costs by pumping waste into rivers and this involves social costs in clearing the rivers.

(*c*) The relations a company should have with political parties.

(*d*) Whether or not to export to particular countries.

The Code of Practice of Scott Bader Co. Ltd, is an example of the modern approach.

We recognise that we have a responsibility to society in which we live and believe that where we have some special talent or interest we should offer it to the wider community. We are agreed that our social responsibility extends to:

(1) Limiting the products of our labour to those beneficial to the community, in particular excluding any products, for the specific purpose of manufacturing weapons of war.

(2) Reducing any harmful effect of our work on the natural environment by rigorously avoiding the negligent discharge of pollutants.

(3) Questioning constantly whether any of our activities are unnecessarily wasteful of the earth's resources.

A final comment is on the trend whereby firms are encouraged to pursue 'socially responsible' policies. The suggestion is made by John Humble who advocates firms to keep a *Social Responsibility Audit*.

This is a checklist of about 14 specific areas of social responsibility against which management action can be reviewed with regards to the effect of policies on the external and internal environment of the firm.

External areas to consider—consumer and community relations, investment and shareholder relations, packaging and pollution, plus the consideration of possible new business opportunities that may reduce social difficulties.

This includes ensuring effective communication of information to shareholders and editors of papers, open-dating and full description of goods which are advertised to high standards. Companies are required to consider social issues in making investment decisions, and this goes so far as to consider *not investing* in other companies which are deemed 'socially irresponsible.'

Internal areas to consider—physical environmental factors (e.g. lighting and noise), working conditions, communications, organization structure and management style, industrial relations and the employment and treatment of minority groups, also education and training.

All of these areas should be periodically reviewed to see that the firm is pursuing socially responsible policies.

Brief comments on this approach are that there is nothing really new in them that firms which are well managed and marketing-oriented will not be doing. There seems to be a duplication or overlap of objectives and some may not be easy to attain. In any case a lot of effort and time will need to be expended in setting and checking on all these objectives—the question to be asked is, is it worthwhile?

Management by Objectives (see p. 36) is not too easy to operate effectively and adding social objectives will add to any difficulties. There is also the feeling of many managers that all this attention to objectives other than profit, or the rate of growth of profit, may not be in the long-term interest of the firm.

REVIEW QUESTIONS

Planning

(1) Briefly review the place of forecasting in business and the techniques which are used in forecasting.
(2) What factors must be considered in forecasting?
(3) What do you understand by the objectives of a business?
(4) Distinguish between specific and implied policies.
(5) What are the obstacles to accurate planning?
(6) Define decision-making and comment on types of decisions.
(7) What steps are involved in making a decision?
(8) What is meant by the word 'synergy'?
(9) Comment on the benefits in considering Management as a System.

BIBLIOGRAPHY

Planning

Ackoff, R., *The Systems Age* (Wiley, 1974).
Ansoff, H. I. (ed.), *Business Strategy* (London, Penguin, 1969).
Argenti, J., *Corporate Planning* (London, Allen & Unwin, 1968).
Bannock, G., and Merrett, A. J., *Business Economics and Statistics* (London, Hutchinson, 1962). Introduction, Chapters 1 and 3.
Brech, E. F. L., *The Principles and Practice of Management* (London, Longmans, Green & Co., 2nd edition, 1963). Part 4, Chapter 2.
Cleland, E. I., and King, W. R., *Management, A Systems Approach* (McGraw-Hill, 1972).
Drucker, P. F., *The Practice of Management* (London, Heinemann, 1961). Chapters 5, 6, 7, 8 and 28.

Drucker, P. F., *Managing for Results* (New York, Harper & Row, 1964).

Ewing, D. W., *Long Range Planning for Management* (New York, Harper & Row, 1963).

Humble, J. W., *Improving Business Results* (Maidenhead, McGraw-Hill, 1968).

Katz, R., *Cases and Concepts in Corporative Strategy* (New Jersey, Prentice-Hall, 1971).

Thompson, S., 'How Companies Plan,' Research Study, No. 54 (New York, *American Management Association*, 1962).

White, D. J., *Decision Theory* (London, Allen & Unwin, 1969).

(For Review problems—see end of chapter on Control.)

3 Organization

Organization is defined in a number of ways. In the study of management it can refer to the structure of relationships among individuals. A less static approach regards organization as a process or an element of management concerned with *change* or *growth* of the structure. The traditional approach will be considered first.

Organizations are primarily complex goal seeking units which in order to survive must accomplish secondary tasks, e.g. they must maintain their internal system to co-ordinate *the human side of enterprise* and must adapt to and shape the external environment.

One area of conflict is the difference between the goals of management and the goals of individual workers. To overcome this conflict, a number of theories have been propounded to allow for mediation of interests. Motivation theories will be considered in more detail later (see p. 103). Elton Mayo and his associates (see p. 294) saw that the human affiliation of man could be a motivating force and viewed the industrial organization as a *social* as well as an economic–technical system. They considered managers should be judged by their ability to sustain co-operation. The interesting point which can be considered is that, once a *primary* group is seen as a motivating force it may be said that a managerial elite will become obsolete, as the work group itself becomes the decision-maker! Decisions being made at the point in the organization where they are most relevant, i.e. where data are available.

Whether or not this is possible, it does appear that a change is needed in inter-personal relations, and it is here that management can help by instilling *values* which permit the expression of feeling and trust and *concern for the individual* (for further consideration of the ideas of R. R. Blake, see p. 268).

A. STRUCTURE OF ORGANIZATION

The organization structure is the basic framework within which the executive's decision-making behaviour occurs. The quality and nature of the decisions made are influenced by the nature of the structure. Organization, as an element of management, is concerned with—the *grouping* of activities in such a manner that enterprise objectives are attained, the *assignment* of these activities to appropriate departments and the *provision* for authority, delegation and co-ordination.

It is important to note that, in order to accomplish any goal, activities must be grouped logically and authority should be granted so that conflicts do not occur.

Organization can be divided into two parts, formal and informal.

1. Formal organization

This can be simply defined as the network of communications in an enterprise; it is the *official* channel through which information passes. Barnard referred to an organization as formal, when the activities of two or more persons are *consciously* co-ordinated towards a given objective. He stated that formal organization comes into being when persons are:

(*a*) Willing to communicate with one another.
(*b*) Willing to act and share a common purpose.

This appears to be too broad and is not generally accepted. W. Brown in *Exploration in Management* said:

I personally believe that the more formalization that exists, the more clearly we will know the bounds of discretion which we are authorized to use and will be held responsible for; and prescribed policies make clear to people the area in which they have freedom to act.

There is concern that formal organizations are inflexible, but there should always be room for individual discretion in a well-organized enterprise.

2. Informal organization

The formal structure theory has been modified by the research of the social scientists who stress informal organization, which cannot be represented on an organization chart. Small groups, working together, form ideas and attitudes as the Hawthorne Experiments showed. The attitude of the groups could help or hinder the company goals, to the extent that these attitudes are subordinated to the purpose of the enterprise.

Management determines the formal structure and the social desires of persons find their expression in the informal structure, which should not be disregarded by management. It is far better if informal relations are put on as formal a footing as possible in order to ensure that they do not go against formal relations. For example, informal meetings of union members may undermine the authority of the union and management.

B. BUREAUCRATIC ORGANIZATION

A sociologist, Max Weber (1864–1920), studied organization structures and he considered that they could be divided into three types:

Traditional—based upon the *head*, or chief's, *authority*.
Rational-legal—based upon *power*, which people recognized and accepted in a given situation.
Charismatic—based upon the *exceptional ability* or personality of someone who has 'charisma.'

Bureaucracy may be defined as a type of organization designed to accomplish large-scale administrative tasks by co-ordinating the work of a large number of persons in a systematic manner. Weber described the *characteristics of a bureaucratic structure* whereby:

(1) Regular activities are distributed in a fixed way and called *official duties*.
(2) Each lower position is under the control and supervision of a higher position (hierarchical principle).
(3) Operations are governed by a consistent system of abstract *rules*, all leading to the attainment of a common goal.
(4) *Duties* are carried out impersonally.
(5) Employment is based upon technical qualifications and promotion is based upon seniority or achievement or both.

Warren Bennis regards bureaucracy as a social invention perfected during the Industrial Revolution to organize and direct the activities of a business firm. It may be useful to summarize briefly *some* of the advantages and disadvantages of bureaucracy.

Advantages	*Disadvantages*
Impartial application of rules.	Confusion and conflict among rôles.
Clearly defined system of authority.	Arbitrary rules.
System of procedures for processing work.	No room for personal growth. Poor communications and numerous informal organizations.
Division of labour based upon functional specialization.	Slow to adapt to new technology.

C. LEVELS OF ORGANIZATION

Small firms have a simple organization structure. There is specialization of jobs, but it is flexible. Often jobs are made to *fit the person available*, e.g. the Sales Manager may have an aptitude for figures and so be placed in charge of Accounts. Relations are informal and the lower ranks can talk direct to the Managing Director about their problems. Rules are few, and decisions are based largely upon experience.

As the firm expands, more specialists and managers are employed. The organization becomes more complex as management levels are more numerous, and therefore need to be more closely defined. Duties, also, may have to be more specific and the qualities and qualifications needed by the personnel for each job are also more closely defined; this tends to lead to appointments becoming less personal. Detailed rules governing all aspects are formulated to guide managers in the running of their departments.

Levels of authority can vary greatly; from two to ten or more. The number of levels depends, among other things, upon the number and type of employees. For example, a company with a large number of manual workers will usually have fewer tiers than a similar sized company with more clerical workers, because the supervisory ratio tends to be greater on the shop floor.

The growing firm, therefore, hires more men, subordinates are given more authority and work is grouped into sections and a manager placed in charge. Thus two levels are made, which will be further increased as the number of subordinates increases.

The simple figure below (Fig. 8) shows the vertical and horizontal dimensions of the structure of the organization. The broad base indicates that lower down there is a greater number of operating employees.

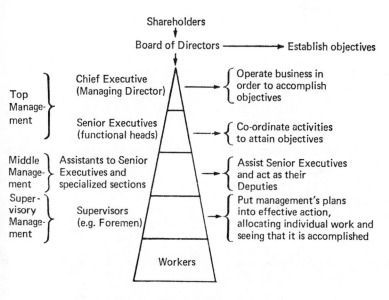

Fig. 8.   Organizational pyramid.

Towards the top, fewer operating workers are needed where more managerial and administrative work is done.

In a complex organization the number of levels may be many and each succeeding lower level represents decreasing authority and status. The practice of delegation creates a 'chain of command' (scalar principle). These scalar levels are important as they provide a framework for transmitting authority and aid communication.

Each of the above levels is responsible to the level immediately above.

Logical steps in forming an organization:

(*a*) Establish enterprise *objectives*, policies and plans.

(*b*) Find out the *activities* needed to execute these plans.

(*c*) *Classify* and group these activities in the best way.

(*d*) *Assign* to these groups the authority needed to perform these activities.

(*e*) Endeavour to *integrate* these groupings through authority relationships, horizontally, vertically and laterally.

D. PRINCIPLES OF ORGANIZATION

Many authorities have published principles and many of these principles are common, but any list can be regarded as inadequate, but they do serve as a *guide* and many are of universal application. The following are some of the main principles:

(*a*) *Unity of objective*

Every part of the organization must contribute to the attainment of the objective of the enterprise.

(*b*) *Span of control*

Consideration is needed to find the number of persons an individual can effectively manage. The number varies for many reasons, but a figure often quoted is that six subordinates is the largest number a person should supervise.

(*c*) *Delegation*

Authority should be delegated as far down the levels as possible.

(*d*) *Unity of command*

Instructions from two or more superiors may conflict. This is why each subordinate should have only one superior. (See section on Direction.)

(e) Scalar principle

Someone must have ultimate authority and a clear line of authority should be in existence to all parts of the enterprise.

(f) Responsibility

The responsibility of a subordinate to a superior for delegated authority is absolute and responsibility should be on a par with the amount of authority given.

It is unlikely that a body of principles will ever be obtained to apply to all organizational problems. Brech considers the primary purpose of principles: 'is to serve as a guide to the correct formulation of a sound framework of integrated executive action.'

H. A. Simon considers principles are essentially useless, but that his study provides:

> . . . a framework for the analysis and description of administrative situations, and with a set of factors that must be weighed in arriving at any valid proposal for administrative organization.

There are a number of principles set out by many authorities, e.g. the American Management Association, Fayol; they all have items in common and many people regard them to be of universal application; others say they are too general and are therefore of limited use. A modern approach is to find out how organizations *work in practice* and then try and generalize about the nature of organization. (See later in chapter.)

E. DEPARTMENTATION

In order to decide upon the method of grouping or division of work, the main objectives of the business must be considered. The grouping of functions or tasks is referred to as departmentation. The main methods are:

1. Functional

This is the most widely-used basis. Three main categories occur in most enterprises, i.e. production (the creation of, or addition to utility, of a good or service), selling (finding customers for goods and services at a price), and finance (obtaining and expending funds). As types of enterprise vary, department names vary, e.g. a wholesaler does not produce, he buys, therefore his departments may be buying, selling and finance. Often the amount of money spent may determine the department and the chief business activity is usually made a separate unit, e.g. auditing department in an accountancy firm. Figure 9 shows this type of classification.

Fig. 9. Departments in a manufacturing company.

Advantages

(*a*) This method is easy and logical to decide and usually effective in practice.

(*b*) It follows the principle of specialization and economies result.

Disadvantages

(*a*) Functions may not be so important as the *area* covered by the firm, e.g. territory may be widespread and another grouping (geographical) may be better.

(*b*) Such specialization may invoke *narrowness of outlook*, i.e. inability to see business *as a whole*.

(c) Management positions need men of wide experience and this is not readily available in a rigid department system which affords poor training grounds for managers.

2. Geographical

As companies grow and are widely spread over the country, it may be found desirable to divide some activities among branches away from the main centre of operations. A manager is put in charge of the area and is given responsibility for all aspects of the unit's activities. Local factors are not now neglected in decision-making. Plants for manufacture and assembly can be so located as to reduce transport costs. Manufacturers of bulky products tend to divide their work on a territorial basis, with a separate plant to serve each area or district.

Advantages

(*a*) Lower cost of operating.

(*b*) Knowledge of local circumstances helps decision-making and aids the creation of customer goodwill.

(*c*) Provides a good training ground for managers.

Disadvantage

Loss of control and co-ordination by head office.

It is possible to envisage each area being completely responsible for all functions. These are independent units with no headquarters services. Usually some activity is centralized, the most common one is finance, as local factors do not appear to have any merit and the economies of centralizing finance appear overwhelming.

3. Product or service

In departmentation by product, a production unit is set up for each good and service. It is mainly adopted by large organizations, but can work effectively in smaller ones. Top management can delegate wide authority to a division or plant which manufactures and sells a product.

Advantages

(*a*) Aids specialization of men and machines.

(*b*) Co-ordination may increase and customers be given better service.

(*c*) Responsibility for profit can be introduced, by setting a standard for a product department with the manager responsible for most of the functions involved.

(*d*) Management is given a wider responsibility. For example, responsibility for a section of a retail store could be given, where all aspects are controlled by one person (i.e. buying, selling, personnel, etc.). It is not usual for *all* functions to form part of product grouping. Usually finance and industrial relations are centralized, central control being deemed imperative.

4. Customer

This may be found in sales departments which have various types of customer, e.g. large and small customers, or wholesalers and industrial buyers. One could envisage, in the extreme case, a bank's having departments specializing in commercial loans to, say, the fruit industry, and dividing each customer group so that each, e.g. apple growers or orange growers, was represented by one department.

The advantage of this method is mainly that it caters for customers of different needs and brings benefit of specialization.

The disadvantages arise in co-ordinating departments.

5. Process or equipment

The purpose here is to achieve economies by grouping activities around a process, or type of equipment which cannot be made in economical small units and must therefore be costly and specialized. The boot and shoe industry is divided into six main divisions of the process of production, e.g. checking, closing, press cutting, lasting, finishing, glossing and cleaning.

Advantages

(*a*) Similar types of equipment and labour are brought together.
(*b*) Departments are separated by *clear-cut* technical considerations.

Any separation of activities creates problems of co-ordination and each of the above methods of departmentation have advantages and disadvantages. A rigid structure is not the answer and *more than one* basis for grouping activities may have to be employed in order to achieve the objectives of the enterprise.

F. SPAN OF CONTROL

The previous paragraphs mentioned that a department was a specific area or branch over which a manager has authority for the performance of specified variables. Departmentation was necessary as a single person was unable to manage 'too many' subordinates, i.e. his span of control was too wide. This span of control or, preferably, span of management responsibility is simply the number of subordinates that an executive supervises. It is important to note that the phrase refers to executive or supervisory subordinates over whom an individual has authority, and not to subordinate *operating* personnel. There are of course other factors than the *number* of subordinates to consider, e.g. the *abilities* of supervisors and subordinates.

Spans of control vary widely from two to over twenty. The number varies with such factors as:

(*a*) The nature of the work, e.g. the more repetitive the work, the greater the number that can be controlled.
(*b*) The ability and training of subordinates and supervisors.
(*c*) The degree of delegation exercised.
(*d*) The effectiveness of communications and also physical proximity.

V. A. Graicunas published a paper in 1933 emphasizing the complexity of managing more than a few subordinates. The more individuals that are added to the span of reporting executives, the greater the increase on the number of relationships. He put his theory in mathematical terms for emphasis and calculated that with six subordinates there were 222 relationships, with seven over 490 relationships. The maximum number of relationships is shown by a formula, but this will never be attained in reality. The actual number of relationships is not so important as the demand made upon a manager's time, and how frequently they occur.

The problem then arises, that, if the span of control is *restricted*, information must then be carried through *several levels* of officials for decision and then back downwards in the form of instructions. This may cause undue delay and lead to the label of 'red tape' being given.

Extremely tall or flat structures are the exceptions and usually growth is directed so that the dimensions are kept in reasonable balance. An important objective of organizational planning should be *simplicity*, this helps communications and can reduce overhead costs.

G. TYPES OF ORGANIZATION STRUCTURE

Four types can be considered for analysis—line, staff, functional and committee. It must be noted that the idea of types of organization serves little useful purpose. Terminology in this area is very confused—functional, for example, has come to mean the same as line and staff in some areas. Modern scholars are critical of formal organization structure and believe it creates a feeling of dependency on the part of subordinates, and stifles initiative.

1. Line organization

This is a type of structure consisting of direct vertical relationships connecting the positions at each level with those above and below. These line relationships are the channels through which authority flows from its source to points of action.

This structure forms a basic framework for the whole organization. The other types of structure are, in effect, modifications of it and must rely on it for authoritative action. It is usually depicted on charts by solid lines connecting the positions.

Line relations or direct or executive relations are those existing between a senior and his subordinates at all levels of command. The senior's instructions are to be complied with as authority is direct.

2. Staff organization

When organization is small, so leaders can effectively direct and control, line structure is usually adopted. All major functions therefore must be performed or supervised by the owner.

As business grows, time must be allocated among many functions and those which the owner prefers are more efficiently performed. The others will sooner or later be given to specialists and their abilities can be included in the organization by applying concepts of (*a*) staff or (*b*) functional structures.

Staff structure occurs in two forms, staff assistant and specialist. The staff assistant performs his work subject to approval of his superior, he has no formal authority to command actions of others and acts in the *name of his superior*.

For example, an assistant to the general manager takes over functions the general manager can do least well. The scalar chain is not lengthened, and the assistant performs work which is subject to the approval and support of his chief.

Staff specialists are a modification of line structure. The structure consists of departments manned by staff specialists, who assist the line, e.g. industrial relations.

It is worth noting that a line commander cannot ignore his superior's staff officers, as the staff officer's suggestion will usually result in formal orders being issued by the line manager's superior. The personnel function has often been regarded as staff. In practice, industrial relations departments have often taken over responsibility for hiring, firing, union negotiations and grievance settlements.

Staff relations arise from such appointments, the staff assistant assists the executive to whom he is allocated, but has no executive authority of his own and acts on behalf of his superior. Often he represents his chief, when he may assume 'representative' authority and responsibility.

3. Functional organization

This type of structure is a method of relating specialists to the line organization. It is necessary to preserve the coherence of specialized sections through the various levels in the organization without subjecting them to control by line managers at the various levels. For example, a personnel manager, in a branch, reports direct to the plant manager, but in personnel matters he is also supervised by the head office personnel officer. Divided loyalties may arise on some questions and it is essential that clear-cut distinctions be made about the rôles and scope of the two supervisors.

Functional organization is often applied to systems where functional managers are responsible for certain activities and are given *substantial executive authority*. Functional departments may, with the authority of general management, set programmes and standards with which operative departments *must* comply.

Functional relations arise when a specialist contributes a service to the line managers, who are the organization executives. This specialist is often called a 'functional' officer, and he has responsibility to see that his special activities are effectively carried out throughout the organization. He advises 'line' colleagues and is responsible for assisting line managers.

If he has a staff of his own, the relationship is then 'direct.' Service, advice and direction are given, but the functional post must not interfere with the application of the operating manager's authority along the line of command.

Lateral (*horizontal*) *relations* are those existing between executives or supervisors at the *same level* of responsibility and holding equal authority. Such co-operation is necessary to aid efforts to reach organization goals and when this relationship operates between executives or supervisors they should act with the knowledge of their line supervisors. This is known as Fayol's 'bridge theory.' There are two types: (*a*) *colleague* relationships, which are those between managers in the *same* department who work together under one superior; and (*b*) *collateral* relationships, which exist between managers in *different* departments and serve to discharge responsibility more effectively.

Neither line nor functional types exist separately in their pure form in most firms. A third type exists, whereby the main operational activities are in a 'line' pattern, but there are specialized activities of a non-operational nature for which a senior executive is responsible and his staff will have relations to him of a line nature.

4. Committee organization

Committees are a controversial device of organization. They consist of a group of persons to which some matter is committed. Some undertake management functions, e.g. policy making; others do not, e.g. operating committees. Some make decisions, others deliberate but do not decide, some have authority to make recommendations to a superior, others are formed purely to receive information without recommending or deciding.

Ad hoc committees are usually temporary, as they are created for a specific purpose, or to solve short-range problems, rather than for administrative purposes. If they are established as part of the organization structure, with specifically delegated duties and authority, they are called *formal.*

Advantages of committees

   (*a*) Actions and ideas of related company units are co-ordinated.
   (*b*) Communications are improved. (See p. 102.)
   (*c*) Judgement and executive talents are pooled and full use is made of specialization.
   (*d*) Responsibilities for decisions are shared, rather than borne by a person.

Disadvantages of committees

(*a*) They are often a waste of time or resources, especially if there are unsatisfactory compromises, or delay by a few members.

(*b*) Executives may hide behind committee decisions and avoid responsibility for their individual actions.

Confusion as to the nature of committees has arisen because of the variation of authority assigned to them. They therefore should have a clear purpose and be effectively led.

Types of committee

(*a*) Board of directors. (See section on Direction.)

(*b*) Works committees; e.g. joint productivity, accident prevention.

(*c*) Cost reduction; usually having representatives from various sections.

(*d*) Joint consultation; see p. 290 in chapter on Personnel.

(*e*) Budget committee; for use where budgetary control is operating.

H. MODIFICATIONS TO STRUCTURE OF ORGANIZATION

1. Matrix organization structure

The idea originated from aero-space technology where this type of structure was used for specific projects. Examples of projects where it is used today are—development of a new product, building a factory.

A more flexible and adaptable system was needed to achieve project objectives. The matrix organization attempts to merge traditional line authority for decision-making with a project-orientated, multi-disciplinary, team-based approach.

Personnel from functional departments are assigned for the duration of the project. *Project* managers define *what* has to be done. *Functional* managers determine *how* to do it. The project manager must integrate the work of functional departments and the project teams. Members of the project team agree to accept the authority of the project manager for the duration of the project. It is interesting to note that more 'senior' persons than the project manager may be in the team. Conventional vertical authority relationships are now changed and day to day working problems may have to be agreed or *negotiated* (Fig. 10).

Project management aims at achieving specified performance within an agreed time scale and budget. The work of the project manager starts at the *procurement and specification stage* where details of performance, time and cost are needed describing ways of meeting the specifications. Every aspect of the project is defined, e.g. quality and reliability, weight, power etc. Other points to consider are design, tendering, manufacture, construction, etc., right up to post-sales services.

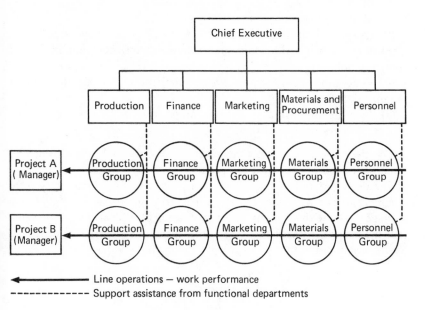

Fig. 10.   Matrix organization structure.

Knowledge required by an engineer for the post of project manager includes a knowledge of the legal bases of contracts as well as professional experience.

After procurement and specification stages, there is the *tender* for the contract, which states how performance and achievement is to be demonstrated. Then a *programme* needs to be compiled (network analysis is used, see p. 136); activities are planned in the right order and departments receive orders in minute detail. Finally there is the *progressing* aspect which needs fast and accurate reporting back of forecasted and actual stage activities.

Advantages

(*a*) Better control of project; greater security.
(*b*) Better customer relations, and higher morale of staff.
(*c*) Lower programme costs, and higher profit margins.
(*d*) Shorter project development time.

(*e*) Aids the development of managers, as the work includes wider responsibilities.

Disadvantages

(*a*) More complex internal operations.

(*b*) Lower staff utilization.

(*c*) More difficult to manage and possible inconsistent application of company policy.

(*d*) Functional groups may neglect their job and let the project organization do everything.

(*e*) Too much shifting of staff from project to project may hinder training of new employees.

The degree of the project manager's authority and relationships to functional departments must be specified.

The degree of authority given to the project manager may vary from company to company and therefore it is very important for the project manager to have the backing of top management. It is also wise to ensure that the project manager reports to at least the same level of management as the functional heads.

Requirements of a good project manager

(*a*) Ability to select and organize a team of persons with a variety of skills.

(*b*) Ability to smooth out difficulties between specialist groups and present facts clearly to management.

(*c*) Ability to understand the nature of technical details.

(*d*) Ability to run meetings and communicate effectively.

(*e*) Ability to deal with contract documents and negotiate with customers.

Project management can be considered an outcome of applying systems thinking on organization.

2. Working groups

There are various types of group working, some are fairly similar in nature, others have quite distinct features. Matrix or project groups have already been discussed and Boards of Directors and Committees are considered elsewhere in the book. Other types of group working are dealt with below.

Group technology

This is a method of organizing small-batch or multi-product production processes so that specialist machines on the shop floor and their operators are grouped into cells. Each cell containing various machines which perform *all* of the operations on a 'family' of products (e.g. drilling, turning, and grinding). This compares with the more usual arrangement where machines are grouped into large shops, each shop containing only *one type* of machine.

Advantages include:

(*a*) reduction of delivery times and delays and reduction of stock and working progress;
(*b*) easier progress chasing and control of quality;
(*c*) social benefits from group working.

Disadvantages include:

organization problems, e.g. adapting payment systems; structure of management and control of stocks.

Autonomous work groups

A great deal of attention has been given to experiments in group working on *assembly line* production. These groups can also be formed in continuous process industries. It is often said that workers on production lines have such a monotonous, boring job that they are dissatisfied, even though other benefits are satisfactory, e.g. wages, welfare, etc. Sometimes it is forgotten that some workers may *not* want to work in groups, obtain recognition, or exercise autonomy. Surveys among workers on flow-line production rarely show that more than 25 per cent are dissatisfied with their jobs. This does not mean that changes to group working may not prove beneficial to most workers as well as management.

Motor-car producers, Volvo and Saab, have not entirely abandoned flow-line working, what they have done is provide for job enrichment (see p. 284) through the addition of certain changes in the work organization.

In chapter 1 it was stated that one must be careful in considering implementing ideas found to be successful in other countries as cultural differences may be so great. Bearing this in mind, some of the *factors to be considered* before going ahead with this idea are shown below.

(*a*) There must be a strong desire for participation by workers, and a positive co-operative attitude.

(*b*) Management must be forward looking and believe in worker participation.

(*c*) There must be a suitable industrial relations mechanism to ensure effective negotiation and consultation.

Benefits from group working include:

For management

(*a*) Group can accommodate labour absenteeism, and turnover of labour is reduced.

(*b*) The more flexible system can deal with frequent changes in production requirements and helps to ensure effective working inter-relationships.

(*c*) Easier to set standards and targets because fewer units are involved.

(*d*) Aid to training newcomers to group.

(*e*) More effective communication and less supervision.

For members of group

(*a*) More variety for individual through job rotation.

(*b*) Possible 'social' satisfaction because of belonging to group.

(*c*) More autonomy in planning is allowed than if an individual.

(*d*) Sharing of responsibility means it is not so easy to blame an individual.

General *disadvantages* are:

(*a*) As added responsibilities are given to workers, if work is transferred from supervisors it may mean the supervisors are no longer needed!

(*b*) Some workers *resist* changes to structure of jobs.

(*c*) Workers may ask for *increased wages*, to compensate for their utilization of further skills and their flexibility and their assumption of greater responsibility.

(*d*) Some unions consider that the power of collective shop floor action may be lessened.

A number of *implications for managers* can be noted if group working becomes more widespread at *supervisory and management levels*. Specialists form part of a team on a project and they may often make decisions and advise their group without reference to their superior; also if the group agrees on a course of action advocated (by say the accountant in the group), it may be very difficult for a senior accountant to alter that course of action. The implication is that specialists in lower levels of the organization may have more autonomy.

Another implication is that specialists in groups will have to have a wider knowledge of other functions and this needs consideration by those responsible for training. A greater knowledge of group behaviour is also needed and this will be considered later.

Clover-leaf structure

This is a newer type of organization structure advocated by B. C. J. Lievegood in *The Developing Organisation* (1973, Tavistock). It has been described as a project management approach applied to the *whole* organization, making use of the ideas of systems thinking and the need to consider worker satisfaction.

In the following diagram the Board of Directors can be seen at the centre co-ordinating and linking with four main areas of organizational management.

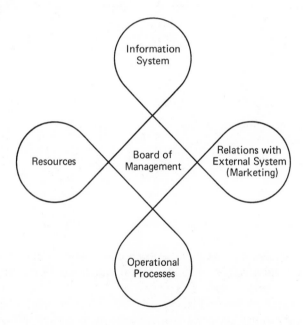

Fig. 11.   Clover-leaf organization structure.

The Board of Directors is not at the *apex* of a pyramid. Directors have interests in all areas and identify overall objectives and policies to carry them out. The importance and practical effect of this new approach will be looked upon with interest.

Circular organization structure

In the book *The Systems Age* (1974, Wiley) Ackoff advocates a structure based upon the hierarchical system, whereby managers at each level work with an *associated board*. This board would be responsible for policy and evaluation of the managers' performance. The composition of each board was the immediate senior manager, who would be chairman, the immediate subordinate managers and the manager himself. It can be seen in the diagram below that every level would have representation on the board of the immediate superior.

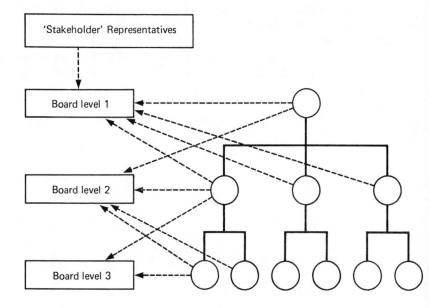

Fig. 12.   Circular organization structure.

A further suggestion was that the top board should contain representatives of stakeholders, i.e. in addition to shareholders—customers and suppliers, investors, public and employees. Ackoff claims this would enable employees to have wider opportunities for participation and allow the organization, to a greater extent, to serve the purposes of its members and its own purposes.

'Linking-pin' structure

Rensis Likert, in *New Patterns of Management* (1961, McGraw-Hill), recommends an overlapping-group form of organization structure in which a 'linking-pin' function is performed to integrate activities of the various sub-systems in the organization. Each supervisor or manager is a member of *two* groups at the same time, e.g. a managing director who is also head of his department. He is a member of the *higher level* group and also a member of his *own group*. He is a linking pin, joining groups together and serves as a channel of communication and influence.

I. AUTHORITY AND RESPONSIBILITY

Authority in the context of organization and administration of a business enterprise has been defined in a number of ways. H. Fayol regarded it as 'the right to give orders and the power to exact obedience.'

H. A. Simon regarded it as 'the power to make decisions which guide the actions of another.'

Research findings in this area of power and authority are limited. It is obvious that authority over people can be effective only when they *accept* it. Many instructions are obeyed because of custom, but acceptance of authority may in some cases be ensured only by resorting to the use of power.

Authority is not power. Power is the product of personality in a specific situation. Sir Frederic Hooper in his book *Management Survey* states:

Authority can be delegated; power cannot. Either it exists or it does not. One may invest a person with authority and with responsibility, but one can no more invest him with power, than one can provide him with imagination and understanding.

Authority can be regarded as the right or power to delegate responsibility and it emanates in a company from shareholders to the board of directors, and down the scalar chain.

Responsibility is an *obligation* to use authority to see duties are performed. It is an obligation to perform owed to a person's superior.

Accountability is concerned with the fact that each person who is given authority and responsibility must recognize that the executive above him will judge the quality of his performance.

By accepting authority, a person denotes his acceptance of responsibility and accountability. The person who is delegating requires subordinates to allow their performance to be reviewed and evaluated and holds them accountable for results.

Kinds of authority

Formal authority is conferred by law or delegated within an organization.
Functional authority is based upon specialized knowledge.
Personal authority is based upon seniority or leadership. Another

method of analysis is to show the kinds of authority which correspond to the structure types, i.e. line, function and staff.

(a) Line authority

This authority can be regarded as the main authority in an organization; it is the ultimate authority to decide upon matters affecting others and is the main feature of the superior subordinate relationship. Line authority is not absolute, it must be applied with discretion, within the limits of delegated authority, and must relate to the performance of jobs which lead to the attainment of the objectives of the organization.

(b) Staff authority

Staff authority is not easy to describe. Its scope is very limited as there is no right to command. It is concerned with assisting and advising and is used where line authority becomes inadequate and occurs in all but the smallest companies. Specialized skills are used to direct or perform those activities which the line manager cannot so effectively perform. Staff authority is subordinate to line authority and its purpose is to aid the activities which are directed and controlled by the line organization. A personnel officer, for example, has line authority over his own staff, but he cannot control production workers, even on personnel matters. Examples of staff departments are legal, public relations and personnel; the heads are staff executives who exercise staff authority. It is worth noting that, if these departments did not exist, or were abolished, their functions would have to be performed in the line, where they originally existed.

(c) Functional authority

This type of authority is subordinate to line authority but, in comparison with staff authority, it confers upon the holder the *right to command* in matters relating to the function. It therefore has a limited right to command and helps the superior to delegate authority to command to specialists, without bestowing full line authority. Where organizations have a central head office and branches or divisions, functional authority is often used. For example, a head office personnel director renders staff functions for the whole company, but he usually exercises functional authority on personnel matters in his relationships with branch personnel officers. This of course ensures uniform policy.

It was mentioned previously that the staff specialist gives advice to his line superior. One modification of this occurs where the superior delegates authority to the staff specialist to deal directly with line personnel. For example, where the staff specialist is showing how to deal with labour problems, he may also *consult* with line executives and aid in putting the recommendations into effect.

True functional authority occurs when the staff assistant is delegated specific authority to prescribe procedures and processes or policy to be followed by operating departments. For example, where a finance director is given authority to prescribe procedures and the nature of the accounting records to be kept by the production sales departments. Such authority should be restricted authority. It is possible for some line managers to exercise functional authority over some process in *another line* department; a sales manager may exercise functional authority over aspects of manufacturing, e.g. packaging.

It is often said that most organizations have *line and staff* structures. This denotes the inter-relation of operational and functional responsibilities. But it is not always easy to determine which department is line or which is staff, as some operations do not conform to specific boundaries and probably only by examining the intentions and actions of the person who is delegating can it really be known. Confusion may occur if a staff executive is given implied authority to act in the name of the delegating executive and it may then appear that the staff executive is exercising line authority. Perhaps the degree of closeness to the primary objectives of a company can be used to distinguish between line and staff functions. For example, the closer to basic activities, e.g. production and selling, the more activities are line; assisting activities may be deemed staff.

In view of the difficulty surrounding the definition and operation of *line and staff* it is better not to use such confusing terms.

In considering the limits of authority, an obvious limitation is that action must conform with the policies and programmes of the company. In many cases, specific limitations are made (e.g. not to take on more staff without the approval of a superior). The reason *why* a subordinate accepts a superior's decision has been considered by many authorities. One line of thought is that there is an 'area of acceptance' wherein the subordinate is willing to accept the superior's instructions.

J. DELEGATION OF AUTHORITY AND RESPONSIBILITY

In a previous section authority was seen to reside with the board of directors and to be delegated to the chief executive and down to all those in the company, until they are given the requisite amount of authority to carry out their allotted work.

Delegation is the *process* whereby an individual or group transfers to some other individual or group the duty of carrying out some particular action and, at the same time, taking some particular decision. It means, in effect, entrusting some part of the work of management to subordinates.

Responsibility is not, though, surrendered, as no manager relieves himself of *ultimate* responsibility by delegating. The work is delegated and the superior holds the subordinate *accountable* to him. The subordinate is responsible for *doing* the job, it is the superior's responsibility to *see* the job is done.

When authority is delegated, all it means is that someone has been granted *permission* to do something; the superior must ensure that the subordinate has *sufficient authority* to do the job and that he has been told *how* the authority is to be used. Delegation can therefore be briefly stated to be a process whereby a manager:

(*a*) *Assigns* duties to his subordinates.

(*b*) Grants them *authority* to make commitments to the extent thought necessary to enable duties to be carried out.

(*c*) Creates an *obligation* on the part of each subordinate for the satisfactory performance of the job.

Responsibilities should be clearly defined at all levels before work can be delegated.

1. Reasons for delegation

(*a*) Lack of time or energy.

(*b*) Complexity of rules and new techniques means specialists are needed.

(*c*) Need for training for management succession.

It is noteworthy that a superior cannot delegate *all* his authority, otherwise he passes his position to his subordinate. When a superior delegates he is taking a calculated risk on the abilities of his subordinate. Supervision is needed but should not be too close as this tends to stifle initiative. Many managers fear to delegate because of the possible incompetence of subordinates.

Delegation is therefore an art and the following points should be noted:

(*a*) A manager should ensure that the subordinate accepts and understands what is involved.

(*b*) After giving an outline of the job, the control limits and the desired standards, a manager should leave his subordinate to do the job himself.

(*c*) Checking should be done periodically, and the superior should be willing to listen to the ideas of subordinates.

(*d*) Authority must be given to subordinates, as a manager cannot make all the decisions himself. He must trust subordinates to do their job, and delegate to them those matters which the subordinate is most competent to deal with, even though the manager can make better decisions than his subordinate.

This is an illustration of the principle of comparative costs as applied to delegation. This principle will be understood by readers who have studied economics.

2. Degree of delegation

(a) Cost of decision

The more costly the action to be decided upon, the more probable it is that the decision will be made higher up. For example, a decision to purchase a computer will be made higher up the scale of authority than a decision to buy a typewriter.

(b) Need for uniformity of policy

The greater the need for uniformity, the greater the amount of centralization. For example, there often is a need to treat all customers alike. But too much uniformity means local knowledge is not used and initiative is stifled.

(c) History of the firm

This could be an important factor as there is a tendency to retain decentralized authority, particularly at first, when a firm amalgamates and consolidates with other firms. Whereas, if a firm has grown up from a small group, there is a tendency to centralize. The philosophy of management is also important, for example, Henry Ford senior, the American motor car manufacturer, was very keen on centralization and, wherever possible, made every major decision himself.

(d) Availability of capable managers

If there are few managers of quality there will be less decentralization of authority. The solution here lies in efficient training and decentralization is a good method of obtaining management experience.

(e) Size of firm

The larger the firm, the more complex the organization and the greater the difficulty in co-ordination. Decisions are more slowly reached and therefore more costly; decentralization can reduce this problem.

(f) Controls available

If control techniques are good, management will be keener to delegate authority. If a subordinate can be controlled easily, a manager is more likely to delegate authority to him.

K. DECENTRALIZATION OF AUTHORITY

This is a situation where ultimate authority to command and ultimate responsibility for results is localized as far down the organization as efficiency permits.

If authority is not delegated it is centralized. The two extremes, centralization and decentralization, have disadvantages and in practice a combination of the two occurs.

Centralization refers to the withholding of delegated authority. Decentralization is closely related to delegation of authority and is concerned with what should be transferred down, what policies are needed to guide actions and the need to train and select people and control their actions.

Centralization is sometimes used to refer to centralizing performance where the operation is under one roof or one location. It often refers to department activities, e.g. *centralization* of office services, such as the typing pool. But, where centralization is discussed as an *aspect of management*, it refers to the withholding of delegation of authority and the way authority and decision are dispersed. Decentralization is closely related to delegation, but it includes all areas of management and requires a great deal more than handing authority to subordinates.

Drucker refers to *federal decentralization*; where activities are organized into separate product businesses, each having its own market and responsible for its own profit or loss. They are, in effect, independent operating units. The other type is *functional decentralization* whereby units are set up with total responsibility for distinct stages of the business. This type is generally applied to management organization, but has certain weaknesses, as the narrowness of outlook inherent in functions and standards set cannot easily be linked to objectives of the business.

Federal decentralization has many advantages, particularly the ease of managing by objectives, whereby the efforts and results of managers and units are easily assessed.

Production and sales are often the first functions to be decentralized and finance and personnel the last.

The degree of centralization to be adopted is not easy to determine. Some decisions must be taken locally and management must decide what are vital decisions and keep these, then delegate the rest (e.g. a price change is a vital decision).

The *degree of decentralization* may be said to be greater where:

(*a*) The greater the number and the more important are the decisions made lower down the hierarchy.

(*b*) Less checking is needed on a decision; especially if few people need be consulted on a decision.

(*c*) The greater the number of functions affected by decisions made at lower levels, e.g. a company which allows financial decisions to be made by branches are invariably greatly decentralized.

Decentralization should not be blindly applied as the size of operations and their complexity may not warrant it. Dangers arise from non-uniform policy and the difficulty of control the more a unit becomes independent, and the whole of the specialized services, e.g. accounting and statistics, of headquarters becoming duplicated, resulting in high cost and less efficient services.

A final comment on this question is that the best balance between centralization and decentralization may *vary in various periods in the firm's history*. The newer the company, the more the need for centralization at first to establish common policies. Once managers know the tradition of the company they are more likely to think and act in the company's way when they are in charge of decentralized units.

L. ASSIGNMENT OF ACTIVITIES TO DEPARTMENTS

Earlier in the chapter it was noted that activities could be grouped in various ways. Another problem is, which activities to assign to each functional department or to a customer, territory, or product department? Activities have to be assigned or moved, and some activities may not be so easy to classify, e.g. should transport be assigned to production or marketing departments?

Guides to assignment of activities

(*a*) Some managers who have a special talent and interest for certain activities may be assigned these activities, especially in the early stages of a company's growth.

(*b*) Those activities which are mostly used by a department may be put under departmental control. This is a simple, logical method, whereby, for example, a production manager, who uses transport for raw materials, for handling in the factory, and for transfer to a warehouse, may be given charge of transport.

(*c*) Activities may be assigned to those departments which will best ensure the attainment of the objectives of the company. For example, the credit control section may be considered best allocated to the accounting department as it may apply company policies better than if control were given to the sales manager who may adopt too liberal a policy.

N.B. Some activities overlap department boundaries and often the same equipment is used by more than one department, but divided control does not work effectively so a choice has to be made as in point (b) above.

(d) Co-ordination of activities is essential and the *point of co-ordination* may be a guide as to the method of departmental integration. For example, if sales, advertising and warehouse sections all report to the marketing manager, these sections may comprise one group.

Organization structure, therefore, greatly aids co-ordination of activities. It is important to note that the *reasons* for co-ordination may vary from executive to executive. The converse to the above must also be considered, where an inspection department may be under the production department and this may mean pressure on inspection not to be too rigid in interpretation of standards, in case production output suffers from too many rejects. By making inspection report to the design department manager, who sets the standards, one may overcome this problem while maintaining quality. The principle here is that an activity must not be assigned to a department whose activities it checks (often called the separation principle).

The above are only guides. Good judgment is required to select from alternatives. The *stage of growth* of a firm is important, as small firms may find the guides difficult to implement in some cases, as economies of specialization may be difficult to achieve. As firms grow, emphasis changes on activities and organization structures need to be altered. The final guide should be the assignment of activities in such a manner that the objective is achieved in the most effective way.

M. AIDS TO ORGANIZATION DESIGN

Many tools, methods and techniques are available and it is essential to place them in their proper perspective. Their value depends upon the skill used by the executive in their selection and application. Relationships can be formalized and communicated to the members of an enterprise in the following ways.

1. Records

If these are kept over a period of time, they give the background picture which can help organizational change. Similarly personnel records enable an accurate evaluation of personnel to aid determination of job selection. In addition, *reports* can be used to see if there are any defects in organization structure. (See p. 114.)

2. Organization charts

No diagram can effectively convey the reality of executive responsibilities or functional inter-relationships. Organization charts are an *endeavour* to record the formal relationships in an organization, showing some of the relationships, the main lines of communication and the downward flow of authority and responsibility through all the levels of the management hierarchy.

Advantages of records and organization charts

(a) *Thought* is needed in constructing charts, as this exercise forces executives to think more specifically about organizational relationships.

(b) Records and charts provide *information* to people who wish to know about the enterprise and are useful in instructing new personnel on company organization.

(c) They form a basis for organization change and by projection into the future can aid the evaluation of organization planning as strengths and weaknesses can be observed.

Disadvantages

(a) They soon become *out of date*.

(b) *Human relationships* cannot be shown on paper, even when they can be defined and described.

(c) They introduce *rigidity* into relationships, as people tend to keep within their charted area and become too conscious of boundary lines. (This is one reason why the American Chrysler Corporation deferred using organization charts for a long time. They wished to encourage the crossing of lines of authority and to retain flexibility.)

(d) *Costs* of preparation, storing and studying charts may be more than their benefits are worth.

(e) They introduce *status* problems. People may not wish comparisons to be made between themselves and others. (The writer recently asked a personnel manager why his company had no organization chart. He replied in one word, 'Politics.')

If the above disadvantages are considered carefully most of them can be overcome and, if the charts are carefully compiled, kept up to date and regarded purely as an *aid*, they can be of assistance to management.

There are certain conventions which are generally in use in the compilation of charts. Line relationships are shown by a continuous line. A position function or unit is often enclosed by a 'box.' Sometimes names of personnel occupying positions are also included in the box. Broken or dotted lines are used to denote functional relationships and vertical and horizontal lines link boxes. Figure 13 shows three types of chart.

Vertical charts (A) are a traditional method.

Horizontal charts (B) make use of the normal method of reading from

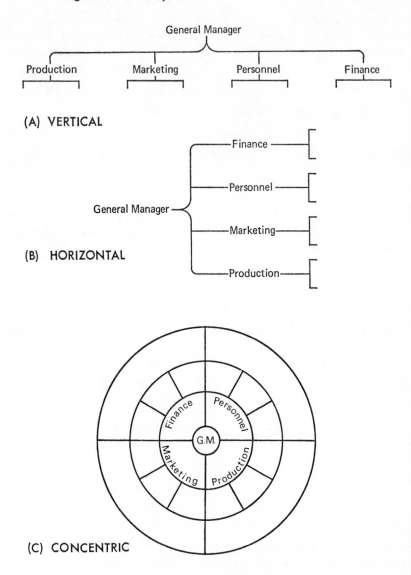

Fig. 13.   Types of organization charts.

left to right and minimize the idea of levels and supe̶rior–subordinate relationships.

Concentric charts (C) consist of circles which indicate echelon levels with the chief executive in the centre. These charts show the dynamic nature of personal relationships and eliminate the status implications of 'above' and 'below.' The distance from the centre indicates the degree of closeness to the chief executive. Sectors show different divisions and no appendages to organization are included.

Organization charts attempt to be a two-dimensional representation of a three-dimensional relationship, and a few recent attempts have been made to portray this third dimension pictorially. This cannot be done on a normal chart, but special planning boards can be used.

An adaptation of all these charts is given in the chart shown in Fig. 14. This chart depicts a consumer-orientated company which sells consumer goods in a highly competitive field through the normal channels of distribution. The phrase 'consumer-orientated' will be discussed in the next chapter on Marketing.

The chart in Fig. 14 has some unusual features:

(*a*) The consumer is placed at the top of the chart, as a reminder that he is sovereign and that it is upon his decision (to buy) that the company's success depends.

(*b*) As the chart is circular, it can be seen that each main department, headed by a director, is closely in touch with the managing director and with adjacent departments. The impression given is of a closely-knit, balanced team.

(*c*) Departments shown are in sequence, showing the flow of information, thought, decision and action.

Market Research feeds facts to the Marketing Department, creating strategy and initiating product planning. The *Design* Department translates product plans into engineering realities—blueprints and specifications. The *Manufacturing* Department translates specifications into finished products. The *Sales* Department then persuades shops to display and stock hoping then that the *Customer* buys.

3. Organization manuals

Some firms have a book or manual which sets out in more detail each position and often includes job descriptions, salaries, relationships, detailed descriptions of activities and duties, responsibilities and functions. It is often compiled by first getting each job holder to fill in a questionnaire. A loose-leaf system is desirable and careful indexing is needed and the manual should be reviewed periodically.

4. Schedules of responsibility

A job title is usually descriptive of the work involved but is inadequate as a *definition* of duties and responsibilities. Schedules are therefore used and the following information is recommended to be noted:

(*a*) Title of job.

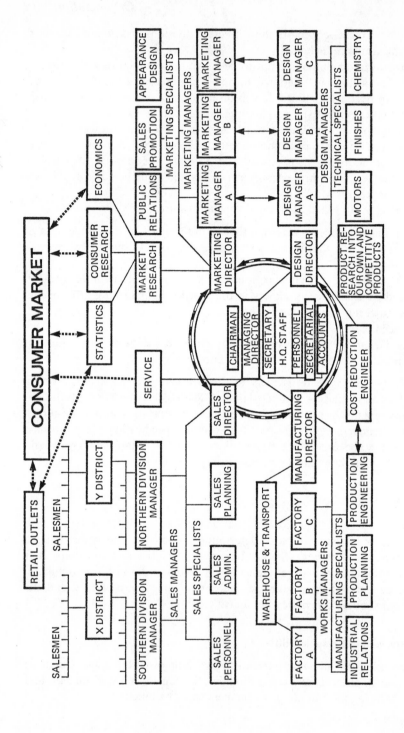

Fig. 14. Organization chart.

(*b*) Date.

(*c*) Code or reference number.

(*d*) Grade of job.

(*e*) Department concerned.

(*f*) An account of duties and an assessment of responsibility carried.

(*g*) Number and nature of employees supervised.

(*h*) Nature of liaison with colleagues.

(*i*) Person to whom responsible.

(*j*) Any special responsibilities.

It should be clear for which activities an employee has executive responsibility and those for which he acts in an advisory capacity. A person should know the limits of his authority, which may be stated specifically, e.g. no authority to purchase equipment over £1000 without reference to a superior.

If the following plan is used to set out such schedules, they will be found to be more easily compiled.

Position Title . . . . .
Responsible to . . . . .
Responsible for . . . . .
Subordinates . . . . .
Special Responsibilities . . . . .
Limitations . . . . .
Code Reference . . . . .
Date of Issue . . . . .
Schedule Reviewed . . . . .

N. ORGANIZATIONAL CHANGE

Changes have occurred gradually, from the methods used by Taylor, to the mechanization and automatic production lines of modern industry. Changes occurred in technology, marketing, and numerous management techniques, some of which were concerned with human problems. Most of the changes were made in a rather disjointed or *piecemeal* manner. The approach emerging today is to use the growing body of ideas and systematic thought to consider innovatory ideas on organization and to adopt a more *systematic* comprehensive look at problems, so that we look at the *whole* instead of looking at *separate parts*.

An individual has a lot of freedom, apart from certain laws of society, but when he joins an organization his freedom is restricted and his effort must be joined with those of others to achieve organizational goals. There can therefore be *friction* between individual and company goals. Some administrative apparatus is needed through which managerial authority is exercised. Therefore a hierarchy is formed which issues policy statements to ensure any discretion that an individual may have in his work is exercised in the spirit or attitude of the company.

The *economic environment* has an effect upon the structure of the organization. The Industrial Revolution brought forth a very competitive, stable environment, and a pyramid structure of authority, whereby a few persons with resources controlled enterprises. This seemed a suitable arrangement for tasks which were basically *routine*. Since then the environment has become less stable and structures are not mechanistic. As science research and technology have grown, there is greater *inter-dependence* between the economic and other sectors of society and particularly between countries (e.g. European Economic Community). All this has resulted in more complicated legal and public regulation and greater competition between firms leading to a merging of resources.

These changes will continue as rapidly as technology changes and firms diversify to an even greater extent. *Other factors* in the change in organizations are:

> The trend of *population growth*, whereby education increases and for example more graduates are employed. The skills in *human interaction* (interpersonal relations) will become more important, because of the need to collaborate in larger projects or concerns.

Further changes in the structure of organization are noted by Alvin Tofler in his book *Future Shock* (1970, Random House). He thinks bureaucracy will be supplemented by a new structure called '*ad-hocracy*' (*ad-hoc* meaning: for a particular purpose). He stresses the need for organizations to respond and adapt to changes in the environment.

The concept of the project team (see p. 62), is considered in depth by two other well-known writers on change in organizations:

E. Trist: In *Matrix Organization*, ed. D. L. Kingdom (1973, Tavistock).

W. G. Bennis: *Changing Organisations* (1966, McGraw-Hill).

The impact of task, technology and structure on the organization

A number of good empirical studies on the above have been carried out in the United Kingdom.

If changes could be made in the *style* of management it can affect the nature of the organization and to this end a number of improvement schemes have been propounded. A brief description will be given here, as they are considered later (under Personnel).

(*a*) R. R. Blake and J. S. Mouton—The Managerial Grid
(*b*) Likert—Systems 1 to 4
(*c*) Management by Objectives
(*d*) McGregor—Theory X and Theory Y
(*e*) Hertzberg—Motivation and Hygiene factors.

McGregor's and Hertzberg's ideas pointed the way towards ideas of more involvement and participation by workers. Blake and Likert are trying to change the style of management and are convinced that when this is done other beneficial changes will occur, e.g. new organizational procedures and structures.

Other forms of organization structure

Glacier Metal Co.

Wilfred Brown argues for retaining the pyramid or hierarchical structure of organization because some persons are better than others at making decisions and as work becomes more complex there are fewer persons able to deal with more involved problems.

Three main features of authority are noted by Brown—managerial authority can: (*a*) veto appointments of subordinates; (*b*) assess their work; (*c*) or transfer them.

Brown advocates a *representative* system of manager and shop floor workers, in the form of a Works Council for each area. W. Brown: *Organization* (1971, Heinemann).

These councils must *unanimously* agree on matters relating to duties and entitlements of members of the company. *No action* is therefore taken if one person disagrees. The management and workers *both* agree not to force any changes, thus strikes are breaches of the constitution and full representation in formulating policies, etc., is allowed together with all information the company can provide.

This structure aims at reducing conflict. There are very clear rôle definitions, a strong managerial line of command and a separate sub-system of consultation and participation.

There are criticisms of this approach to management and although the company's procedures and record of industrial action is good this is no indication that this type of organization could be used with *similar* success elsewhere.

Further, consideration must be given to a series of investigations at the Glacier Metal Company. Continuous analytical observations were made by a team led by Elliott Jacques. They hoped to find the real nature of managerial relationships. *Kinds of work* were distinguished, i.e. managing an operational or primary activity, or specialist or advisory work, and managerial work was claimed to be either partly 'prescribed' or 'discretionary.'

The *prescribed* content contained those elements in which the worker has no authorized choice. This is always specific, e.g. check all documents before posting them.

The *discretionary* content consists of those elements in which the choice is left to the operator's judgement, e.g. adopt the best method of control.

This distinction makes possible a more critical appreciation of managers' tasks and can help to improve their work.

It is upon this discretionary content that people feel the weight of responsibility and this is deemed measurable by finding the maximum period during which a person is relied upon to use his own judgement. The term 'time-span of discretion' therefore refers to the longest period that can pass before a superior makes an effective check on a person's work. This theory has two important implications, one regarding *delegation*, the other regarding a realistic *wage basis* for all workers. As far as delegation is concerned, if a superior has a clear idea of a subordinate's time-span of discretion and his level of responsibility, he may feel he can delegate *more freely*. The subordinates will be more ready to accept their assignments knowing the differentials are fair and reasonable and that they are remunerated accordingly.

Scott Bader Ltd

This company has been owned collectively by the employees since 1951. The company in Northamptonshire was a market leader in polyester resins with a turnover of about £5 million in 1970.

Any employee over 18 who has worked in the company for over one year can join Scott Bader Commonwealth Ltd; this is a company limited by guarantee and owns all shares in Scott Bader Company Ltd.

Employees can participate in policy making through the Community Council which can make recommendations to the Board of Management on company policy.

Points to note are that there is increased opportunity of participation in policy making; common ownership; more autonomy for work groups, and, by introducing more project groups, a weakening of line management structure.

Whether this company has been 'successful' or not is not easy to say, but the absenteeism and strike record is very good.

The company's Code of Practice makes interesting reading (see p. 47). A question to consider is—could the company exist if it was not commercially successful—even though they have agreed to share available work in a downturn of trade?

Finally, it is worth considering two interesting research studies on organizational analysis. In 1958 Joan Woodward (in her book *Industrial Organization: Theory and Practice*) supported Drucker's analysis of the different organizational needs of *different types of production processes*. Her investigations of 100 firms showed that, when grouped into types of production, i.e. flow, batch and single units, and process, the successful firms each had a *similar* pattern of organization which was *related to the technical methods* employed.

Burns and Stalker published, in 1961, a study of companies, *The Management of Innovation*. The electronics industry, which was in a period of rapid change, was compared with a routine producer of rayon filament yarn. The comparison suggested that the *amount* of change affecting the organization influenced its flexibility. Two types of management system were described, 'mechanistic,' which is suitable for stable conditions, and 'organic,' suitable for changing conditions.

Briefly, in the *'mechanistic'* type of management, everyone knew his job and its limits, little consultation was needed and work flowed through clearly-defined channels. Management in such stable conditions can be treated as a mechanical structure.

The *'organic'* type of management had flexible work boundaries and there was more consultation and interaction with others and less command. There was a greater sense of freedom and a great deal of lateral communication compared with the 'mechanistic' type.

This report and others, make it clear that there is *no one ideal form of organization*. Burns and Stalker noted that most structures lie *between* the two extreme types, some companies containing elements of both and may change from one type to another, depending upon their stability. Furthermore, it was management's responsibility constantly to review their objectives and aims and adapt the organization structure suitably.

O. ORGANIZATION AS A SYSTEM

Traditional theorists attempted to devise an organization which would allocate and co-ordinate resources efficiently. Various positions were given authority and responsibility to accomplish tasks. Stable structures, e.g. military or public bureaucracies, were taken as guides. Certain principles of organization were considered which were aimed at establishing clearly lines of authority and relationships:

(*a*) Specialization of task, led to departmentation and division of labour.

(*b*) Scalar principle, established hierarchical structure and refers to vertical division of authority and responsibility with duties assigned along the 'scalar chain.' This emphasized the supervisory–subordinate relationship with authority and responsibility flowing vertically from the highest to lowest levels. Organization charts today still illustrate this principle.

(*c*) Authority, responsibility, accountability, unity of command and span of control, complete the main ideas of traditionalists.

Line and staff functions as we have seen are traditionally the basis of differentiating managerial activities. This enabled activities of specialists to be integrated. As organizations became more complex, *staff rôles* have become more important. The idea of line having command authority and staff only advising, is not always true, as the expertise of *some* staff rôles may be considered a source of authority in organizations. This occurs when staff have functional authority, e.g. industrial relations department has functional authority over aspects of personnel practice in *all* departments. An interesting point is made by Etzioni in *Modern Organisations* (1964, Prentice-Hall) where he mentions that the rôles of staff and line may be reversed in certain areas, for example, in hospitals, research laboratories and universities. A main factor in the change in staff and line form relates to companies who are in changing or dynamic environments and who find it more difficult to accept the traditional approach. The more stable the environment, the more acceptable is the traditional approach.

An organization can be considered as a single *system*. It is an open system, i.e. open and in interaction with its environment. Traditional theories were closed-system views, because they considered the system concerned was self-contained, concentrating upon the internal operation of the organization and believing it could be suitably analysed *without* reference to the external environment.

An open-system view recognizes that the social system is in a *dynamic* relationship with its environment, whereby *inputs* are received, trans-formed and *outputs* are passed on. This is a continuous cycle. (Figure 2 on p. 25 can be referred to again here.)

E. L. Trist and his associates at the Tavistock Institute hold the view that the organization can be viewed as a *socio-technical system*. Organiz-ation is the structuring and integrating of human activities around various technologies. The inputs to and outputs from the organization are affected by various technologies, but the effectiveness and efficiency in using the technologies is determined by the *social system*. The various approaches to organization and management tended to emphasize parts of the system (i.e. sub-systems); for example, the technological sub-system or the social sub-system. The importance of other sub-systems was not considered in the old approaches. The modern approach views the organization as a structured socio-technical (open) system which considers *all* of the sub-systems and their interactions between each other and the environment.

The older approach has *rigid* boundaries defining the areas and these are a barrier to interaction between people within the boundary and those outside. Management must link the various sub-systems together to ensure integration and co-operation, acting as a boundary agent between the organization and the environment. The area of contact between one system and another is called an *interface*.

Emery and Trist in *Management Sciences* (1960, Rerga Press) suggest that the idea is for an organization to reach a state where the system remains in dynamic equilibrium and can adapt to changes in its environ-ment; this is called a *steady state*. In social organizations, managers are working at the boundary of the system (interface), trying to maintain a state of *dynamic* equilibrium between the system and the environment which is constantly changing.

REVIEW QUESTIONS

Organization

(1) What is meant by formal and informal organization?
(2) Are there any accepted principles of organization?
(3) Outline the findings of recent studies on the different patterns of organization to be found in this country.
(4) Consider the methods of grouping functions and tasks and their advantages and disadvantages.
(5) 'The span of control principle is unimportant.' Discuss.
(6) Describe the types of organization structure.
(7) What factors determine the delegation of authority?
(8) Are there any guides to the assignment of activities to departments?
(9) 'Organization charts serve no useful purpose.' Discuss.
(10) What is meant by the phrase 'Matrix Organization'?
(11) What benefit is it to study the systems approach to Organization?

BIBLIOGRAPHY

Organization

Ackoff, R., *The Systems Age* (Wiley, 1974).

Argyris, C., *Intervention Theory and Method. A Behavioral Science View* (Reading, Mass., Addison Wesley, 1970).

Barnard, C. I., *The Functions of the Executive* (Cambridge, Mass., Harvard University Press, 1938). Chapters 6–9.

Beishon, R. J., and Peters, G. (eds.), *Systems Behaviour* (The Open University Press, Harper and Row, 1972).

Brech, E. F. L., *Organization: The Framework of Management* (London, Longmans, 2nd edition, 1965). Chapters 5–8.

Brown, W. B. D., *Exploration in Management* (London, Heinemann, 1960). Chapters 10–15.

Child, J. (ed.), *Management and Organization* (Allen & Unwin, 1973).

Clark, P. A., *Organizational Design and Planned Change* (London, Tavistock, 1971).

Cleland, E. I., and King, W. R., *Management, Systems Approach* (McGraw-Hill, 1972).

Drucker, P. F., *The Practice of Management* (London, Heinemann, 1961). Chapters 16–18.

Gamson, W. A., 'Power and Discontent,' in Bennis and Thomas (eds.), *Management of Change and Conflict* (Penguin, 1973).

(For Review problems on Organization, please refer to end of chapter on Control.)

4 Direction

In order to direct subordinates, a manager must lead, motivate, communicate and ensure co-ordination of activities so that enterprise objectives are achieved.

A. NATURE OF DIRECTION

A simple definition is that direction entails ensuring employees do the jobs allotted to them. All firms use the combined services of human beings, who must be directed, through communication and orientation, to carry out assignments with the utmost co-operation. Working relationships are involved at all levels and these must be governed to see they are effectively executed. Proper motivation is needed to encourage them to work and various techniques may be used to this end.

1. Principles of direction

(a) Harmony of objectives

There must be harmony between the objectives of a subordinate and those of the firm. This may not be easy to attain, as goals may not be *identical*, but, if individual motives can be directed to achieve group goals, the work is easier. The aim should be to see if the subordinate's needs can be satisfied and at the same time contribute to enterprise objectives.

(b) Unity of command

This refers to the need for subordinates to be responsible to only one superior. F. W. Taylor did not do this, as he allowed eight foremen to give orders to one worker. If one person directs, it is easier to co-ordinate plans and select the best techniques to be used to achieve group goals.

Direction is aided by delegation of authority. Orders may be issued formally or informally, and may be general or specific. They should be all enforceable by the employment of sanctions. Delegation can be regarded as a more general form of direction than issuing orders. In some cases *detailed* authority may be granted (e.g. to do a specific job); in others it may be *broad* (e.g. to discipline subordinates). It will of course be broader at the top of the pyramid of organization and more detailed towards the bottom.

The personnel function (see chapter 8) usually deals with the method of introducing and informing newcomers in the ways of the firm. The supervision of this orientation should be done by management. The subordinate should know his own job, its scope, purpose and position in the organization; the methods of control used, how jobs inter-relate and what facilities are available to help him (e.g. service departments). This is a constant job using all methods of communication to aid co-ordination of activities. Managers, as well as subordinates, must come under this plan of orientation.

2. Board of directors

The directing authority is a person, or a group of persons, who represent the owners and who bear final responsibility for the formulation of basic policy and the direction of enterprise. In a public company the board of directors is a committee elected by shareholders and responsible to them.

(a) The duties of a board of directors

These duties comprise:

(i) Laying down general policy and broad sectional policies.

(ii) Seeing legal requirements are met and the company is operating in accordance with its Memorandum and Articles of Association.

(iii) Sanctioning capital expenditure and the method of disposal of profits.

(iv) Ensuring sufficient capital is available and maintaining an efficient system to control the affairs of the company.

(v) Appointing a managing director and seeing he creates a sound structure, maintains co-ordination among the chief executives and develops good morale.

The board is vitally interested in the appointment of the senior managers, and determines their salary structure and the nature of their 'fringe benefits.' (See chapter 8 on Personnel.)

The board should also be interested in management succession and in this connexion training schemes for managers should receive their close attention.

(b) Chairman of the board of directors

He is usually elected from full-time members. Often the managing director is also chairman. This term is used to denote a person in charge of functional executives and who is also on the board.

The position of the general manager is not the same, as this term strictly means he is only an executive and has no seat on the board. In practice, most general managers are also managing directors and, for convenience, will be treated hereafter in this way.

It is not considered entirely satisfactory for a managing director to be chairman of the board as he acts as an executive (a manager) on the one hand, and when appearing on the board acts as a director and this may lead to a conflict of interest. If a director is divorced from the duties of managing director he can take a more detached view. The German system shows this 'separation of powers' by having a separate supervisory board, which appoints the actual management.

N.B. The duties of chairman were set out in the previous chapter on Organization and apply to all chairmen.

(c) The managing director

He is appointed by and responsible to the board of directors and often is also chairman of the board. He is the link between the formation of policy and its execution by managers and is responsible to the board for the effective management of the enterprise, within the framework of policy laid down.

Duties of the managing director. The duties of the managing director can be summarized as follows:

(i) He represents the board of directors, interprets policy and ensures it is carried out by all members of the company.

(ii) He formulates programmes to attain objectives and establishes a structure of delegated responsibility to ensure effective control of operations.

(iii) He submits statements to the board and keeps all activities (e.g. design, sales, production, quality, new techniques) of the company under periodical review.

(iv) He sees that staff are content as regards salaries, promotions, etc., and ensures that morale is high.

(d) Appointment of directors

Articles of Association often recommend that directors shall be appointed only if they hold a specified number of shares in the company. This may be a nominal holding or a substantial one: such a share qualification varies widely. The Companies Act provides that a Register of Shareholdings be kept and remain open for inspection. Articles often provide for one third of directors to retire yearly, but shall be eligible for re-election. Upper age limits are often set (e.g. sixty-seven years), this is some guarantee that persons with new ideas will be obtained.

Functional executives, e.g. production and manufacturing section heads, are often appointed directors. Directors are also appointed who have no executive function, these may be full-time or part-time.

(e) Size and composition of boards

Boardroom organization varies greatly in Great Britain, from management by committee to virtually one-man rule. If one person is in command, authority is centralized and unity of command upheld, but problems arise, particularly of succession.

The Companies Act provides for at least two directors in a public company and at least one in a private company. Large firms have many directors, e.g. Imperial Chemical Industries have twenty-four, seventeen of whom are full-time executive directors and seven non-executive directors. In some companies part-time directors are employed and these can bring specialized skill and experience and a more objective approach to deliberations. If too many executive directors are appointed, they may tend to have too narrow a viewpoint. In addition, they may not be able to accomplish the two jobs of managing and directing. As the jobs are of a different character, one person will find it very difficult.

Difference between direction and management of a company

Direction is concerned more with the long-term affairs of the company and the *obtaining* of resources. It is concerned with deciding the *broad* course of action to be followed and then decisions made are operative over a number of years.

Management, by a full-time executive, is concerned with the day to day affairs and the *detailed allocation* of resources obtained. Procedures adopted are more specific than general and decisions made are effected immediately.

A recent survey of the top 120 companies in Britain (i.e. top by market capitalization) showed:

63 per cent have chairmen, who are also chief executives.
21 per cent have part-time chairmen.
11 per cent have three or more managing directors.

Another feature brought out was that compared with many U.S.A. companies there generally was not a clear-cut position as deputy, i.e. someone who would take over in succession to the chairman. General Motors of U.S.A. had a person who moved to chairman automatically; but Imperial Chemical Industries had to choose from their four deputy chairmen plus outsiders. It is preferable for succession to be certain in most cases.

There are companies where most of the directors also hold full-time executive posts and situations may occur when an individual director may feel that *he* is entitled to formulate policy and give rulings on policy, or to interpret a policy decision in his own way that has been made by the board as a corporate decision. This practice could lead to directors in different sections of the company carrying out their own ideas which may vary from the corporate decision.

Boards of directors therefore need to *examine* periodically their own *composition*, as well as the ways they conduct their affairs. This is pointed out very clearly in *Managing for Revival* (1972, Management Publications Ltd.), E. F. L. Brech suggests that boards should reassure themselves of two factors:

(*a*) that the board is so composed that objectives of performance, productivity and profitability can be correctly and firmly set, and policies formulated that can be expected to achieve successful outcome;

(*b*) that the board has a managing director knowledgeable and competent to undertake the programme of action and improvement that will attain the new objectives.

Surveys constantly show that in many companies there are more executive directors than outside directors and the majority of time spent in board meetings is devoted to matters of functional (executive) practice, with little time for strategy and other important considerations.

This distinction, between direction and management can take the form of organizing the board as a two-tier or two-part board. To show which board is senior it is often called a 'supervisory' or 'management' board. This senior board is concerned with devising policies, setting objectives and evaluating results, whereas the second board is responsible for translating objectives into tangible plans.

It is possible for some members to serve on both boards but they may work more effectively if such an overlap in membership is limited. The Fifth Directive of the Council of European Communities (C.E.C.) (1972) recommends a new form of company, for countries in the European Economic Community (E.E.C.). This emphasizes the authority of the supervisory board and goes as far as to recommend that the members of the management 'organ' may be *dismissed* by the supervisory organ.

The majority of directors on boards, especially full-time directors, have a dual rôle which tends to generate *conflicts of interest*. A head of a division, for example, who has to ensure his operations keep up to schedule and keep his men happy, may then move to a meeting of the board which is discussing changes in output and staffing, which could mean harsh decisions are required. The two-board structure would at least give the two rôles to separate persons—the policy board for long-term considerations, the executive board for everyday operations.

The policy board would probably consist of a chairman, non-executive directors and the managing director who would be co-opted to give all relevant information to enable the policy board to make major decisions, e.g. mergers, or large amounts of capital expenditure. Membership of the executive board could consist of the managing director as chairman, and all the heads of functions and divisions, but *no* outside directors.

One major point to consider carefully, is the question of whether the information received by the policy board is sufficiently adequate and *unbiased* for them to make decisions. In the above example, only the managing director is the common member. This could presumably be overcome by holding meetings of the two boards and periodically co-opting executive members to the policy board. As long as the boards (however they are organized) trust each other and operate in an environment where information is freely exchanged, their chances of success will be higher.

3. Worker participation

A starting point in considering to what extent (if any) worker representatives should be on boards of directors is to note the Fifth Directive of the C.E.C. which states that 'at least *one-third* of the members of the supervisory organ shall be appointed by the workers or their representatives.'

There are, though, many ideas as to what is meant by the words *worker participation* so that the comments made by D. McGregor (*Human Side of Enterprise*) are worth quoting:

'Participation is one of the most misunderstood ideas that have emerged from the field of human relations. It is praised by some, condemned by others, and used with considerable success by still others.

'Some proponents of participation give the impression that it is a magic formula which will eliminate conflict and disagreement and come pretty close to solving all of management's problems. These enthusiasts appear to believe that people yearn to participate . . . that it is a formula which can be applied by any manager regardless of his skill, that virtually no preparation is necessary for its use, and that it can spring full-blown into existence and transform industrial relationships overnight. Some critics of participation, on the other hand, see it as a form of managerial abdication. It is a dangerous idea that will undermine managerial prerogatives and almost certainly get out of control. . . . It wastes time, lowers efficiency and weakens management's effectiveness.

'A third group of managers view participation as a useful item in their bag of managerial tricks. It is for them a manipulative device for getting people to do what they want, under conditions that delude the "participators" into thinking they have had a voice in decision making.

'A fourth group of managers make successful use of participation, but they don't think of it as a panacea or magic formula. They do not share either the unrestrained enthusiasm of the faddists or the fears of the critics.'

It is therefore very important to specify exactly what is the main object of any scheme for participation. It is concerned with *sharing* power to allow employees to influence decisions. This may be *specific* (i.e. relating to an *individual*—his career, promotion, remuneration, etc.) or *general* (i.e. representing *groups* of employees who are involved in decisions affecting sections of the workpeople) and may refer to participation in profit sharing, ownership of assets and decisions that affect the career or remuneration of employees.

There are, therefore, many possible levels of involvement in participation. A wide or a narrow approach to participation could range from, on the one hand, little information being given to employees and, where some suggestions are allowed, to decisions being decentralized and employees participating in setting company objectives, worker representation on the board and perhaps eventual transfer of ownership.

There are many ways of devising schemes of participation where management and employees commit themselves to voluntary or legal agreements. The main point to consider is 'what is participation designed to achieve?' It could be considered to be either:

(*a*) to improve the material well-being of employees (e.g. profit sharing and bonus schemes);

(*b*) to improve the efficiency of the company (e.g. to set up works councils, planning and consultative committees);

(*c*) to own the enterprise (e.g. worker representatives on board and transfer of ownership schemes);

(*d*) to safeguard position of individuals.

(It is important to ensure that group decisions do not unduly affect the individual worker's own position to determine his own well-being.)

It was mentioned earlier that *mutual confidence* between management and worker is of paramount importance. If this is not present it is very doubtful if this can be installed by legislation. It requires *employees* to look at the needs of the enterprise as a whole and not to pursue sectional interests, and *management* to believe participation is beneficial to the enterprise, and the employees have a *right* to be consulted and kept informed.

The Fifth Directive of the C.E.C. lays down certain rules regarding the percentage of employee representatives on the two boards (supervisory and management). In the German system, one-third of the board must be appointed by workers or their representatives, or on the proportion of workers or representatives. The Dutch system aims at a balance of representatives from both sides and co-option for the whole supervisory board including any worker representatives. At the present time in Great Britain, the Trades Union Congress and the Labour Party are considering possible legislation, amending the Companies Act to incorporate the idea of the trade union worker-director. They propose a two-tier board with 50 per cent trade union or nominated representatives, 50 per cent shareholder elected directors and an independent chairman on a top supervisory board. A lower board would carry out daily management functions and policies laid down by the supervisory board. No one should belong to both bodies. Opposition to this idea of two-tier boards is from the Confederation of British Industry, who are opposed to anything that they feel will interfere with collective bargaining. They are not actually against the idea of worker participation in principle.

A final comment on this important area which has evolved more quickly in recent years is, that there is a real problem in considering the reason why an individual should be appointed as a director. Is the appointment because of personal qualities, experience and professional abilities, *or* should they be elected to act as *delegates* who represents certain sectional interests? There is a strong feeling that there is a conflict of interests, *gains to employees* may occur at the *expense of customers, shareholders and suppliers*, because the worker representative would have to give priority to the interests of the employees.

B. LEADERSHIP

Leadership is a means of direction. A leader's actions are devoted to helping a group to attain its objectives. *Leadership* is the ability of management to induce subordinates to work towards group goals with confidence and keenness. Leadership also implies that the leader accepts responsibility for the achievement of the group objective and it is therefore essential for trust and co-operation from both sides to be in evidence all the time.

It must be noted that leadership is not synonymous with administrative ability and that numerous attempts have been made to analyse the nature of leadership. One is to contrast authoritarian and democratic leadership.

1. Types of leader

The authoritarian leader gets others to do things by giving them little scope to influence decisions. He uses fear, threats, and his authority and personality to get his way.

The democratic leader seeks to persuade and considers the feelings of persons and encourages their participation in decision-making.

Studies have shown that the democratic method gives followers greater job satisfaction and enables them to co-operate better, but there is doubt as to whether decisions taken under this sort of leadership are better. Recent studies are more doubtful about democratic leadership because outside influences, e.g. government, consumers, exert pressure and, if a leader becomes *too* employee-centred, production may suffer and morale fall.

Leadership can be *formal*, i.e. having delegated authority, and can exert great influence. *Informal* leaders can initiate action, but do not have the same authority. The choice of leader, therefore, should be based on an accurate diagnosis of the environment, i.e. its reality, noting that effective leadership depends upon *many* conditions.

2. Qualities of a leader

No two persons would ever agree on the desired qualities, as almost every human strength or virtue will be quoted. The elements of persuasion, compulsion and example may be considered to be essential to effect leadership. It has also been said that a leader should make it his job to be *known to all* and that it is more important to be *recognized* than to be popular.

Lord Montgomery in his book, *Path to Leadership*, describes a leader as:

> . . . one who can be looked up to, whose personal judgement is trusted, who can inspire and warm the hearts of those he leads, gaining their trust and confidence and explaining what is needed in language which can be understood.

Chester Barnard in *Functions of an Executive* considers a leader should have the following attributes—skill, technology, perception, knowledge, physique, memory, imagination, determination, endurance and courage.

It must be carefully noted that the leadership qualities that are needed in a particular situation are not usually found in any one individual. From this it can be seen that, if a particular vacancy has to be filled, the strengths and weaknesses of the person who is being appointed should be considered, along with those of the people he will be working with.

The successful leader therefore can be considered to be perceptible and flexible and able to act *appropriately*, i.e. in one situation he is strong, in another he is permissive. It is worth noting also that the *formal status* of an individual does not indicate the ability he has to influence others, as such ability is rather a combination of his *position* and his *personality*.

3. Leadership styles

A well-known approach to leadership styles by D. McGregor in the *Human Side of Enterprise* (1960, McGraw-Hill) has been discussed and criticized a great deal. His assumptions of human nature and behaviour were expressed in an analysis of two theories of leadership, called Theory X and Theory Y.

He considered people were being treated to a Theory X approach, which he considered wrong. This approach assumes:

(1) The average person dislikes work and will avoid it if possible.

(2) People therefore must be coerced, controlled and directed and threatened with punishment in order to get them to work towards organizational goals.

(3) The average person prefers to be directed and wants to avoid responsibility, he has little ambition and desires security above all.

McGregor considered this approach was based upon wrong assumptions about motivation and Theory Y was preferred, i.e.

(1) Expenditure of physical and mental effort in work is as natural as play or rest. Work can be a source of satisfaction.

(2) People can exercise self-direction and control to achieve objectives to which they are committed.

(3) Commitment to objectives is a function of the rewards associated with their achievement.

(4) Under proper conditions people can learn to accept and seek responsibility.

(5) Ability to use imagination and creative thinking is widely distributed in the population.

(6) The intellectual potential of the average person in industrial life is only partially realized.

The practical manager can be helped by analysing various approaches to leadership styles, but he must come to his own conclusions and adapt to the actual situation.

Research into leadership by F. Fielder in Ohio, U.S.A., has been summarized in his book *A Theory of Leadership Effectiveness* (1970, McGraw-Hill). Leaders are placed on a scale depending upon whether they are *task-orientated* or *people-orientated*. R. Likert was also involved in these investigations and the findings appear to confirm research by others. These are, when foremen created an atmosphere which contributed to discussion of work problems in a relaxed, natural way, when they had time to discuss personal problems and stand up and support their men, the result showed the workers had a higher satisfaction and low absenteeism.

Research by Fielder can be of practical advantage to managers. He gave advice on what should be the *appropriate* leadership style or behaviour in various situations. He suggested that the extent to which a manager should be democratic or authoritarian in his leadership style related to:

(*a*) The *authority and power* he had in his position as manager (i.e. right to hire, dismiss, reward).

(*b*) The extent and nature of the *interpersonal relations* between the leader and members of the group (i.e. high—as on a conveyor assembly; low or unstructured—as on an investigation, needing wide discretion).

In this *contingency theory of leadership* he suggests that where relations between members and leader are good and the task basically unstructured and the power of the leader weak, his style should be more democratic and considerate. If the converse was the case then a more authoritarian style would appear to be appropriate.

For many years writers have considered the qualities or traits needed for a leader and brief summaries of these are on p. 96. Research into these areas has become more specific, and is not just a listing of personal abilities. Modern trait research is more scientific. These tests have shown that:

(*a*) Leaders show better judgement, they are better adjusted psychologically, they interact more socially than non-leaders.

(*b*) Leaders tend to ask for and give more information and take the lead in summing up or interpreting a situation.

This approach is still not considered really satisfactory. One objection is that the degree to which a person exhibits leadership depends not only on *his characteristics*, but on the characteristics of the *situation* in which he finds himself. A person, therefore, may show better leadership in a hostile situation than in a group which is friendly and co-operative. There are people who arrive at a senior position through their abilities, but these abilities may *not* act to their advantage when they are there. This seems to reflect the approach taken by Laurence J. Peter in his book *The Peter Principle* . . . which states 'in a hierarchy, each employee tends to rise to his level of incompetence: Every post tends to be occupied by an employee incompetent to execute his duties.' He illustrates this by suggesting that usually competent workers became incompetent supervisors, and competent junior executives became incompetent senior executives. The fact is, that there *are* competent persons at the top of each hierarchy, but only because there are not enough ranks for them to have reached *their level of incompetence*. This idea has wide implications, particularly for management training, but must not be considered a universal statement applying to all companies or persons.

Some abilities as a leader may take a person to the top but may not be to his advantage when he is there. From this approach there is a point of view which suggests that in a group almost *any* member may become a better leader if there are circumstances that enable him to perform the needed functions of leadership, and *different* persons may contribute in different ways to the leadership of the group. This implies that leadership is an 'organizational function' rather than a personal quality.

4. Systems approach

A *systems* approach to leadership would regard the leader, the follower
and situation as inter-dependent units, all engaged in the production of
desired outputs, and would consider—what are the relationships involved
and to what extent are they aimed at mutual goals? Several key factors
interact in a leadership–group situation and a modern approach is to
consider that the leader and the group adjust their behaviour dynamically
to each other.

It is not easy to summarize briefly the various approaches, but it appears
that no one type of person, or set of personality characteristics, can be
associated with successful leaders. Factors which were considered important were found by examining the *type of task* personality, whether the
leader is elected or appointed, and any *special* competence of the leader.

Further aspects of leadership will be mentioned in the following
chapters, especially regarding the management of change and the need
for an 'integrator' in modern organizations.

C. CO-ORDINATION

Co-ordination and leadership are intimately bound; as each affects the
other. One cannot achieve co-ordination without effective leadership:
together they ensure that all efforts are channelled effectively towards the
right goal.

Some authorities, e.g. Mooney and Reiley, regard co-ordination as the
first principle of organization. Others—Koontz and O'Donnell—prefer to
regard it as the *essence* of management and regard *each* of the managerial
functions as an exercise in co-ordination.

No matter how a firm is organized, its functions must be effectively
co-ordinated.

1. Definition

Co-ordination is the process whereby the effort of a group is synchronized
so that the desired goal is obtained. Responsibility for co-ordination rests
mainly with the board of directors and chief executive. The need for a
common purpose or goal is imperative as, if there is more than one
purpose in people's minds, co-ordination of effort is not possible.

As people cannot be compelled to co-operate, the right environment for
the exchange of information is required. There are many conflicts which
can arise between management and workers, and these must be smoothed
out and, if, to use Fayol's phrase, *esprit de corps* can be attained, problems
can be more easily overcome. Often departmental interests and goals are
regarded as ends in themselves, e.g. deliveries required to be made by the

marketing department may be considered secondary to the production manager's production programme.

2. Problems in co-ordination

As concerns expand, many functions and activities have to be delegated to many people. In addition, larger concerns tend to have a greater number of specialists.

Co-ordination problems are essentially those of communication which will be dealt with at the end of this section. Difficulties lie in horizontal and vertical communication and a big problem is that when the elements to be co-ordinated are *human* the variables emerging are numerous.

In many firms, *routine* questions are presented to a far higher authority than necessary for the decision. This is not co-ordination and may often be due to the desire of the individual to be noticed.

3. Ways of achieving co-ordination

In order to be successful, co-ordination must not be directed in an autocratic manner, but rather encouraged in a democratic manner, everyone participating in a unified way. It operates vertically as well as horizontally and should be effected at the most appropriate time. In addition to these points, Mary Parker Follett suggested three more factors of effective co-ordination:

(*a*) By *direct contact* between the persons immediately concerned.

(*b*) It must commence at the *earliest stages* of planning and policy-making.

(*c*) It must be a *continuous* process.

It is apparent that everyone is influenced by their colleagues and by the total environment; co-ordination will be easier to achieve if they understand each other's jobs and they will compromise more if information is exchanged. The ideal is for arrangements for *co-ordination* to be such that problems can be *anticipated* and therefore more easily prevented.

As previously stated, co-ordination exists horizontally and vertically, and it is essential for authority and responsibility to be *clearly delegated* so that department heads know the limits of permissible behaviour. It can be appreciated that as more functions are self-contained the number of organizational relationships will be reduced and less co-operation will be required.

If authority *overlaps*, co-ordination generally will be more difficult; but this may be permissible in some cases especially if the objectives of each department concerned were different.

4. Techniques used to achieve co-ordination

(*a*) *Committees*

Committees aid co-ordination in that they:

(i) Pool resources to solve problems.
(ii) Co-ordinate overlapping or conflicting functions.
(iii) Ensure prior consultation and lead to greater acceptance of decisions.
(iv) Enable executives to be trained.

(*b*) *Staff meetings*

These meetings are useful, particularly if they are informal. An agenda is preferable and these meetings should:

(i) Give a sense of unity to the work of the organization.
(ii) Provide an opportunity for subordinates to question superiors and provide a forum for discussion.
(iii) Inform staff of new developments and problems.

(*c*) *Conferences*

These are another method of making a group decision. They aid free discussion and help to improve understanding of company matters and this 'face to face' communication is an important factor in effective co-ordination.

(*d*) *Programmes*

Programmes are instruments of co-ordination, i.e. a timetable, a production programme, enables results to be compared with standards and action to be taken where necessary. These programmes register and communicate decisions, and hence allow them to be delegated.

5. Co-ordination outside industry

There are other areas in which co-ordination is achieved. The Cabinet has various devices to aid co-ordination, e.g. the use of committees (*ad hoc* and standing) and the civil service hierarchy. Some departments are co-ordinating departments, e.g. the Treasury; the town clerk in local government acted as a co-ordinator between specialist departments and chief officers. Under the present system the numerous council activities are effectively co-ordinated by a professional manager who may have a greater effectiveness to co-ordinate successfully than the town clerk; he is called 'chief executive'.

D. MOTIVATION

A large part of a manager's task is getting things done through people; he must therefore try and understand people's motivation.

This aspect of the management element of direction is concerned with inducing people to work to the best of their ability. All aspects of motivation of employees cannot be provided by management as other influences occur *outside* the working environment, e.g. community and family pressures.

Motivation refers to the way urges, aspirations, drives and needs of human beings direct or control or explain their behaviour. It may simply be described as, keenness for a particular pattern of behaviour.

1. Why people work

It is worthwhile taking a closer look at theories of motivation and one approach which is widely known by managers is clearly set out by Abraham H. Maslow in his book *Motivation and Personality* (1970 edn., Harper & Row).

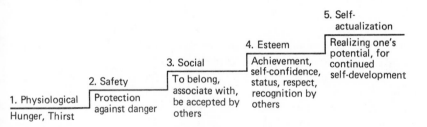

Fig. 15. Hierarchy of needs.

Maslow's theory of motivation claims that human motives develop in sequence according to five levels of need (Fig. 15). This theory assumes needs follow in sequence and when one need is satisfied it decreases in strength and the higher need then dominates behaviour. This leads to the statement that a satisfied need is not a motivator. There is a doubt whether this really applies in practice to the higher needs as it is likely that self-esteem requires *continual* stimulation and renewal.

Few attempts have been made to test the validity of Maslow's ideas. A big problem is that people do not necessarily satisfy higher-order needs through their *jobs* or occupations, and this cannot really be tested. Another point is that he viewed *satisfaction* as a major motivator and this is not *directly* related to production. He also does not mention the time period between various needs—does a person *immediately* turn to a higher need or is it after a few years?

In 1968 Hall and Nougaim studied a company in America and used four of Maslow's need categories (2 to 5 above). The survey of 49 young managers in an organizational setting only provided modest support to his theory, but stressed the importance of environmental factors in the development of a person's needs towards the top of the hierarchy.

It was not until F. V. Hertzberg in his book *Work and the Nature of Man* (1968, Staples Press) presented his two-factor theory of motivation that differences between higher and lower needs were elaborated. Here again the outcomes related to satisfaction rather than productivity. He stated that factors which create satisfaction (satisfiers or motivators) are those stemming from the *intrinsic* content of a job (e.g. recognition and responsibility, meaning and challenge)—these satisfy higher needs; factors which create dissatisfaction (dissatisfiers or hygiene factors) stem from the *extrinsic* job context (e.g. working conditions, pay, supervision)—these satisfy lower needs. An important point in the theory is that as dissatisfaction stems from lower needs not being satisfied, when these are satisfied, this only *removes dissatisfaction*, and does not increase motivation. If the hygienic factors did not reach a certain standard (e.g. salary, working conditions, job security, poor supervision) they felt *bad* about their jobs, and were unhappy. Positive motivation and a feeling of well-being could only be achieved, *not* by just improving these hygiene factors, but by improving *genuine motivators* such as recognition, achievement, responsibility, advancement and the work itself.

The theory has been criticized by other researchers; one criticism is that Hertzberg omitted other behavioural criteria, such as performance, absenteeism and labour turnover, another is that he only concentrated upon satisfaction and dissatisfaction. Researchers since Hertzberg's studies have generally agreed that extrinsic and intrinsic factors do separately contribute to satisfaction.

Another approach recognizes that people will act *only* when they have a reasonable expectation that their actions will lead to desired goals. They will perform better if they believe that money will follow effective performance. So if money has a positive value for an individual, higher performance will follow. This is called *Expectancy Theory*, which places emphasis on performance noting that there must be a clearly recognized goal and relationship between performance and outcome. Motivation (M) is a function of the Expectancy (E) of attaining a certain outcome in performing a certain act multiplied by the Value (V) of the outcome for the performer.

$$M \propto E \times V$$

Outcomes that are highly valued and having high expectations of being realized will direct a person to make a greater effort in his task. Outcomes with high expectations which are less highly valued (or even disliked) will reduce effort expended.

Other studies on expectations on job performance emphasize the greater importance of intrinsic motivation factors, e.g. Hockman and Porter (1968) and Lawlor and Porter (1967), *Managerial Attitudes and Performance* (1968, Irwin). All of these studies show that money, if properly used and tied to performance, can help to increase *motivation*—whether or not or to what extent it increases *performance* can only be surmised.

In looking at the *job* of work, studies agreeing with Hertzberg indicate that to improve the job, it must be enlarged, that is, to make it more interesting, giving more responsibility and discretion for decision-making. But Hulin and Blood (*Psychological Bulletin*, 1968) point to the mixed reaction to job enlargement. They find that many persons *prefer* working on routine jobs and wish to avoid responsibilities, and also that there are great differences between those responding to job enlargement and those who do not. Workers who accept middle-class values (e.g. hard work and achievement) and come from small non-industrial areas are favourable to job enlargement. Whereas those from large, urban, industrialized communities, are alienated from middle-class work values and are not so favourable to job enlargement. (For further consideration of job enlargement see Personnel chapter, p. 233.)

It is not easy to summarize all the research evidence, but it appears that people desire a variety of outcomes, a *combination* of extrinsic and intrinsic. They will respond to a greater degree to jobs which optimize the outcomes, and will try and combine favourable characteristics of each. On balance, job behaviour and satisfaction depend more on the *content* of work than on the conditions surrounding it.

2. Requirements of a good system of motivation

Some requirements of a good system are as follows:

(*a*) Subordinates must be *induced to work* and produce more.

(*b*) A good system must be *comprehensive* in providing for the satisfaction of all needs.

(*c*) The system must be *flexible* in order to account for varying requirements of people who need different stimuli, e.g. some would work harder for more pay; others for status only.

(*d*) Provision must be made for financial *opportunities* particularly those giving more personal freedom, e.g. shares in the company.

(*e*) *Security* is a vital element. It means more than the promise of a job and a wage. A recent survey showed that if people knew the situation in their industry, i.e. where they stood in relation to the firm, and if more information were made available by managers, *morale* would be higher.

The confidence of workers must be won by management and one important factor is the right environment to create the right physiological climate, e.g. equitable arrangement of work flow, rest periods, heating, lighting and ventilating, etc.

Government regulations have helped in this respect (e.g. Factory and Offices, Shops and Railway Premises Acts), and have also, to a large extent, ensured that the primary needs are catered for (e.g. Contracts of Employment Act and Redundancy Payments Act). The working environment is now safer and a person's livelihood is safeguarded to some extent. People now are more interested in secondary needs (e.g. a worthwhile job, good conditions and promotion) and this may be seen in trade union negotiations.

The desire for social relationships is often a neglected consideration. The need of a job which gives a person a respected position in society and enables social relationships to develop is very important and must be recognized by managers.

Basic needs can be attained only if the job is secure; this coupled with a good level of wages is needed. Other needs, e.g. self-respect, group participation, can then be developed. In this promotion, job descriptions (reflecting status), e.g. rodent inspector not rat catcher, all have a part to play. Self-esteem is helped by letting subordinates participate in the work of decisions of the superior. Status can be shown by extra holidays, job title, method of payment (monthly or weekly) (note—there is a trend towards staff status for manual workers), provision of a firm's car, parking and travel facilities.

E. MORALE AND DISCIPLINE

Morale can be a combination of many factors. A simple definition is that it is the state of a person's (or a group's) feelings and attitudes. In a more military sense, it is the *quality* that exists in a group of men, which arises from faith in their efficiency and discipline, and in the competent and fair way with which they are led. A rather broader meaning is given when it is used in business management—it is the collective attitude of workers towards each other, their work and management.

When morale is high, work is done willingly, and with less supervision; when it is low, work is of poor quality and problems arise, e.g. with a high labour turnover and absenteeism. When groups emerge in industry, each person must sacrifice some part of his individuality, as he in effect joins the group to serve the group purpose, thereby (impliedly or otherwise) *agreeing to obey* those who are in charge. Each group has a particular kind of acceptable behaviour, which is implanted in the member's thoughts, and this participation tends to give the members a feeling of superiority over non-group members. Craftsmen often adopt this attitude over non-craftsmen.

Team spirit

If a group can constantly work towards the common purpose, morale can be maintained. The purpose of the *group*, e.g. to win a race, or to produce an article, becomes accepted as the purpose of the *individual*. Individual interests, though, must be subdued to the group interest and, if this can be done, morale will be high. If morale is good, team spirit should be good as this arises where all members of the group know every member is working to achieve the group goal and obeys internal authority. But, if some members are aware that others are more interested in *personal* success, morale will be low and team spirit will be low.

In industry, for example, the manufacturing department may not achieve its target because of lack of material, and the planning department may be blamed. Many similar cases occur daily, in business—morale may be high (as everyone is trying to achieve the desired goal), but team spirit may be low because people (rightly or wrongly) are aware that some members are not pulling their weight.

The remedy for lack of team spirit is to give staff better education and knowledge of the other person's or section's problems and to make them aware of the fundamental inter-relations between departments.

Discipline

A basis for effective discipline is good motivation and sound, clearly-given instructions. It is essential for good communications to be used in order to let staff know what they are required to do.

Ideally, discipline should be based upon co-operation and a high morale, which will ensure rules and conditions are obeyed willingly. By virtue of his position, a superior has the right to command and enforce obedience, if necessary. This gives him the right to punish, because of the harm which may be done to the group's purpose.

Discipline can be obtained by rewards as well as by punishment, but usually punishment is expected if accepted norms of behaviour are not upheld.

Disciplinary action should contribute towards improved behaviour, but certain matters must be noted:

(*a*) Behaviour expected must be *made known* and this is best done in the period of induction.

(*b*) Discipline should be exercised *fairly*, with no favouritism or excessive penalties, and as *soon after* the breach as possible. (Some methods of disciplining are by reprimand, downgrading, suspension, refusing a wage increase, transfer or dismissal.)

(*c*) Management should *not break rules itself*. A good example is essential.

(*d*) The quality of discipline can vary with the type of leadership and the understanding of the common purpose of the organization.

F. COMMUNICATION

It has been said that management is concerned with the way jobs are done *through other people*. Communication therefore is the means whereby people in an organization exchange information regarding the operations of an enterprise. It is the interchange of ideas, facts, and emotions by two or more persons by the use of words, letters and symbols.

Every aspect of management requires good communication but it is particularly important in direction and will be treated in this section for convenience.

It is widely considered that the organizing element of management should concern itself with the system and environment within which communication functions. Management of the communication process requires not only attention to the media of communications, but to the *personal inter-relationships of people in the organization*.

Chester Barnard stressed the need for communication to occupy a central place in organization theory 'because the structure, extensiveness and scope of organization are almost entirely determined by communication techniques.' Communication can be regarded as the foundation upon which organization and administration must be built. Barnard again stressed that 'the first executive function is to develop and maintain a system of communication.'

Communication is a process which links various parts of a system and problems of communication have been divided into three aspects:

(1) *Technical* problems of how accurately the symbols can be transmitted.

(2) The *semantic* problem of how precisely the symbols convey the desired meaning.

(3) The *effectiveness* problem of how effectively the received meaning affects conduct in the desired way.

Cybernetics (see p. 22) has helped to answer problems in group (1) above. Information, in *information theory*, is the quantitative measure of the amount of order in a system. If the properties of a system are known, the maximum rate at which a communication system can transmit information can be calculated. The more probable a message is, the less information it gives and the more uncertain a situation is, then the more information is needed to describe it completely. (See Shannon and Weaver, *The Mathematical Theory of Communication*; 1949, University of Illinois Press.)

As far as (2) above is concerned—that is the meaning a message has to the receiver—a person may *say* one thing but may hear something different, even though the same words were sent and received. A manager must try and check whether the *meaning* of the communication has been understood.

In (3) above, it is usually found that the more *direct* the communication, the more effective it is. The more levels of the organization it passes through affects the action that is eventually taken. So the problem is really to consider how the receiver actually *accepts* the communication. It depends upon his needs, past experience, the complexity of phrases used, the distinction between facts and opinions and the environment in which the communication takes place.

Formal communications are planned to meet the specific requirements of an organization, but informal communications are very important. One informal channel is the 'grapevine,' where rumour passes quickly around. It is not an accurate method, but can be used to the advantage of management at times. It can be considered to serve the social needs of individuals in the organization.

Another approach is to view communication as a pattern of interconnecting lines or *networks*. Examples are as shown on page 110 (Fig. 16).

1. Problems and barriers of communication

The following cover most of the elements in a faulty system of communication:

(*a*) Lack of sound *objectives*, words which are vague, imprecise, omitting necessary information.

(*b*) Faulty *organization*; such as lack of definition of responsibilities, too long chains of command and too wide spans of control.

(*c*) Too many *assumptions* made by a receiver, who may be too quick in evaluating the meaning because of his inability to listen carefully.

(*d*) *Use of technical jargon*, particularly in new specialist fields, e.g. computers. In addition, the *different* educational and social *backgrounds* of recipients do not aid effective understanding.

(*e*) The *atmosphere* or environment may not be normal, and innocent remarks may be given wrong interpretations.

(*f*) Failure by subordinates to *judge accurately* what should be in *reports* to superiors or failure to communicate at all.

(*g*) If every *instruction* is not *written* down, people may use this absence

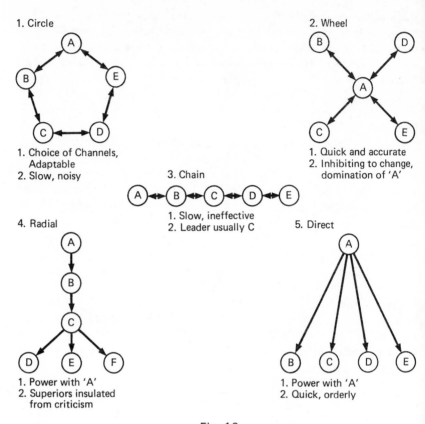

Fig. 16.

of any written instruction and do nothing, using it as an excuse for not using their initiative.

(*h*) *Lack of informal or formal opportunities* is a barrier to upward communication, and feelings are not made known. Management has more ways to communicate than workers, who often have only their union, which generally confines its activities to wages and grievances.

N.B. Appraisal and development interviews are a good means of two-way communication. (See Personnel, chapter 8.)

Barriers to communication can be classified in another way:

(1) *Transmission* problems, distorted messages because of imprecise or inadequate words due to narrow interpretation of specialists. Remedy is to widen understanding of managers (e.g. by job rotation).

(2) *Filtering* or sifting data so only parts are transmitted, to a superior. Good relationships with subordinates, encouragement to them to report problems and a more efficient control system all help to overcome this.

(3) *Irrelevant data* tend to block communication systems. Too much data, too long reports, slow the actions of managers. The remedy is to ensure efficient passing of only relevant, good quality data, by careful sifting.

Communications are aided by good morale. Other points which help are to try and ensure the goals of individuals and the company are similar, and to recognize the benefit to the company of the work of the employees. One of the best ways of removing conflict is by good communications. For example a change to a computer system from a manual one should be explained clearly to employees, well before the implementation. If this is delayed and rumours go round, the issue may be distorted. Good communications can help to minimize conflicts and prevent unnecessary misunderstandings.

2. Principles of communication

The following points should be considered carefully:

(a) Clarity

The language used should be clear and concise, the user should bear in mind the objectives of the communication.

(b) Attention

Attention should be paid by the recipient of the communication—lack of careful attention is a human failing.

(c) Integrity and sincerity

The more workers are told of the company and its future, the more they will respect the integrity of management and morale will be raised and harmony of working encouraged. Any changes should be carefully explained at an early stage. Communications should wherever possible also be sent down the accepted line of authority, because if people are by-passed they lose status and resent the action.

(d) Choice of media

It is important to choose the most appropriate media:

    (i) *Face to face*—for interviews, meetings and conferences.
    (ii) *Oral*—telephone, radio, inter-communicating systems.

(iii) *Written*—letters, books, periodicals, circulars, manuals, newspapers, advertisements, suggestion schemes.

Correct timing is also essential and the use of the right language is vital. In this connexion the use of financial terms is helpful as they form a type of common denominator.

In his book, *Changing Culture of a Factory*, Elliott Jacques considered that the effectiveness of communication does not depend alone upon the executive's skill with language, but rather on:

(*a*) A known and comprehensive *communication structure*.

(*b*) A *code*, governing relations among people occupying various rôles.

(*c*) A *quality of relationship* among people immediately connected with each other.

3. Media of communication

The following cover most of the methods and media used.

(*a*) Company publications

These may take the form of a company magazine or newspaper. But a competent editor is essential and individuals who participate should be as widespread as possible. A definite purpose for the publication is essential.

A handbook or manual can be used to welcome new members. This book should be written in a friendly manner and can be used to explain regulations and interpret rules. It may also give details of company history, organization structure and products and the benefits, opportunities and services which the company has to offer.

Financial information is now more frequently being given to employees to help them to see the results and the position of the company's finances, to understand the company's affairs and stop rumours or misconceptions. The annual reports and accounts may be summarized and presented by charts, graphs, pie diagrams, histograms, etc. These may include sales £1 analysis, sales turnover, return on capital employed; a breakdown of main cost headings, labour costs, depreciation; cost of employee services, reserves and dividend, profit and loss.

(*b*) Notice boards

These should be in a prominent position, e.g. near time clocks. They should have a special section for official notices, e.g. job vacancies, and should be regularly checked to see that old notices are not left on the board.

(*c*) *Pay packets*

Notices can be inserted in pay packets. This must not be done too often as its value diminishes rapidly.

(*d*) *Staff meetings*

These meetings, e.g. yearly meetings to discuss position of company and last year's results, are useful. In addition regular monthly meetings of, for example, first line supervisors can be held.

(*e*) *Suggestion schemes*

Such schemes enable workers to feel they are taking some part in making the company more efficient. They are a channel, a system, for exchanging ideas for changes in organization and are *mainly* a one-way form of communication, i.e. upwards.

(*f*) *Committees*

These are a means of obtaining inter-departmental communication and this type of communication is essential and should be encouraged.

As stated before, in downward communication, management has access to numerous methods; there are fewer methods for upward communication. Horizontal communication among specialized departments is essential, but can cause difficulty as barriers are set up. Strictly communication should be via the line of authority, but use of Fayol's bridge theory is time-saving and more accurate than using the chain of command. But, there must be an understanding that these relationships are encouraged by superiors, that subordinates refrain from making any policy commitments beyond their authority and that they keep their superiors fully informed of all these inter-departmental activities.

Written communications, are more accurate and more carefully formulated and are used for legal records, minutes, contracts, etc. But they may be poorly phrased and are expensive.

Oral communications, are quick and allow questions to be asked if incorrectly understood. Some are a waste of time, e.g. some conferences, and are not suited to lengthy communications. *Note* also that oral transmission is decreasingly accurate; it has been calculated that at the most only 50 per cent of information is retained.

Accurate information is essential and firms should have access to a good abstracting service, e.g. Anbar. The need for a good library service should be considered.

Good techniques are *not enough*, because communication is a co-operative, or two-way process; the attitude of the recipient and his skill in listening and ability are as important as the skill, clarity and accuracy of the manager's words.

(g) *Reports*

There are numerous types of reports. These can be from executives to their seniors, from committees to their appointing bodies, from directors to shareholders.

The function of a report is to present facts and perhaps make a recommendation. The object is to give the person to whom it is presented, sufficient information to enable him to take suitable action, if necessary. Facts must be stated fairly and accurately, be set out in logical order and in a concise manner. Sufficient detail must be given and this may be presented in an attached schedule; what must be avoided is obscuring the main facts by too much detail. Those reports that require a recommendation, as in some organization and methods reports, should show the reasoning leading up to the recommendation. The terms of reference for a report must of course be observed.

One type of report is in a similar form to a business letter. It is addressed to the person asking for the report (e.g. the board of directors). The salutation may be, 'Gentlemen,' and end 'yours faithfully' and be signed; the report should be in the first person.

Other reports may not be addressed to a specific person; these may be written impersonally, as in the case of a committee report, e.g. 'the committee found.'

The salutation and end must not be shown. This is sent with a covering letter to the person requiring the report. This is appropriate where these reports are submitted to a higher authority.

A report consists of the following stages:

Collection of data.
Collection of particulars.
Writing the report.

As far as writing the report is concerned, the custom of the body concerned must be followed, otherwise, the following are good rules.

The title should be clear and brief.

The opening paragraph should state any terms of reference.

Some reports, e.g. an organization and methods report, may give a summary of any recommendations at the beginning.

The body of the report should be set out in clear numbered paragraphs and side headings may be shown.

Recommendations, if required, may be given at the end of each section, or at the end.

The report must be signed and dated.
Appendices, reference and an index may be required.

A *company report* takes the form of the annual report to be submitted with the accounts, it is usually signed by the chairman of the board. The Stock Exchange has asked quoted companies to prepare interim reports on their progress. The report must include information as to the state of the company's affairs, the amount, if any, which the directors recommend should be paid by way of dividend, and the amount, if any, which they propose to carry to reserve.

The report and accounts may be the only information shareholders receive as to the company's activities and results, therefore, careful attention is needed to ensure the presentation of facts so that the average reader can understand. Statements of accounts should be easy to read and may be illustrated by showing a breakdown of information detailed in the accounts, e.g. bar chart or 'pie' diagram.

Finally, a periodic review of all reports is needed in order to see whether it is still required, or whether it has to be modified, continued or scrapped. This is similar to forms control and can effectively be done at the same time.

REVIEW QUESTIONS

Direction

(1) What are the main duties of the board of directors?
(2) Consider the types of leaders and the qualities a leader should have.
(3) Define co-ordination, and consider the ways in which it may be achieved.
(4) What are the requirements of a good system of motivation?
(5) 'Discipline should be based upon co-operation and high morale.' Discuss.
(6) What are the problems and barriers of communication?
(7) Consider the methods and media used in communication.
(8) What do you understand by the term 'worker participation'?
(9) What is meant by 'leadership style'?

BIBLIOGRAPHY

Direction

Black, S., *Practical Public Relations* (London, Pitman, 3rd edition, 1970).
Brown, J. A. C., *The Social Psychology of Industry* (Baltimore, Penguin, 1954).
Drucker, P. F., *The Practice of Management* (London, Heinemann, 1961). Chapters 21–23.

Fielder, F. E., *A Theory of Leadership Effectiveness* (New York, McGraw-Hill, 1967).
Follett, M. P., *Freedom and Co-ordination* (London, Pitman, 1949). Chapters 5 and 6.
Fox, A., *Man Mismanagement* (Hutchinson, 1974).
Hollander, E. P. and Julian, J. W., 'Studies in Leader Legitimacy', in Berkowitz, L. (ed.), *Advances in Experimental Social Psychology* (Academic Press, 1970).
Likert, R., *The Human Organization: its Management and Value* (New York, McGraw-Hill, 1967).
Likert, R., *New Patterns of Management* (New York, McGraw-Hill, 1961).
McGregor, D., *The Human Side of Enterprise* (New York, McGraw-Hill, 1960).
Moonman, E., *Communication in an Expanding Organization* (London, Tavistock, 1970).
Simon, H. A., *Administrative Behaviour* (New York, Macmillan, 1957).
Spence, A. C., *Management Communication—Its Process and Practice* (London, Macmillan, 1969).
Tannehill, R. E., *Motivation and Management Development* (London, Butterworths, 1970).

(For Review problems, see end of chapter on Control.)

5 Control

Control is an element of managerial tasks and involves the measurement and correction of the performance of subordinates to make sure that the objectives of the enterprise and the plans devised to attain them are accomplished efficiently and economically. Control involves:

(*a*) Setting standards.
(*b*) Measuring performance against standards.
(*c*) Feedback of results.
(*d*) Correcting deviations from standards.

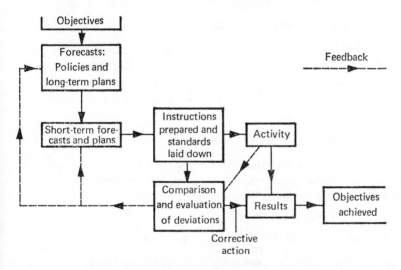

Fig. 17.   Planning–control feedback cycle.

Figure 17 shows the Planning–control feedback cycle and the connexion between planning, with its determination of instructions to be used as directives for activity, and standards for comparison. Control comes from the comparison with standards showing the need for corrective action, and analysis of deviations so future plans can be readjusted. There are many types of control, for example, control of quality of products, morale, etc. There must be, in all cases, clear and unambiguous plans to enable managers to carry them out efficiently and effectively.

Standards are an expression of planning goals and may be of many kinds, e.g. physical (numbers produced) or monetary. Some goals cannot easily be expressed in quantitative form, e.g. morale of a group, and may be measured only in a qualitative manner.

The more jobs move away from the assembly line, the more difficult, and the more important, becomes the control of them.

A. PRINCIPLES OF EFFECTIVE CONTROL

To maintain effective control certain principles must be adhered to:

(1) Controls must be set according to the nature of the job to be performed.

Small firms need different systems of control from large firms. It is important to note that although the same techniques are universally used, e.g. budgets, break-even charts, financial ratios and standard costs, one must never assume any of the techniques can be used in a given situation.

(2) Deviations should be reported immediately.

In an 'ideal' situation, notification is made before deviations occur. In practice, such information is usually supplied too late to be of immediate use, and can be used only for future planning. Electronic accounting machines have speeded up data processing; this will mean more recent data will be available.

(3) Controls must conform to the pattern of the organization.

If the organization pattern is clear and responsibility for work done is well defined, control becomes more effective and it is simpler to isolate persons responsible for deviations. It should be noted here that the correct choice of cost control centres is vital.

(4) Controls should show exceptions at selected points.

The 'exception' principle, whereby only exceptions to the standard are notified, should be adopted. Note must be taken of the varying nature of exceptions, as small exceptions in certain areas may be of greater significance than larger exceptions elsewhere.

(5) Controls should be flexible and economical in operation.

A system should be sufficiently flexible to allow or provide for alternative remedies where failures occur. (See p. 121, flexible budget.) A system of control should not cost more than it is worth. For example, a complete system of standard costing may be installed, where in fact a simpler system would have been cheaper and more suitable.

(6) Controls should be simple to understand and should indicate corrective action.

Presentation of control information in a way management can understand is vital. Some controls, e.g. of a mathematical nature, such as complex break-even charts, are not understood by many managers. In this con-nexion, management training schemes are important, to familiarize management with these techniques. If deviations are detected, this is not very useful in itself. It is essential that the results point the way to causes, e.g. *where* the failures are occurring, *who* is responsible for them, and *what* shall be done about them.

B. TYPES OF CONTROL

1. Budgets as a control device

Budgeting is the word given to the formulation of plans for a given future period, expressed in quantitative terms. Budgets can be stated in financial terms, e.g. capital and revenue expenditure budgets, or in non-financial terms, e.g. units of production.

(a) Purpose of budgeting

Taking the structure of the organization into consideration, one then breaks down the numerical statements of plans into constituent parts; this enables the budgets to correlate planning and allows authority to be delegated without loss of control.

Plans reduced to specific figures show where money is going or where physical input and output have taken place. With this knowledge, a manager can delegate authority more easily in order to make plans effective, within the budget limits.

(b) Method of budgeting

In order to locate responsibility it is necessary to divide a business into areas which coincide with functional responsibility. Examples of normal divisions are: production or manufacturing, selling and distribution, administration, research and development. In addition to functional budgets there must be departmental budgets. The areas selected here should comply with the normal responsibilities of supervisors and are known as budget or cost centres. Department budgets are an integral part of the functional budget. All the functional budgets are then co-ordinated in a master budget.

Co-ordination is essential, and means viewing the system as a whole and harmoniously fitting the various budgets together so that all restraining factors are noted and the policy of the company is followed. A restraining or key factor, for example, may be the fact that finance is in short supply.

The budgets are also used as checks on the actual results of a business. Deviations from pre-determined plans are seen by comparing actual and budgeted performances and costs. The subsequent analysis of the differences or variances and the action taken are a vital part of the control mechanism.

An integral part of the budgetary control is the recognition that performances and costs can be traced to the people concerned, e.g. manager or foreman. In variance analysis an attempt is made to isolate any controllable variances from the budgeted costs; they are controllable if they can be traced to a person or group and if they are influenced by factors internal to the firm.

A system of budgetary control enables members of the management team to work together according to a clearly-defined financial policy and to authorize specific expenditure to executives. Requirements more than the budget would necessitate special authority and would have to be carefully examined. In this way control can be centralized and responsibility and authority delegated.

Where budgeted and actual figures agree, no action is normally required. Only exceptions are reported, thus enabling corrective action to be taken.

The procedures to be followed in designing and operating a budgetary control system vary from business to business, but a brief summary of the usual forecasts which would be made is as follows.

    (i) Sales.
   (ii) Production.
  (iii) Stocks.
  (iv) Costs—broken down into production, administration, selling and distribution.
   (v) Capital expenditure, including research and development.
  (vi) Cash.
 (vii) Credit—debtors and creditors.
(viii) Purchasing.
  (ix) Master forecast, incorporating forecast of profit and loss and balance sheet.

In building up the master budget, alternative combinations of forecasts are considered and note of the restraining factors is taken. These forecasts are possible plans and when they are co-ordinated in the master plan, they become budgets.

The period covered by a budget can vary from months to many years. Obviously the longer the period, the less reliable will be the figures in the budget.

(c) Budgetary control

Budgetary control concerns itself with total costs for each department; each variance is the responsibility of the official in charge of the department in which it arises, he must therefore explain the variance and take action to stop its recurrence.

(d) Standard costing

This is a method of pre-determining the cost of each product, by breaking down the product into each element of cost, i.e. labour, material and overheads. These costs are the standard costs representing what they *should be* under stated conditions and volume of output. The use of a flexible budget allows standard costs to be set for different levels of output.

As the work proceeds actual costs are compared with the standard and the variances (if any) are analysed.

Under suitable conditions, budgetary control and standard costs may be used in conjunction with one another. Planning and control can be more effective if this can be done; one helps to strengthen the other. The *detailed* analysis and control provided by standard costing and the *overall* co-ordination and control of budgetary control can be most effective, if wisely used.

(e) Variable or flexible budgets

These are designed to vary usually with sales or production volume and so are largely limited in application to expense budgets. Expense items are analysed to see how individual costs *should* vary with volume of output. Alternative budgets may be prepared for varying levels of operation, e.g. high or low, each department being told which budget to use.

(f) Points to consider on budgeting

(i) *Too much detail* in budgetary control renders it meaningless and is expensive. Too rigid and too detailed control may mean the cost of budgeting exceeds the cost controlled. Some flexibility of action must be given to managers.

(ii) Budgets may hide *inefficiencies*. If an expense is allowed in one budget, it may always be provided for in the future, whether it is essential or not. As budget requests are usually scaled down, managers often ask for more than they need. A constant re-examination of standards is therefore needed.

(iii) Budgetary controls must not supersede company goals. Department goals may take precedence, as the department budget limits appear very important, but they must not override the main objectives of the company, e.g. sales department should not be refused information because the cost of getting it would exceed the budget of the accounting department. Common sense must not be replaced by strict budgetary rules.

(iv) Too much dependence may be placed upon the budget by management; the scope and limitations must be noted.

(v) *Inflexibility* is a danger, as numerical terms appear very definite. Sometimes certain expenses must be incurred, in excess of the budget, in order to increase profits.

(g) *Marginal or direct costing*

This is a recognition by accountants of basic economic principles—that is, many costs vary in whole, or in part, with volume of output.

A marginal cost is the amount by which aggregate costs are changed if the volume of output is increased or decreased by one unit. It includes direct wages, materials, expenses and variable overheads. Fixed costs are disregarded when considering product cost; these are met by the difference between sales revenue and marginal costs, which difference is called the 'contribution.'

A problem is that some costs are semi-variable and the ascertainment of the fixed and variable elements is not usually easy. The marginal cost approach can help price-fixing, but the difficulty lies in knowing if the estimated changes in revenue expected from a course of action are correct.

(h) *Planning, programming and budgeting systems* (*P.P.B.S.*)

This is a system which analyses and classifies expenditure according to the policy ends the expenditure is to achieve. Government and public authorities do not find it as easy to formulate such precise objectives as industrial and commercial organizations. The output of various government activities is not easily measured or evaluated as no market is involved. Choices have to be made in planning public expenditure and allocating money among various parts of the public sector. The purpose of P.P.B. systems is to provide an improved framework of information analysis to enable decisions to be reached about the allocation of resources and establishing just what a department is trying to achieve.

A sequence of stages begins with:

(*a*) Identification of *strategic problems*.

(*b*) The definition of *objectives* (e.g. the *reason* for services for the aged).

(*c*) Each major objective is broken down into groups of activities or *programmes*, which are identified as closely as possible with policy objectives. Proposed, as well as current activities are to be shown and they should not be constrained by departmental boundaries. An analysis of the programme may involve calculation of financial costs and revenues and possibly cost-benefit analysis. These are aids to decision taking.

(*d*) A budget so formed is called a *programme budget* and may be prepared for a few years ahead. Benefits expected are shown and expenditure on different policy objectives can be compared.

(*e*) The programme plan provides a guide to check against actual performance by *periodical reviews* (usually annual reviews).

P.P.B.S. strengthens decision-making by:

(i) emphasizing *outputs* of programmes rather than inputs and helps to encourage consideration of effective performances.

(ii) As programmes are grouped together to achieve an objective, relationships between departments and also between the authority and outside bodies are highlighted.

(iii) The full cost implications of current and past policy decisions are known and information obtained helps to re-define objectives.

This emphasizes the need for an inter-departmental approach to planning, programming and budgeting.

2. Non-budgetary controls

There are many devices for control which are not directly connected with budgets. Brief consideration will be given to ratio analysis, break-even charts and statistical data and reports, and use of audit, in a wider sense than accountants generally use.

(*a*) Ratio analysis

This term is used to describe significant relationships which exist between various figures shown in the accounts. Ratio analyses can serve many purposes:

(i) They provide a means of showing inter-relationships between groups of figures and can be used as a measure of efficiency.

(ii) They enable a large volume of data to be conveniently summarized.

(iii) They can be used in forecasting and planning.

(iv) They can serve as an aid to communication, as people can more easily see changes in a business.

(v) They can be used to assess solvency, overtrading and profitability.

Ratios must be carefully compiled, presented quickly, bearing in mind the department head who is to receive them, e.g. sales managers will not usually be interested in ratios other than those relating to sales.

Many ratios can be used, and a single ratio by itself may often mislead. Another point is that one cannot assume that standard ratios can be established for all types of business.

There are three main categories of ratios:

(i) *Financial*, or balance sheet, ratios, showing the relationship between items in the balance sheet, e.g. liquid ratio, current and stock ratios.

(ii) *Operating* ratios, derived from the profit and loss account (e.g. turnover and expense ratios).

(iii) *Inter-related* ratios show relationship between the financial and operating ratios, e.g. capital or earnings ratios.

A full description of *all* possible ratios is outside the scope of this book, but the following ratios are in common use.

Return on capital employed (*or primary ratio*). This compares net profit with assets employed and is a reflection of the overall efficiency of the business. 'Capital employed' can have different meanings, but is generally taken to mean the fixed assets and working capital of the unit. Care must be taken in comparisons to note changes in money values over time. A low return may indicate capital is under-employed or that capital is fully, but inefficiently, employed.

Liquid (*or quick*) *ratio*. This ratio is calculated by dividing liquid assets by current liabilities. *Liquid* assets comprise cash in hand and debts realizable easily; current liabilities are amounts due for payment in the near future. This ratio should be at least 1:1 in most cases.

Current ratio. This ratio is often called 2 to 1 ratio. It is calculated by dividing current assets by current liabilities. This shows how much working capital is available. As stated above, the ratio should usually be 2:1, but again this depends upon the nature of the firm (e.g. seasonal trades will have a great variation in liquid resources).

Sales ratios. Sales/Debtors—showing the rate cash is received from credit sales, e.g. if payment is made monthly, ratio would be 12:1.
Sales/Fixed Assets—showing efficiency achieved in using fixed assets.
Sales/Working Capital—showing efficiency achieved in using working capital.

Stock ratios. These may help to indicate efficiency of stock control. Stock problems vary from company to company, e.g. some firms have little work in progress and in job production, there should be no stock of finished goods. Ratios can be only a guide in controlling stocks and some useful guides are:

(*a*) Raw Material/Total Sales Turnover—shows stockholding in relation to amount sold.

(*b*) Work in Progress/Total Turnover—shows stockholding in relation to amount sold.

(*c*) Raw Material/Purchases—shows number of times stock is 'turned over.' The average stock of raw material is divided into total purchases for the year.

Cost ratios. There are many cost or expense ratios. They must therefore be used intelligently and are a useful tool with which to measure relative efficiency. They show the trend of costs in relation to important factors, e.g. sales. Some cost/sales ratios are:

Factory Cost/Sales.
Administration Cost/Sales.
Selling Costs/Sales.
Distribution Cost/Sales.
Research and Development Costs/Sales.

Other ratios. Ratios need not be limited to financial figures as above. Physical quantities may be the basis for calculations. These are used often in standard costing (e.g. Standard Hours of Actual Output divided by Standard Hours for Budgeted Output × 100—this is Activity Ratio). Many others are used.

Published accounts are now showing some of these ratios in the annual report and this trend will surely increase. Trends can more easily be seen and company progress observed over periods of years by using ratios wisely.

The Centre for Inter-firm Comparison (C.I.C.). The C.I.C. is a body established in 1959 to which many firms contribute financial data, in confidence. The centre prepares a brief report which is sent to the contributing firms showing data indicating the average, for the type of industry, and the range of performance of contributors. The information enables management to determine the efficiency of their organization as compared with other similar businesses. An attempt is made to show *why* results vary between firms in similar categories. Great use is made of financial or cost ratios. The Centre:

(*a*) carries out research to enable the best methods of comparison to be made available;
(*b*) offers specialist advice to firms and trade associations;
(*c*) arranges seminars on the use of ratios and inter-firm comparison.

Management can draw conclusions from the figures which may enable it to see the areas where efficiency could be raised. Comparability between firms is not easy to obtain as firms contributing may not prepare their returns in the same way. It is therefore important to define carefully what items are to be included, in what categories and particularly ways of valuing and depreciating assets. Some firms are reluctant to give information in case competitors may use it against them.

The C.I.C. recognizes that too many ratios become confusing as all ratios do not suit all trades and industries, therefore a selection of relevant ratios is taken.

The use of a 'pyramid' structure, showing the ratios in order of importance, is in current use. The most important—the return on capital—being at the apex of the pyramid and the detailed breakdown of how this is determined being shown underneath.

(b) Break-even point analysis

The chart in Fig. 18 shows the relationship of sales and expenses in such a way as to show at what volume revenues exactly cover expenses.

It can be seen that, at a lower volume, a loss would occur and, at a higher volume, a profit.

Break-even analysis is an extension of marginal costing (briefly mentioned on p. 122).

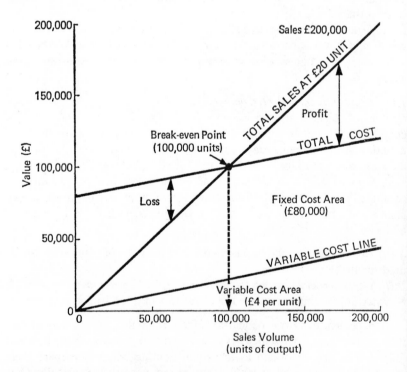

Fig. 18.   A break-even chart.

The break-even point coincides with the volume of output at which neither profit nor loss appears.

Problems which may be solved by break-even analysis

(i) The determination of the price which gives the desired break-even point and profit.

(ii) The volume of sales needed to cover return on capital employed, dividends and reserves.

(iii) The calculation of costs and revenues for all possible volumes of output and the calculation of variable cost per unit.

A few criticisms of chart

(i) As costs do not vary directly in proportion to output, the total cost line should not be shown as a straight line (i.e. linear relationship). The same variable cost cannot be attributed to *each* unit sold.

(ii) The sales–revenue line may similarly be incorrect.

(iii) Each *product* should preferably have its own break-even chart.

(iv) The chart usually depicts *past* results, i.e. it is static.

If these criticisms are borne in mind, the chart (and the many types), are very useful in planning and control as they emphasize the marginal concept. Ratios tend to overlook the impact of fixed costs. The break-even chart does emphasize the effects of additional sales or profits and shows clearly the effects of additional expenses or changes in volume, bringing to the manager's attention the marginal results of his decisions.

(*c*) *Special and routine reports and analyses*

In addition to routine reports and statistical data, special reports are needed.

Data are collected, stored, processed and transmitted and information from all sources is provided for management control. The subject of reports is dealt with in the previous section on Communication. (See p. 114.) Control reports can be functional, i.e. those on department progress; personnel, e.g. staff appraisal; investigations, e.g. on a new machine.

In the section on Office Management, the need to review forms is considered, similarly there is a need to view any report which is of a routine nature.

(*d*) *Control by Audit*

(i) *Internal auditing* is an effective tool of managerial control. The term is often limited to the auditing of accounts. It should be considered in a wider aspect, that is involving the appraisal of all operations, e.g. appraisal of policies, procedures, quality of management. The concept of internal auditing could be broadened as there is no reason why the actions of management should not be audited.

(ii) The term *management audit* has been given to this approach. It can be regarded as a procedure for systematically examining and appraising a management's *overall* performance.

The *object* is to determine the present position of the business by assessing the results of its operations in specified areas, in relation to accepted standards. Imperfections found can then be remedied.

In the U.S.A. the American Institute of Management goes very deeply into audit and lists ten areas of appraisal, and awards points for each area. The results are used to compare the efficiency of various organizations. This goes further than normal ratio analysis. These detailed audits as used in the U.S.A. are not accepted by all, but they do attempt to define the nature and components of management ability.

Appraisers must be qualified in various fields, e.g. finance, production, and such a team should preferably be composed of outside persons, who can be more objective in their assessment of management efficiency. The team would of course be responsible to the board of directors. The team has to define the problems and suggest solutions.

Items to be *appraised* usually include questions on capital and organization structure, management policies and practices. They may cover:

Effectiveness of delegation, channels of communication, effectiveness of organization (e.g. Is organization structure appropriate for its purpose?).

Effectiveness of co-ordination, adequacy of planning and control methods, effectiveness of use of management data, executive competence (regarded as the most important), consideration of company's products and markets (e.g. What products contribute most to profits, etc?).

It can be seen that any method used to put management on a more 'correct' or 'effective' path must be considered and new methods must be carefully considered and assessed, before being dismissed as unimportant or pointless.

C. ADVANCED CONTROL TECHNIQUES

1. Operational research (O.R.)

Management action must be quick and flexible to take advantage of changes in environment; which changes could be economic, political or social. Newer techniques are available to give a more scientific approach to the control of problems. As only a brief outline of these new techniques is possible, readers are referred to the bibliography at the end of this chapter for further books on the subject.

The use of electronic equipment and more accurate programming enables information to be classified so that management can have sufficient information to act quickly. It is, though, necessary to ensure that management knows *how to use* the information and this means that management training must be sufficiently thorough. (See chapter on Personnel.)

(a) Background

Operational research has a military origin. Mathematical theory was applied to army problems, and military applications, such as the optimum convoy size, were the main areas of development at first. Later, it was applied to industrial problems.

A feature which distinguishes operational research from other research and engineering investigations is that it analyses operations *as a whole* and employs people of *various specialities*, e.g. chemistry, logic, mathematics, physics, psychology. It usually uses an inter-disciplinary approach, although most of the present business applications are concerned with mathematical and statistical analyses of the results of possible alternative actions in specific areas.

(b) Approach

Trained researchers, using tools of various sciences, consider a problem and often a conceptual or mathematical model is constructed to represent the system to be studied. There are usually equations or formulae developed to relate important factors of the operations studied. These factors can be mathematically operated upon to determine the effects of changing the value of the variables. One main factor is the *optimization* (i.e. best, highest or lowest) of some criterion. This is a measure by which results can be evaluated, for example, the ultimate object may be net profit, cost, or return on investment.

Techniques and tools used include statistical methods and computers and, in particular, the following have been developed—linear programming, game theory, simulation, sequencing and replacement theory.

The procedure in *applying* O.R. is similar to the steps involved in planning, i.e. formulate the problem, construct a model, derive a solution, test the solution, provide controls for the model and solution; then put the solution into effect.

(c) Definition

A simple definition of O.R. is that it is a scientific method which assesses alternative courses of action in a system, providing an improved basis for management decision-making.

The definition used by the Operational Research Society is more specific:

> The attack of modern science on complex problems arising in the direction and management of large systems of men, machines, materials and money in industry, business, government and defence.
>
> The distinctive approach is to develop a scientific model of the system, incorporate measurements of factors such as chance and risk, in order to predict and compare the outcomes of alternative decisions, strategies and controls. The purpose is to help management determine its policy and actions scientifically.

(d) Position in organization

Existing staff could be trained to operate an O.R. section which when formed, it must be noted, usually acts in an *advisory* capacity. The position in the organization varies and often it is placed as part of the function of production. This may cause friction and a better place is probably to require the section to report direct to a senior executive, preferably the managing director. If there is a management services department, responsibility to the head of the department is usually satisfactory.

Like the organization and methods section (see chapter 9) the O.R. section must be accepted by the staff of the other sections and usually the work it is first given is of a minor nature, with a high probability of success. For example, the congestion at a small unit store, or production scheduling for a single product. This enables confidence to be gained so that wider-ranging, more important, problems can be considered.

Personnel in the team must have a knowledge of O.R. techniques and an understanding of the theory of probability. In addition to knowledge of a specialist nature they must have an interest in management problems and be able to communicate well.

(e) Uses of O.R.

When O.R. was applied to industry, the first problems tackled were mainly in the field of production where measurement was comparatively easy and objectives reasonably clear. It is now carried out in all functional areas, marketing, finance, personnel, research and development, purchasing and overall planning.

The following are brief details of the fields in which O.R. has been used.

(i) *Production*
    Sequences of jobs, machine loading and work scheduling.
    The best 'mix' of products and the correct amounts to produce to maximize profit.

(ii) *Marketing*
    Location of warehouses and factories and retail outlets.
    Scheduling of vehicles, minimizing transport costs.
    Problems of excessive queues at arrival and departure points.
    Stock or inventory control.
    Optimum size and best allocation of a sales force.

(iii) *Purchasing*
    Economic purchasing quantities.
    Decisions to make or buy.

(iv) *Research and development*
    Priorities of projects.
    The life and reliability of projects.

(v) *Overall planning*
    Systems of communication.
    Policies of diversification.

One important point is that particular assignments usually cover one small part of the organization and that any scheme to 'optimize' this small area may not be optimum when taking into account the whole of a firm's operations. This *concept of 'sub-optimization'* is clearly dangerous as the consequence of departmental inter-relations cannot always be fully explored. The recognition of inter-dependence of the activities of an organization is called the *systems* approach and more will be said of this in the last chapter.

(f) Limitations of O.R.

    (i) Lack of mathematical knowledge among managers and lack of managerial knowledge among O.R. men.

    (ii) Can be very expensive to have detailed O.R. analyses and computer usage.

    (iii) Many decisions involve intangible and unmeasurable factors which, therefore, cannot form part of a model. Judgements must therefore be non-quantitative and are more likely to be wrong.

The study of O.R. often follows similar lines and the following areas are chosen for consideration.

Stock or inventory control; replacement policies; queuing or waiting—line problems; competitive strategies (game theory); sequencing problems; linear programming; critical path analysis.

Most of these will be discussed further after the next section on Simulation.

2. Simulation

Before discussing in more detail the various applications of O.R. it is worth considering first the nature of simulation, which people have used for a long time in one form or another. Simulation is now thought of as a branch of O.R. but the origins are closely connected with probability theory.

(*a*) *Nature*

If we abstract from reality in order to create an image this will aid us in thinking about something. If these abstractions are in quantitative form or can be mechanically manipulated, they are called *models*. These are widely used in the physical sciences. Simulation models are used to investigate the facts about a system or compare systems, or examine the relationship within a system and to understand the effect of change.

A *management system* comprises many systems of activities and functions. A knowledge is needed of possible changes on the existing system and such an assessment is not easy as many factors interact. Uncertainty and risk are basic elements in our environment and the ability to detect changes and adapt an organization to minimize adverse consequences and maximize opportunities is particularly valuable. In this connexion, models facilitate effective planning.

A road map is an abstraction from a physical road network; the conditions of roads and the distances between points are shown. Such an abstraction can be of use to some people, but not to others. A motorist would find it interesting, but not a sociologist, who would prefer a *different* type of map, showing, for example, population density. An abstraction is not very detailed and is small, but is more flexible than reality, and enables relationships to be more easily understood. To simulate is to manipulate a model to help us to find out things about the complex systems in reality.

Abstraction is not a new idea. Accountancy systems record results of operations; these are synthesized into financial reports and create an abstraction of one element—the financial structure of a firm.

N.B. An abstraction becomes a model only when it can be manipulated in quantitative terms.

It is worthwhile noting that a group of techniques exist called analytical models, e.g. linear programming. These are not simulation models because:

(i) These systems often contain decisions for which there are not yet mathematically precise rules.

(ii) Information about the system is not *sufficiently* complete.

(iii) As optimization is a main object there is a tendency to over-simplify the *complex* goals in a large management system.

(b) *Examples of simulation*

(i) *Game simulation*
This is part of a competitive model (see 3, below). This is rather a tool of exploration giving an insight into *broad aspects* of problems, and its purpose is rather to produce ideas than quantitative solutions.

(ii) *Training simulation*
The flight trainer, or simulator, has been a great success for training pilots as it reproduces in great detail the conditions and environment of an aircraft flight.

(iii) *Computer simulation*
The availability of computers and the application of mathematics have increased the scope of simulation. Economic models for a country can be built whereby small elements in an economy can be changed and the effect analysed.

(c) *Problems of simulation*

Training and judgement are required in developing systems.

Models may be over-simplified or even over-simulated, i.e. *too many* factors included resulting in loss of flexibility and greater expense.

As the simulation is an abstraction from the real world, the results have then got to be *interpreted back* into the existing real system.

3. Competitive strategies (Game Theory)

This is a branch of mathematical analysis and simulation techniques are used. It is an extension of decision theory where one's choice of action is determined by the possible alternative actions of an opponent who is playing the same game. Usually action is taken by one person after the opponent has made his move, and various rules have been formulated. The *minimax rule*, for example, gives the maximum assurance of a loss not greater than a certain minimum.

Usually in a given situation one can choose a certain mixture of strategies so that, whatever the opponent does, he cannot do better than attain a result which is *calculable beforehand,* and this foreknowledge is very important in such competitive situations.

This theory can be applied where firms are in direct opposition, where any extra customers must come from the competing firm. One example of its use is in the correct timing of an advertising campaign.

4. Sequencing

Briefly, these problems involve deciding what is the best order for tasks in a process to be performed. The order must bear in mind technological feasibility, e.g. plant limitation, regarding the number of machines available. Or to optimize from a particular criterion, e.g. lowest amount of production time per article.

The use of a computer in selecting the 'best' order of salesmen's routes can be seen in chapter 6.

5. Stock or inventory problems

The problem of holding the minimum amount of stock necessary to satisfy production requirements and yet not be too high is a typical problem. Stock control is concerned with the relationship between:

(*a*) Cost of holding stock, i.e. capital tied up, deterioration and obsolescence and cost of warehouse space.

(*b*) Loss of profit in being unable to meet demand through shortage of materials.

(*c*) Amount and variability of demand.

(*d*) Cost of placing order.

(*e*) Discounts obtainable by ordering large quantities.

Models have been developed for different combinations of the above conditions.

Many firms, though, have given insufficient thought to solving this problem and many stocks are far too high. They tend to play safe by keeping high stocks. One reason for this might be that decisions about what are safe stock quantities are *made too low* in the level of the organization, such personnel being afraid to be out of stock.

Statistical methods can be used to evaluate the level of stock needed, while providing an acceptable level of protection. If the delivery period for replacement is short, the percentage of possible out-of-stock items may be calculated and a decision to risk being out of stock may be made, if there is a low probability of the events occurring.

Advanced stock control systems need good sales forecasting techniques to be successful. Research in this field has produced techniques for evaluating errors between forecast values of sale and actual values; these errors are 'fed-back' to adjust the original equations which determined the original forecast value. This is the cybernetic approach, where mistakes made are noted and the system is adjusted automatically.

An example of this is *exponential-smoothing*; where the estimated value of a time series is modified by a proportion of the amount by which it was most recently in error, thus giving a new forecast.

More recently, a method called *Box-Jenkins* has been developed, whereby the forecast adjusts the last observed value by an amount which is the sum of proportional, first difference and cumulative terms. Again, the deviations operated upon are the past errors of prediction and, in essence, the forecast controls itself.

6. Queuing theory

Queues form everywhere. Members of a queue may arrive in a random manner or a prescribed manner, in groups or individually; they may be served individually (as in a dentist's surgery) or in groups (as passengers in a train).

A manager may have a number of people waiting to see him or a storekeeper a number awaiting him to be served. If, therefore, the causes of queue formation can be discovered, a remedy may be forthcoming to save the time wasted.

Queuing theory is a branch of probability theory and has been used regarding serving customers in retail stores, loading and unloading ships in port, setting up a balanced assembly line, where output rates of machines vary.

It is of interest to find the average length of waiting time of the queue and then try to reduce it. Simple queues are solved by many simultaneous equations; more difficult queues by statistical probability and simulation.

Monte-Carlo methods (a branch of simulation) can be used to find the time spent in a queue, by setting up a *model* of the real situation. Variables are selected at random, from tables of random numbers.

7. Linear programming

Programming is concerned with the determination of optimum allocation of resources in complex situations. The use of a mathematical model is to set out the necessary computations, so that the optimum is reached without any limitations being exceeded. For example, one limit in transporting goods is the size of the lorry.

(a) Definition

Linear programming is a technique for determining the optimum combination of resources to obtain a desired goal. It is based upon the assumption that there is a linear, or straight line, relationship between variables and that the limits of the variations can be easily determined.

(*b*) *Examples of problems solved*

It is used in all parts of the transport industry and the fuel industry, where a solution is designed to minimize distance travelled and costs incurred or to maximize profit. (This is a typical resource allocation problem.)

(i) *Transport example*
Assume six warehouses supply four shops. A specific number of barrels are known to be in the warehouses. Orders from two shops are made and road haulage charges are known. The problem is how should managers of the business satisfy the wants of the two shops while minimizing transport costs.

(ii) *Product mix example*
If the problem is to make a type of food of lowest cost, with a protein content of say forty to forty-five units per ton, the many ingredients that could be used and their cost have to be considered. Calculations can be done by computers to determine the lowest cost for a mix of the required protein content. There are similar problems in the petroleum industry to give petrol blendings of the required ingredients.

N.B. There could be more constraints of course than protein content and cost.

8. Network analysis

In the early part of the twentieth century, H. L. Gantt used a chart system which showed time-relationships between 'events' in a production programme. He recognized that total programme goals should be regarded as a series of inter-related plans (or events), that could be followed easily. This simple theme has been developed and some of the new methods show which elements of a plan are the most important or the most urgent.

Many projects of a complex nature, e.g. building a motorway, or the recent Victoria Line underground railway, can be more effectively planned, co-ordinated and controlled by using network techniques. Two common methods are critical path method (CPM) and programme evaluation and review technique (PERT).

They evolved from two different sources almost simultaneously. CPM was developed about 1957 by an American company which wished to improve the planning, scheduling and co-ordination of its new plant construction programme. In 1958 PERT was used to aid the United States missile development programme. Their common factor is that they both use a planning network; they are different in that they include different combinations of facilities. In a simple exposition there is little to gain by differentiating between the two: the term PERT will be used to embrace both methods.

(*a*) *Basic terms*

An *activity* is an operation requiring time or resources which has a definite beginning and end. It is portrayed by an arrow and represents the smallest unit over which control is desired.

An *event* is a significant point of time within the project. It is portrayed by a circle and represents the beginning or end of an activity. No expenditure of resources is associated with an event.

(*b*) *Construction of a network*

The first stage in a PERT control system is to define the project in terms of a network model; this will illustrate the dependencies existing between the activities in the project. Each of the activities has certain constraints regarding its starting time—either they can begin as soon as the project begins, or their start is dependent upon the completion of another activity or group of activities. Clearly, most activities will be of this latter nature (for example, parts cannot be assembled unless they have been ordered and received).

In the construction of a network it is usually best to begin with the final activity in the project and work backwards, determining which activities must be completed before a given activity can begin. Normal PERT and CPM systems require events to be numbered. This facilitates computer processing by making it possible to refer to an activity in terms of its beginning and end events.

(*c*) *Estimating time*

The network, therefore, forms a framework relating important characteristics of activities contained in it. Total project time is very important and in PERT three estimates of the time required for an activity are needed. These are:

'optimistic'—which assumes everything goes well;
'pessimistic'—assuming every possible hindrance;
'normal'—the most likely time.

In the CPM approach only a single time estimate is required. Where there is a high degree of uncertainty, numerous time estimates are needed (as in research and development for which PERT was originally designed). PERT can also be applied to maintenance and training programmes and sales campaigns. Network methods are best applied to the development and achievement of specific tasks, not repetitive work (e.g. flow production).

(*d*) *Procedure in PERT analysis*

(i) List all jobs or activities in a project noting their inter-relationship.
(ii) Estimate the time for each activity.
(iii) Draw the network diagram.
(iv) Analyse the network.

(*e*) *Simple illustration of a network*

Figure 19 provides a simple illustration of a network.

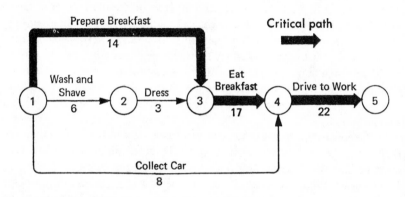

Fig. 19. Simple illustration of a network.

Assume that a person, A, is helped to go to work by his mother, who prepares breakfast, and his sister, who collects A's car from a nearby garage, and that their duties commence when the alarm bell rings in the morning. The ringing of this bell is the starting event and allows the initial activities to begin—i.e. prepare breakfast, wash and shave, collect car.

To ensure that the end result (arrival at work) is reached on time, A must wash and shave, dress, eat breakfast, and drive to work—and we shall assume that he always performs the tasks in that order. Thus he can start dressing only when 'wash and shave' is finished; 'eat breakfast' depends upon *two* activities being completed, preparation of breakfast and dressing. 'Drive to work' is dependent upon eating breakfast and collection of car.

Minimum project time. Time durations can be obtained for the activities and these are—

wash and shave — 6 minutes
dress   — 3 minutes
prepare breakfast—14 minutes
eat breakfast   —17 minutes

collect car   — 8 minutes
drive to work   —22 minutes.

These are inserted on the network.

There are three routes through the network and the times of these routes can be calculated. These are—

1–3, 3–4, 4–5   —53 minutes
1–2, 2–3, 3–4, 4–5—48 minutes
1–4, 4–5   —30 minutes.

The greatest time, 53 minutes, is the *minimum project time* and the corresponding route is the *critical path*, i.e. 1–3, 3–4, 4–5. (*N.B.* Event 3 is reached in 14 minutes; add duration time for activity 3–4, making a total of 31 minutes; and the 22 minutes for driving to work brings the total to 53 minutes, when the last event is reached.)

All activities on this path are *critical* and must be completed on time if the whole project is not to be delayed.

Any *spare time* available in performing other activities is called float. Fetching the car, for example, requires 8 minutes and may be performed at any time within a period of 31 minutes (i.e. 14 + 17). The difference between 31 and 8 is 23 minutes and represents *float*. Also, washing, shaving and dressing takes 6 + 3 = 9 minutes and there is a float of 5 minutes between this total and the 14 minutes needed to prepare breakfast. A could stay in bed 5 minutes more and still be ready when breakfast was; the time along the critical path would not be affected.

This *knowledge of float values* is therefore very important where resources are limited. For example, if the car could not be collected because the sister was ill, the mother could, after preparing breakfast, collect the car herself and still the car would be ready for A by the time he had eaten breakfast (14 + 8 = 22 minutes; there are 9 minutes to spare before the 31 minutes to event 4 elapse).

These principles can be applied to thousands of activities and, usually, when more than about 100 activities are involved, a computer is used. Finding the critical path will identify those activities which must be completed on time to avoid project delay. Progress can be *reviewed* by comparing achieved figures with original estimates of durations, and a systematic use of float values ensures that resources are allocated to the best advantage.

In the case of a contract containing penalty clauses the contractor, faced with delay on the critical path, can make an objective choice between paying the penalty and incurring additional costs (e.g. by working over-time). Vital activities can be seen, and so can those activities which may safely be delayed.

(*f*) *Management action*

As typical PERT analyses run into tens of thousands of events, computers are used and vast amounts of data are obtained. Discrimination is therefore essential and a useful method is to pre-define certain events of particular management interest, and give a *summary network* to the managers concerned. The information can also be portrayed in a graphic form by the computer. A good reporting system attracts management's attention to areas which threaten scheduled progress.

If the schedule cannot be met, a new plan is needed, which may require answers to the following questions:

(i) Can sequential activities be performed in parallel?

(ii) Can manpower or resources be diverted from activities with larger float?

N.B. If the critical path is now shortened, there may appear another critical path; contemplated changes may be processed on a computer and this network is now, in effect, a *simulation model*.

By focusing management attention on activities lying on the critical path, management by exception is facilitated.

(*g*) *Advantages of PERT*

(i) Managers are forced to plan in making up a network.

(ii) All departments must co-operate in planning.

(iii) Attention is concentrated on critical elements.

(iv) Control can be immediate and enables corrective action to be taken.

(v) Management is given the ability to plan the best possible use of resources to achieve a goal, within the limitations of cost and time.

(vi) Inter-dependencies and problem areas are revealed which are either not obvious or not well defined by conventional planning methods.

(*h*) *Disadvantages of PERT*

(i) The project must not be nebulous, i.e. it must be specific enough to time accurately.

(ii) It is not practicable for routine planning, e.g. flow production.

(iii) If emphasis is purely on time and not cost, its value diminishes. Certain adaptations of PERT are rectifying this matter. (See PERT/Cost.)

(*i*) *Applications*

Network analysis can be used in the office, e.g. in completing a balance sheet by a certain date and noting the numerous inter-dependent activities, or in the installation of a new accounting system. It can be used for planning and controlling auditing programmes, and on the marketing side it is being applied increasingly to the launching of new products. Some kinds of administrative project—an office move, for example—are well suited to critical path methods.

9. PERT/Cost

The construction and process industries have successfully used a *cost extension of CPM* to determine the optimum combination of manpower and costs to meet a directed project completion date. PERT originally had time as the only relevant factor and the importance of cost was such that it had to be included and this was introduced in 1962 by the American government.

Estimated costs are collected for small groups of related activities. Labour, material and overhead costs are noted and, as the project continues, actual accrued costs for each cost collection point are gathered and revised estimates submitted if needed. Time and cost data are available, enabling management to identify activity groups contributing to over-runs of time or cost. A projection of *manpower needs* for each category of job can be obtained by computer and the number of man-hours needed can be broken down over the months in each category and, if demand for a skill exceeds supply, overtime can be worked, or more personnel hired, or activities can be *re-scheduled*.

10. Resource allocation and multi-project scheduling (RAMPS)

PERT and CPM do not take complete account of resources and often, when a number of projects are being carried out simultaneously, there will be fairly severe restrictions on available resources. RAMPS was developed to tackle such problems. Based on the network model, it allows various restrictions to be placed on resources and copes with the *planning of a number of projects* that need to be carried out *simultaneously*. The aim is to minimize the total cost, by allocating resources where alternatives exist.

REVIEW QUESTIONS

Control

(1) What are the principles of effective control?
(2) Distinguish carefully between budgetary and non-budgetary controls.
(3) What can operational research contribute to effective management?
(4) Give examples of the use of simulation techniques.

(5) What are the main factors to consider in stock control?
(6) What do you understand by queuing theory?
(7) Give examples of the problems solved by linear programming?
(8) How can network analysis aid the optimum allocation of resources?
(9) What is meant by Planning, Programming and Budgeting Systems?

BIBLIOGRAPHY

Control

Battersby, A., *Network Analysis for Planning and Scheduling* (London, Macmillan, 1964).

Broad, H. W. and Carmichael, K. S., *A Guide to Management Accounting* (H. F. L. (Publishers) Ltd, 1965).

Brown, W. and Jacques, E., *Product Analysis Pricing* (London, Heinemann, 1964).

Bursk, E. and Chapman, J., *New Decision-making Tools for Managers* (New York, Mentor Books, 1965).

Duckworth, W. E., *A Guide to Operational Research* (London, Methuen, 1963).

Franks, J., *Corporate Financial Management* (London, Gower Press, 1974).

Grass, M. (ed.), *Control of Working Capital* (London, Gower Press, 1974).

Institute of Cost and Works Accountants, Various publications.

Jones, F. H., *Guide to Company Balance Sheets and Profit and Loss Accounts* (Cambridge, Heffer, 1963).

Lockyer, K. G., *An Introduction to Critical Path Analysis* (London, Pitman, 3rd edition, 1969).

Rose, T. G., *The Internal Finance of Industrial Undertakings* (London, Pitman, 1963).

Smith, K. M., *Critical Path Planning* (London, Management Publications Ltd, 1971).

Woodgate, H. S., *Planning by Network* (Business Publications, 1964).

REVIEW PROBLEMS ON MANAGEMENT PRINCIPLES

(1) Set out in detail the rôle of chairman of the board of directors. Distinguish this rôle from that of managing director. Comment on the practice among medium-sized firms of appointing the same person as chairman and managing director.

(2) How would you apply the principles of organization structure when examining an enterprise? What common weaknesses in organization are found in business? Classify these weaknesses under:

(*a*) Definition of responsibilities.

(*b*) Span of supervision.

(*c*) General management.

(*d*) Functional specialists.

(*e*) Co-ordination.

(3) Chester Barnard said: 'the first executive function is to develop and maintain a system of *communications*.' Discuss this view, dealing in particular with:

(*a*) The common sins of communication.

(*b*) The guiding principles for a manager wishing to improve his communication skills.

(*c*) The nature of communication in a business environment.

(4) One of the *basic principles of planning* is that policies establish the framework upon which planning procedures and programmes are constructed. Discuss what is meant by policies and show how policies are formulated and developed. One broad classification of policies deals with functions of the business—sales, production, finance, etc. Take any one of these functions and give the major policy questions in this area, showing the factors to be considered in making policy decisions thereon.

(5) Many businesses are now engaging in *long-range planning* of their production and marketing effort. Why have they become conscious of the need for long-range planning? What benefits can be anticipated from such planning? In the planning process definite goals must be set in five fields. What are these fields?

(6) Discuss, in depth, the composition of *boards of directors*. Cover the following points in your study:

(*a*) The number of directors on the boards of companies of different sizes, histories and trades.

(*b*) The frequency with which directors are appointed.

(*c*) The considerations to be weighed in making each appointment to the board, and the relative importance of each.

(*d*) The proportions on different boards as between executive and non-executive directors.

(*e*) The extent of the share-holdings of the director.

(*f*) The number of directorships held by individual directors.

(7) There is a danger that a modern manager may become so interested and expert in the art and technique of being a manager as to forget the purpose of the business enterprise he is managing. Discuss this statement with particular reference to the management of specialist functions. There are many possible objectives for a business and many requirements which it must meet. List ten such objectives and/or requirements showing in two cases how you would measure achievement.

(8) Outline the process of *decision-making* in industrial management. Show the stages of the process which will be assisted by the use of an electronic computer. Illustrate with an application to a specific problem in the top management field. What difficulties might arise in practice from dependence on computers?

(9) A company has for many years been trading as a wholesaler of children's toys. The company was founded by Mr X who owns 50 per cent of the shares, the balance of which are held equally by his two sons, who have run the company for the last five years. Owing to the rapid expansion of business in the last two years the sons find they can no longer efficiently organize the detailed functioning of all the departments of the firm.

Outline a scheme for the consideration of the directors of the company (Mr X and his two sons) stating how the company should be organized so that the two sons will retain control over policy and general organization.

(10) Discuss the relative importance of specialist expertise, administrative ability and skill in human relations for a chief executive.

Indicate how these qualities may be developed.

(11) What would be the major factors you would wish to consider if you were drawing up a 5-year corporate plan for *one* of the following organizations:

(*a*) Hospital   (*c*) Bank
(*b*) Car manufacturing company   (*d*) Nationalized industry.

(12) You have been selected to be the first manager of a new department which will commence operations in two months' time. The managing director has now asked you for a report indicating how you mean to set up this new department, especially stating (*a*) the departmental organization structure and (*b*) the objectives of the department.

The new department can be any *one* of the following:

(i) Production   (iv) R & D
(ii) Personnel   (v) Marketing
(iii) Accounts   (vi) Data Processing.

Draft your report accordingly.

(13) Explain whether or not you would expect the work motivation of salaried staff in an organization to differ from that of wage-earning 'shop-floor' workers.

(14) Discuss the following views:

(*a*) Good organizations are living bodies which grow to meet new problems and fresh opportunities.

(*b*) In the best organizations senior executives see themselves working in a circle as if around a table. Leadership passes from one to another depending on the particular task being attacked.

(15) Often, rather than instruct others in detail, the manager's task is to make it possible for them to get on with their job. Explain the implications of this, and give suitable examples.

Does this approach apply to one type of activity rather than another? Is there a case where it will not apply?

(16) What are the functions and responsibilities of a company director? State the particular contributions the board should expect from a non-executive director.

What action may a director take if he is dissatisfied with: (*a*) the policy, and (*b*) the performance of his company?

(17) Discuss the proposition that budgetary control is of limited use to managers in that it:

(*a*) indicates the existence of some problems rather than suggesting their solution;

(*b*) may concentrate on expenditure whilst tending to neglect income; and

(*c*) may direct their energies to activities which do not improve the efficiency of the company.

Part Two
Management in Action

6 Marketing and Sales Management

In small firms the person in charge of marketing may also be responsible for one or more of the other functions, for example, finance. As the firm grows, delegation of certain duties is needed and usually one person is given the responsibility of marketing.

This term should be correctly used. It may be simply defined as—bringing the right goods and services to the customer in the most efficient and profitable manner.

The Institute of Marketing uses the following definition:

> Marketing is the creative management function which promotes trade and employment by assessing consumer needs and initiating research and development to meet them. It co-ordinates the resources of production and distribution of the goods and services; determines and directs the nature of the total effort required to sell profitably the maximum production to the ultimate user.

Effective marketing is the means whereby all the activities of a business are drawn together to a common goal, with the full co-operation of other departments—production, research and finance.

The term sales manager is often used in place of marketing manager. To be more specific the term sales manager should be confined to the organization and control of the selling and distribution activities. The wider duties of the marketing manager can be seen from the following schedule.

A. MARKETING ORGANIZATION AND ADMINISTRATION

1. Schedule of responsibilities of marketing manager

The schedule might include:

(a) Advising board of directors on marketing policy.

(b) Within the limits of policy laid down, the marketing manager will plan and execute all the activities for assessing and creating consumer demand and for the sale, storage and distribution of the company's goods.

(c) As concerns market research, he will keep the market under review, noting the extent of the market, his firm's share and the share of the market held by competitors and all aspects of changing demand.

(d) Sales promotion—advertising and display, pricing policy, discounts and credit terms.

(*e*) Budget preparation—preparation of sales budgets in liaison with production and finance departments.

(*f*) Control of distribution—this involves selection of channels of distribution, warehousing and transport facilities.

(*g*) Control of personnel—in collaboration with personnel manager, selection and training of selling, clerical and warehouse staff.

A more detailed schedule of responsibilities would include an indication of any special duties and possible limitations in his authority, for example: 'the authority of the managing director is required if credit is to be allowed.'

2. Marketing objectives

In selling, most emphasis is on actual sales: in marketing, the needs of the buyer are considered and a product to satisfy these needs should be the aim.

The ideal position could be said to be where the planned volume of goods is produced, which is then sold to give the planned profit.

(*a*) *Marketing policy*

This involves the appraisal of many factors in order to decide the broad principles which the company is to follow. Correct answers to the following important questions are needed:

  (i) What is the nature of competition and the present position in the 'life' of existing products? (See Fig. 25, p. 173.)

  (ii) What are the most effective methods of distribution and advertising?

  (iii) What methods of transport, wholesaling, allocation of sales quotas, sales training and control of personnel should be adopted?

N.B. It is sometimes preferable for a committee comprising heads of production, finance and marketing to determine policy, to ensure complete co-ordination.

(*b*) *Marketing plans*

Whatever plans are made to direct and control the marketing operation, they must be flexible, as there are many outside factors which can easily affect the plans, e.g. government legislation. These plans can be set up for each aspect of marketing, e.g. media strategy, sales promotion, budget appropriation.

Marketing policy should be known by all the staff; this enables them to act in a unified manner with wholesalers, retailers and customers. A firm's reputation is largely built up on its selling policy, e.g. Marks and Spencer's —the lowest price consistent with product quality and reliability.

It is worthwhile considering an example of the need for careful fore-casting. There is a current trend to build hyper-markets on the outskirts of urban developments, where land is low in price and the site is convenient for consumers who are more mobile than in the past. Some of the points that will need to be considered include estimates of:

(*a*) The growth of the country's economy (Gross National Product).

(*b*) Availability of suitable sites and their cost.

(*c*) Changes in spending habits of consumers.

(*d*) Attitude to self-service.

(*e*) Population trends and the rate of urban development.

(*f*) Local plans for road building.

(*g*) Availability of motor transport, especially for housewives.

(*c*) *Public image*

It is important that a company should decide, as an important matter of policy, what type of *public image* is required. To this end, all policies—marketing, manufacturing and personnel—should reflect this overall policy of image. Then a basic public relations policy can be put forward to ensure that the public are influenced to react to the company in the desired way. There are a number of publics, e.g. shareholders, customers, employees (potential and present), suppliers and government. The various 'publics' can be influenced by good public relations to regard the organizations as:

(*a*) public spirited with a civic responsibility,

(*b*) a good organization to work for, or invest in,

(*c*) a company whose products can be purchased with confidence and reliability.

It is also important to increase morale both inside and outside the company. If employees are proud of the organization, its achievements and service to the community, employees must be aided in their daily work. This can, for example, help salesmen to be more confident in their approach to selling.

Effective public relations can also be of help in the promotion of products (see p. 172). The purpose being to back up advertising and to ensure the customers are more favourably disposed towards the products of the company which are to be advertised. So in effect, public relations promotes a company and its products to a wider range of public than normal advertising and sales promotion. There is a problem in trying to measure the effectiveness of public relations as its results may not be too evident or capable of measurement.

Management must ask itself a basic question about the present business of the company and its future plans. A close watch is needed on existing product stages, to consider whether they need to be revitalized, dropped, or new products introduced. The answers obtained will form the basis for product planning decisions for the future profitability of the company. The various elements of product planning have to be modified or changed during the various phases of the cycle, for example, policies for pricing, research and development, market research, packaging, advertising, sales promotion schemes. The right mix of the marketing ingredients is vital.

(d) The marketing mix

This refers to the combination of policies and procedures adopted from time to time by a company in its marketing programme. It involves the integration of the elements of a marketing programme that will best achieve the objectives of a company in a given time period. Success can be measured by a company producing most profit from a mix of the following variables: product planning, pricing, branding and channels of distribution, selling, advertising and promotion, packaging and display, servicing, physical handling, fact-finding and analysis. There are other forces beyond the control of the marketing manager in the short term, e.g. buyer and trade behaviour, the position and behaviour of competitors, and also government action. Each variable intercuts with another, they can be broken down further; for example, distribution may be direct, or through intermediaries, exclusive dealers, part-owned dealers or franchise.

The position of the product life-cycle has an important bearing on the marketing mix. It is therefore important not to ignore the change in marketing strategy when phases 2, 3, and 4 are reached (see Fig. 25, p. 173).

3. Marketing organization

It has already been stated that policy must be formulated in conjunction with finance and production. Proper co-ordination is essential and techniques such as budgetary control are most useful. The actual composition of the sales organization varies greatly between firms. Current trends in marketing organization reflect the following points:

(*a*) Many functions, formerly considered non-marketing, are being assigned to or co-ordinated with marketing, e.g. product development.

(*b*) Market research has assumed greater importance.

Companies which manufacture electronic equipment will have different marketing problems from motor-car manufacturers. If a company is part of a group, individual company policy may be subordinated to group policy. Some firms buy goods for the market, others manufacture goods and then pass them to separate marketing bodies.

Figure 20(*a*) shows a grouping of various specialist managers, under a marketing manager. In large organizations, it may be advisable to appoint product managers, who would co-ordinate marketing activities relating to single products or groups of products.

Figure 20(*b*) shows such a grouping under products. Other groupings can be chosen depending upon, for example:

(*a*) The market—electricity is sold to home and industrial users. Two sales managers may be needed, for home and industrial.

(*b*) Applications of products—similarly, where oil, for example, is used for heating and also for cars, etc., two managers, one for each use, may be required.

4. Marketing philosophy

A principle of the utmost importance is that a firm should be consumer-orientated.

Many firms were, and many still are, production-orientated. After the Second World War, many products were sold in large numbers because of the high demand and little regard was paid to the real needs of the consumer. Later, more firms competed for the customer's money and firms found they had to take heed of the customer's requirements in order to keep, or increase, their hold on the market.

Firms that treat their customers as being of the utmost importance, so that products are made with the needs of the customer in mind, are said to be consumer-orientated.

The application of this principle can be seen in the organization chart in Fig. 14 (see p. 80).

B. ORGANIZATION OF THE HOME TRADE

Goods are produced and must find their way to a buyer. The ideal may appear to be to sell direct from producer to consumer. This is not always possible or profitable, as many factors must be considered. Intermediaries are used in most cases, i.e. wholesalers and retailers.

As can be seen from Fig. 21, the main channels of distribution for manufactured goods are:

(*a*) Direct sales, e.g. sale of a computer to a firm.
(*b*) Distribution to retailer direct.
(*c*) Distribution via wholesaler to retailer.
(*d*) Via agent, wholesaler and retailer.
(*e*) Via agent to retailer.

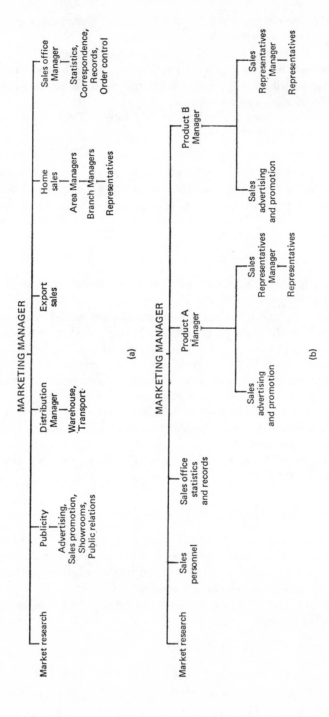

Fig. 20. (a) Organization chart for medium to large company;
(b) Organization chart—emphasizing products sold.

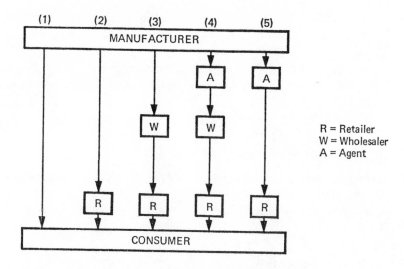

Fig. 21.   Main channels for manufactured goods.

1. Wholesale trade organization

A wholesaler is generally a merchant who buys goods in bulk from manufacturers in his particular trade, selling them in convenient quantities to retailers. By buying in bulk and paying promptly, he can obtain trade and cash discounts from the manufacturers. From these allowances he must provide warehouse accommodation and a selling and delivery service. He tries to obtain a quicker turnover to minimize loss through deterioration or obsolescence. If he keeps too narrow a range, some customers may go elsewhere, so he may stock slow-moving lines to retain their custom.

He delivers at varying times; in some trades he expects cash on delivery, in others he extends credit to his customers. Some manufacturers act as wholesalers and may also buy other firms' goods. There are also large retailers who act as wholesalers for smaller shops in an area, and make a profit by receiving quantity discounts.

Any manufacturer who decides to *omit the wholesaler* must take over his functions. This will mean opening warehouses in suitable areas and engaging more staff. Deliveries may be later than before and only his lines will be sold. It has been found that in many cases the cost to the manufacturers is rarely less than when the original wholesaler was used.

'Cash and Carry' wholesalers

The main features are:

(*a*) Retailers collect from wholesaler's warehouse and provide their own transport.

(*b*) No credit facilities or delivery services are given.

(*c*) The wholesaler has lower occupancy costs as the warehouse is outside the city centre.

(*d*) Retailers pay less for their purchases.

2. Retail trade organization

Figure 21 shows the main retail trading outlets in this country. It is important to note that there is a tendency for these to merge and overlap, e.g. department stores combine to form groups in the fashion of multiple stores.

3. Other trading outlets

(*a*) House to house selling and travelling shops.

(*b*) Voluntary groups, e.g. retailers' co-operatives, such as 'Spar.'

These are independent retail shops, participating in a reciprocal arrangement with a wholesaler to obtain economies of purchasing. Each retailer agrees to take a percentage of the goods from the wholesaler. The tendency is for groups to develop their own lines and brand names. Group advertising is possible, e.g. on television, which would not be practicable for an individual retailer. In addition, services such as shop conversion and help in display are given to retailers.

4. Trading stamps

These are a method used by retailers to attract customers. Stamps are given in accordance with the value of purchases made. The stamps can be exchanged later for gifts by a trading stamp company. The retailer buys the stamps in bulk from the stamp company and distributes them. They can be regarded as retail sales promotion on a long-term basis. The *cost to the retailer* is approximately 2 per cent of his turnover, plus time spent in distributing them. It is expected that increased turnover will more than pay for the cost of the stamps.

Retailers who do not issue stamps may find they lose custom to competitors who do issue them. Many independent grocers saw stamps as an opportunity to offer a counter-attraction to the lower prices of the supermarkets and chain stores.

Today, many retail outlets issue stamps. This means increased sales may not occur and the trader must pay the cost of the stamps from reduced profits. He cannot easily withdraw if his competitors are still issuing stamps.

Supermarkets took up stamp trading as a means of offering customers a discount without breaking the Resale Prices Act; some have now abandoned stamps in favour of giving straightforward price reductions. Some large companies campaigned vigorously against stamp trading, e.g. Sainsbury.

The Trading Stamps Act, 1964, was passed to control stamp issues and the regulations therein must be observed by all stamp issuers.

5. Resale price maintenance

Resale price maintenance is the practice whereby a manufacturer fixes the price the retailer is to charge the customer. The passing of the Resale Prices Act, 1964, was intended to restore competition in the distributive trades and keep prices down.

The Act:

(*a*) Renders *void* any condition imposed by a supplier for the maintenance of a minimum resale price, unless the supplier has claimed exemption for the class of goods concerned.

(*b*) Renders *unlawful* any withholding of supplies from a dealer on the ground that he has sold or is likely to sell the supplier's goods at less than his fixed or recommended resale price, unless he has sold them as 'loss leaders.'

It is recognized by the Act that, for some goods, price-cutting may be to the detriment of the consumer, e.g. making it difficult for the retailer to provide an efficient service. So a supplier may register a class of goods with the Registrar of Restrictive Trading Agreements and, until the Restrictive Practices Court examines the applications and orders otherwise, the goods will be exempted from the provisions of the Act. Exemption will only be granted if the supplier can show:

(*a*) Public detriment would otherwise result.

(*b*) There would be a reduction in the number of varieties or quality of goods, or number of retail establishments, or in necessary sales or after-sales service, or increase in danger to public health, or an eventual price increase, outweighing the detriment arising from a continuance of Resale Price Maintenance.

N.B. The Act does *not prohibit* the fixing of maximum prices or of recommended minimum prices.

Where a supplier is entitled to maintain prices, he makes it a condition in his agreement with wholesalers and retailers. Compliance can be enforced by withholding similar goods, or sueing the retailer for damages for breach of contract.

C. DISTRIBUTION

This word is used in a different sense from the economic meaning of the word, which deals with the rewards to factors of production. In the marketing context, it means the transfer of goods from producer to consumer.

1. Selection of channels of distribution

Some of the main channels of distribution are shown on the chart in Fig. 21, on p. 155.

Five main channels are shown, but the problem of selecting the most satisfactory channel for each product is complex.

Selecting a channel of distribution

The selection of a channel should involve consideration of the following:

(*a*) *Nature of product.* In this connexion, the distinction between industrial and consumer goods should be considered:

(i) Industrial goods include capital equipment and raw material for further processing. These are usually sold direct to firms. Distribution policy for such goods is usually simpler, as outlets are smaller and average values per sale are greater; there is less need for a large sales force and average overhead marketing cost to sales is lower.

(ii) Consumer goods are mainly purchased by the public and are goods in constant demand, e.g. food, clothing, cars. They are sold through many dispersed retail outlets.

Direct sale to a consumer usually occurs when the product is of a technical nature, necessitating expert knowledge. If sold through inexperienced retailers, this would be harmful to the manufacturer. For example, a computer or accounting machine would not be sold through a retailer, although a typewriter would, as little knowledge is needed to explain its operation.

(*b*) *Financial position of manufacturer.* The fewer the number of organizations in the chain, the smaller the financial burden on the manufacturer. Expenditure on distribution through alternative channels must be noted.

(*c*) *Variety of products to be sold.* A wide variety may necessitate numerous channels. Some producers may run their own retail outlets if the volume is sufficient, e.g. Boots. They may also sell other firms' products.

The actual selection may fall into the established pattern for the trade, which has proved satisfactory. A manufacturer who introduces a new product will usually adopt the customary method; he should of course consider changes.

For a comparison of the main methods of distribution see Fig. 23.

2. Warehousing

Whatever efforts marketing managers make to regulate consumer demand, it is very difficult to equate demand to manufacturing programmes. Warehousing is therefore needed to store finished products.

Transport is costly, so a decision has to be made as to whether warehouses are to be centrally situated or decentralized.

(a) Function of warehouses

(i) They act as a buffer for holding goods between the production process and the user, as many goods are not made directly against customer orders.

(ii) They can be used to change bulk and reduce transport costs.

(iii) If located in a suitable position, they can provide a source for quick supply to customers, e.g. spare-part warehouses.

The 'best' number of warehouses for a particular firm depends upon a number of factors. The right balance between the factors depends more upon the optimum loading of transport units than the actual distance from producing point to user.

(b) Factors in warehouse planning and organization

Design and layout. This is of great importance. Ideally, a single floor allows for better movement of goods. A stock rotation system is needed to avoid possible deterioration of goods. Goods which are moved most frequently should be in a conveniently accessible place.

Warehouse space can be given a financial value and can be allocated according to the earning capacity of the goods. This principle is used in retail stores for counter space allocation.

Mechanical handling. This can mean a vital saving in costs, but consideration should be given to future needs before buying equipment. The maximum use should be made of height.

Type	Description	Trading Pattern	Other Features
Department Store (e.g. Selfridges)	Large shop (Annual Sales over £100,000) carrying great variety of merchandise under one roof. There are many departments each specializing in one type of good.	They give good personal service—credit accounts and delivery services. They have reputation for good window displays and special offers.	Good quality personnel. They are flexible and benefit from specialized buying, office staff and centralized management.
Multiple Shop (e.g. Burton)	Group of shops, each dealing with similar product, e.g. shoes, under central control.	They deal in small range of goods and offer standard quality and price. Control is strong and flexible. They react quickly to consumer demand.	Benefit from centralized administration and decentralized selling. Large-scale operation justifies use of special equipment, e.g. computers. Bulk-buying and use of warehouses enable them to integrate wholesaling with retailing. Standardization and restricted stock range ensure good stock control.
Variety Chain Store (e.g. British Home Stores)	Similar features to Multiple Shop. Each shop in group sells a larger range of products, usually of lower value.	Minimum service is given. Large range of cheaper goods offered which are in strong consumer demand. Stock turn is high.	Benefit from centralizing buying and central control. Wage costs are lower, because young female assistants are employed, who have restricted range of duties. Close contact with manufacturers. Marks and Spencers benefit from good quality produce, which is rigidly inspected.
Co-operative Stores	Association of individuals organized on voluntary basis to supply goods and services to members.	Pattern varies. Could be any of above types. Slow tendency to modernize, now including more self-service shops.	Restricted range of goods has been a handicap. Over 50 per cent of goods are supplied by Co-operative Wholesale Society. Management committees are elected by lay members (part time), centralized buying, urged by 1958 Gaitskill Commission, to produce

	merchandise, particularly food and household requirements.	niques to encourage trade. Little service is given, cash trade only.	Problems are pilfering and marking of over 6000 items.
Mail Order (e.g. Freemans)	A method of retailing whereby goods are sold by description and illustration—they are advertised in magazines, catalogues and press. Goods are delivered by post.	Credit or hire-purchase terms are usually offered and a guarantee of satisfaction or money back is given. Many agents are used, they receive a percentage commission (about 10 per cent of cash received). Fairly wide range of goods, not so many as Department Store.	Bulk-buying, centralized delivery and payment, and close co-operation with suppliers give worthwhile economies. Very convenient to public. Costs of catalogues are high and so is expenditure on transport. Steady growth in volume of trade in recent years.
Discount Houses	Self-service store dealing in non-food items at reduced prices. Usually having area of 10,000 to 18,000 sq. ft. Similar to supermarket.	Situated on outskirts of city centres, easily accessible large open building. Little service is given; customers take goods away. Low cost because of low overhead charges and very low rent. Goods mainly consumer-durables.	Goods mainly non price-fixed goods. They may increase now resale price maintenance is falling away. High rate of stock turn; low capital investment cost, minimum expenditure on fittings. (*N.B.* Not same success as in U.S.A. probably because of, fewer cars per head, R.P.M. Acts and general suspicion of retail trade.)
Auto-vending	Sale by machine	Mainly in populated central areas. Often additional facility given by shops.	Growing steadily. High cost, so must be justified by high sales. Mainly liquids, cigarettes and chocolates sold, but extended to clothing and other good items as technology develops.
Independent Retailers	Single units, or small group of shops under private ownership. Generally only one owner.	Very personal service. Some may have numerous small departments.	Trend is to groups of retailers, to get more efficiency in all aspects of management.

Fig. 22.   Summary of main retail trading outlets.

(*c*) *Choice of sites*

The following points should be considered:

(i) Study past records of shipments and future marketing plans.

(ii) Consider the possibility of a shift in population and industry.

(iii) Examine size and type of existing and future orders, availability and cost of transport, cost and time in obtaining stock replacements.

(iv) Speed and efficiency in processing customer orders.

3. Transport

One can own or hire transport, or use public transport; it is not easy to compare costs, but a decision has to be taken. Figure 24 shows a plan of alternative supply routes open to a manufacturer.

Transport is closely linked to location policy. A manager is usually placed in charge of this section and he may come under the sales or production manager's authority.

Time, size and weight are important factors. Fast transport is more costly and it should preferably be used for light and perishable goods.

Method of transport

Some factors to consider in deciding upon a method of transport include:

(*a*) *Own transport.* A firm which sells on a large scale direct to other industrial users, or direct to its own retailers or independent retailers who are widely spread, may prefer its own transport system. In such a case the following factors need consideration:

(i) Control of cost of vehicles is essential. Standard costing may be used.

(ii) Work must be *planned*, so that vehicles are effectively employed.

It may be good policy to employ a smaller fleet than necessary and to use outside contractors for extra work. Waste from half-empty lorries and empty return journeys must be avoided.

(*b*) *Outside transport.*

(i) *Relative costs* of different types of transport are important.

(ii) Goods which deteriorate rapidly, or which are required promptly will need *fast transport*, e.g. air or road.

(iii) The *nature of the product* may require a special type of transport.

Close co-operation between all departments concerned is needed to minimize transport costs and the following two examples illustrate this point:

(i) Links with purchasing department may lead to vehicles picking up

Method	Advantages	Disadvantages	Remarks
Indirect 1. Wholesaler to Retailer to Customer.	(a) Large orders dealt with resulting in lower delivery and packing costs. (b) Fewer representatives needed. (c) Fewer accounts required, hence reduction in bad debts.	(a) Lower profit margin on goods sold. (b) Producers must rely on wholesalers to promote goods. No guarantee wholesaler will promote his lines.	Nature of product must be considered. If goods are in regular demand at low price—the low profit margin will not allow expensive selling campaigns; so wholesaler may be used for staple goods, e.g. soap and clothes.
2. Retailer to Consumer.	(a) Profit margin larger. (b) Shorter chain to consumer enables producer to have more say on sales promotion. (c) Closer link aids knowledge of consumer attitudes.	(a) Needs large sales force. (b) Greater costs of packing and delivery and bad debts. (c) Extra costs if retailer is assisted, e.g. by displays.	Similar goods to above method. Particularly perishables, e.g. bread.
Direct 3. Producer to Consumer. (a) Canvassing.	Direct control over selling methods, by using own salesmen. Better supervision of discounts, etc. Saving in salesmen's salaries.	Higher selling costs.	Useful for specialized goods, e.g. accounting machines.
(b) Mail Order.	Great convenience to customers especially if away from shops.	No personal contact by salesmen. High cost of printing catalogues, packing and advertising.	All non-perishable goods.
(c) Manufacturer's own shops.	Good control over sales methods.	High costs of delivery and purchase of sites.	Examples, shoes, confectionery.
(d) Direct Services (Nationalized Industries).	Centralized control.	Great volume of work may lead to some inefficiency in distribution.	Examples, gas, electricity, water.

Fig. 23. Comparison of main methods of distribution open to manufacturer.

material to use in the factory, instead of returning empty after deliveries to customers.

(ii) Design of packaging may enable greater amounts to be handled by making sizes easier to handle.

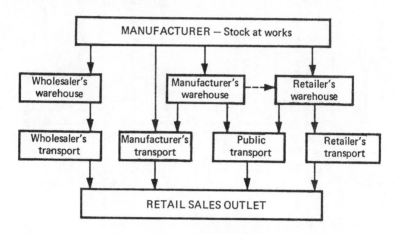

Fig. 24.   Plan of alternative supply routes.

Operational research is valuable in improving aspects of distribution procedure. The following problems can be solved by simulation techniques, i.e. by the mathematical representation of the whole distribution system, noting transport rates, warehouse operating costs, customer's demand and buying patterns, factory locations, production capacity, etc.

(i) How many warehouses should there be, and where should they be located?

(ii) What customers should each warehouse service?

(iii) What volume should each warehouse handle?

(See Control, chapter 5.)

(*c*) *Stock levels.* Records must be up to date and quickly accessible, particularly where demand fluctuates rapidly because of weather, fashion, etc. The right levels of stock must be fixed. Most firms carry too high levels of stock and any firm which is attempting to reduce stocks must note the factors dealt with in chapter 5 under Stock or Inventory Problems.

4. Physical distribution management

For many years, production inefficiencies have been criticized and scrutinized in order to increase productivity. There has been little close examination of possible savings in the area of physical distribution. There

is a movement towards a closer analysis of all aspects of physical distribution. This is particularly important where selling and distribution costs
are high (e.g. 35–40 per cent of total costs spent on salesmen, transport,
warehousing, insurance, packaging, deterioration and obsolescence of
stocks, order processing and handling, size of customer's orders and
delivery). All factors referring to the above can be considered as cogs,
which in the past were treated separately, rather than the present emphasis
in which they are joined and affect each other in a unified system.

Whatever savings are considered, it is important to note that the *total*
cost of distribution is the relevant figure. Cost reductions in some areas
may mean a higher overall cost in a subsequent activity. Actions taken,
for example in selecting one method of distribution, may only show cost
reductions in the long term, and may show cost *increases* in the short term.

Distribution costs are important, but it should be noted that they are
only one element (a sub-system) of the marketing function.

D. MARKET RESEARCH, ADVERTISING AND PUBLICITY

1. Market research

The assessment of the nature and level of demand for products and services
must be accurate, if economic resources are not to be misused. It is the
purpose of market research to find out, as accurately as possible, present
and future market requirements.

More complex manufacturing techniques involve larger capital investment, and planning has to be made farther ahead. Personal incomes have
levelled-up and this affects consumer requirements, so information must
be up to date in order that correct decisions be made.

Ideally, market research should provide information to enable a manufacturer to design a product in accordance with customers' preferences,
to manufacture it in quantities that can be sold, to pack it suitably, making
appropriate arrangements for effective advertising and distribution. In
this ideal case, over-production and losses in typing up unsaleable stocks
will not occur.

(a) Types of research

The finished product of a firm usually passes through two phases before
reaching the consumer. The first is from producer to distributor, the
second is from distributor to consumer.

(i) *Distributor research.* It is important to know the reason why goods are
'slow movers,' or why dealers are not keen to distribute them. Research
can vary from a few questions to a complete investigation. These retail or
shop audits should preferably be continuous, using trained investigators.

Such investigation should show, among other items, the answers to the following:

What is the popularity of competing brands?
What proportion of each brand is stocked?
From which channels are supplies received?

A useful information service is run by A. C. Nielsen & Co. This firm prepares reports at regular intervals and sends them to subscribers periodically. A representative sample of grocers and chemists is taken. Subscribers can be given an analysis, covering sales of one's own brand and competing brands, broken up into area, type of shop, etc.

(ii) *Consumer research.* As in distributor research, surveys can be continuous or *ad hoc*.

An *ad hoc* survey is designed for a specific purpose and the questionnaire is designed around main issues, and may try to find:

Which class of person buys the product, what sex, age group, how often, how many, etc.

By continuous survey the questions try to find information to assess the movement of demand of goods. A well-known survey by independent organizations is called the Brand Barometer. It is designed to measure the movement of branded goods.

Regular figures are provided to manufacturers who subscribe. These figures show, for example, details of total purchases of all brands in various groups in regions, etc. Trends can be seen and suitable action taken.

A Consumer Panel consists of a large number of persons who agree to record carefully their purchases, preferences, actions and to answer periodic questionnaires. The constitution of the panel must be carefully drawn up to avoid bias. This method is expensive, but gives continuous detailed information about consumers' buying actions to price changes, advertising changes, etc. (e.g. B.B.C. Listeners' Panel).

(iii) *Product research.* Product research or product testing is designed mainly to test the acceptability of a product and to check features of a product already marketed, if sales fall below the required standard. Briefly, various types of an article are given to the co-operator to use. These products look the same, but are specially marked. The reports of these persons are analysed. Again, care must be taken in drafting questions or inferences may be incorrect.

(iv) *Advertising research.* This can take many forms—it covers all the media used in advertising. It is invaluable to know what the impact is of advertisements. A good method is the continuous research available from readership surveys, e.g. those published by Hulton Press and I.P.A. The popularity of various newspapers, magazines, details of readers, their social classification, etc., is given.

(v) *Motivation research.* Strictly, this should form part of consumer research, but it is so important that a separate heading has been given to it. The term is used to embrace techniques or methods used in the field of social psychology, in order to try to determine *why* people buy one brand rather than another. Many answers in surveys have been found to be false or incorrect. Often a socially acceptable answer is given, e.g. the number of cigarettes smoked is far greater than the number ascertained by consumer research.

Motivation research is founded upon the assumption that consumer behaviour *may* be influenced by factors, the existence of which an individual may not suspect or may be unwilling to reveal. These facts must be studied and examined to obtain an accurate understanding of consumer behaviour. The information obtained helps in designing the product, packaging, pricing and advertising. This knowledge is very important, particularly from the advertising point of view, as all advertising 'copy' is based upon certain assumptions, as to *why* people purchase products. In the past, intuition and inspired guesses were used: today, systematic surveys form the basis of decisions.

Techniques used in motivation research may briefly be considered:

Group discussion is based upon the theory that, if rapport can be established between a small group of persons, then individual members of that group may be encouraged to express themselves more freely and fully than they might do if questioned alone.

Depth interview is an attempt to find a way beneath the more superficial levels of consciousness, by asking questions in such a way as to encourage the maximum amount of free expression.

Some attitudes cannot be uncovered by direct questioning, so subtler techniques are needed. These are most valuable where the respondent will not supply information on matters where social stigma or prestige are connected, e.g. frequency of cleaning one's teeth, or washing one's hands. Methods used are the completion of pictures or cartoons; or the interpretation of an indefinite picture. In these cases the results of the tests are analysed and interpreted by an experienced psychologist.

2. Advertising and publicity

These terms are often used synonymously. Strictly, publicity has a wider significance. It includes all forms of advertising and all activities which attempt to inform the public about a firm; this includes public relations.

The rôle played by advertising in the marketing activities of firms varies greatly. Advertising can be direct or indirect. The object of most advertising is to present information about a product, arouse interest, build desire and get customers in a favourable frame of mind to buy the product. Firms usually have their own advertising department, but usually they ask an advertising agency to help.

An *advertising agency* is an independent business organization, staffed by specialists, which develops and places advertisements in advertising media and assists in overall planning. The agency obtains facts, plans campaign strategy and the media to be used. The final plans are presented for approval by the firm. The agency acts as a middleman between the advertising firm and the suppliers of the advertising media, e.g. television companies, and they are paid by the owner of the media employed and not by their client.

An *advertising consultant* offers a different service. He is normally a one-man business who, for an agreed fee, prepares the advertising plan and dictates its general direction. He continues to watch over the operation and give further advice.

There are a number of points to consider in communicating to the public by an advertisement. This should be *specific*, expressing clearly thought ideas and have *authority* and *impact*. It must be so *distinctive* as to impinge itself on the memory. It must be *believable* and *acceptable* and related to the *needs of the recipient* and must be presented at the right *time*. A person should be made aware of the product or service and understand its advantages, be *convinced* of its value—this should then, ideally, bring a *response* or action to look at or to take steps to purchase.

It may be worthwhile now to consider briefly beliefs which are often quoted. One is that any price reduction which is made possible by using the amount of money spent on advertising, would induce the consumer to buy more. The price reduction, if spread over a wide range of products would be rather small and hardly noticeable to consumers.

Another belief is that advertising is done to avoid direct price competition. This, though, does not take into consideration that a lot of advertising is made to *support* price reductions. Advertising makes price promotions much more effective by making customers aware of reductions.

A third example of wrong beliefs is that price by itself is the determining factor in sales. This ignores the fact that they may buy for the brand image, distinction, e.g. Rolls-Royce, and the fact that an article is *expensive*, rather than for a lower price.

(a) *Principal forms of advertising*

Below are the principal forms of advertising:

(i) *Direct mail.* Information is sent direct to prospective customers. It can be used as the main advertising method. Mailing lists can be compiled from certain directories and year books; or the aid of certain professional organizations, which provide lists of firms in particular trades, graded in size and status, can be obtained.

(ii) *Press.* This includes all newspapers and journals and specialized magazines. Payment is made by the vertical column inch and varies according to circulation or net sales, position in the paper, status of the paper, use of colour, etc. It is important to note that readership is more important than circulation figures, e.g. newspapers may be read by a few people, magazines may be read by many in a family.

(iii) *Posters.* Sites are mainly in the hands of bill-posting contractors who grade their sites according to position. A bill-posting contract is on a rental basis—this includes fixing, inspecting and renewing if necessary. This method is useful to *supplement* a press, television, or radio, campaign, as the effects last over a period. It also allows concentration of advertising in a particular area, e.g. on transport vehicles.

(iv) *Cinema and television.* Costs are heavy, particularly on television, but displays are 'live' and seen by many in a favourable environment. Consideration is needed for declining cinema audiences and their more youthful nature.

(v) *Other methods.* Special displays and exhibitions, e.g. motor shows.

(b) Sales promotion

This term is often used to describe a wide range of marketing activities. In this book, it refers to the provision of special buying incentives for a limited period of time. They are more often used in consumer goods advertising than in industrial advertising.

They are supplementary to normal advertising and encourage dealers to open accounts or increase stock levels and, if used judiciously, are an invaluable aid to marketing.

Co-operation from distributors is vital and timing is very important. In addition, the period of the offer must not be too long. Problems could arise; for example, if the special offer is very attractive the regular stock will move at a slower rate. It is convenient to divide promotions into dealer and consumer.

Dealer promotions. These are designed to encourage dealers to participate. They are offered some of the following: *cash discounts*, which are either in cash or deducted from invoices on orders over specified amounts; or *gifts and prizes*, awarded on basis of sales or display.

Consumer promotions. These may be divided into the following:

(i) Temporary price reductions, e.g. '4 pence off' the usual price; these will be prominently displayed on special packs. Distributors obtain the same gross margin as on the regular pack and sales usually increase. Success is usually judged by the number of new users who are persuaded to buy.

(ii) Coupons are given to consumers, who then can obtain a reduced price when they are handed over to a dealer. The costs incurred are in the printing, mailing, or delivering by hand, the coupons. The allowance to the dealer is a fraction of a penny per coupon. The effect of this method is reduced if competitors offer similar coupons.

(iii) Premium offers—there are various types of such offers—

Self-liquidating; if a box top plus cash is sent, an article well below market price is obtained. As the company buys in bulk, no loss is made. Such articles must be widely desired and consumers must be able to check market price—this aids the success of the offer.

Box top premiums; cut out tops are sent for a gift—this helps to retain consumer loyalty to the product.

Container premiums; here the jar container itself is useful.

Enclosed premiums; within the packets of the product are gifts, e.g. toys.

(iv) Bargain packs—Often two products are banded together, the products being usually produced by the same company, e.g. soap and toothpaste. It may be, though, a product from another source, e.g. soap powder and clothes pegs. The problems here are mainly in packaging, transport and stacking on retailers' shelves.

(v) Contests—An example of this method is the completion of a coupon which shows ten features of a car in order of importance. It is policy to add a further contest, e.g. involving coining a slogan, in case more than one person is correct. It is essential that the main prizes be attractive if sales are to be increased. The manufacturers of the prizes obtain good indirect publicity and usually offer good buying terms. Contests can offer smaller value prizes of greater number, which are often aimed at children.

A most successful offer was the free offer of a plastic rose with each purchase of a packet of a detergent. Distribution was over 90 per cent among grocery outlets, 70 per cent of wholesalers and retailers bought over the average level and had specially-arranged displays and increased sales. It must be noted that the sales were backed up by excellent distribution and display and an adequate stock build-up. Such co-ordination is essential to success.

(c) Branding

Many goods originally sold in bulk are now sold in packets with a 'brand' or distinctive name, e.g. Typhoo tea. This also occurs in manufactured articles, e.g. Black and Decker drills.

This practice was introduced by manufacturers who wished to distribute products nationally, using national advertising. Such a product establishes its individuality and gives the manufacturer a good control over prices. A manufacturer can then advertise his particular brand of cigarettes, not cigarettes in general. Brand names are also used by department and multiple stores; as rival brands are advertised wholesalers and retailers have to stock more in order to meet consumer demand. Such goods usually carry a smaller profit margin than unbranded goods as they are deemed easier to sell.

Branding is a *grading device*. A purchaser will assume the quality will also be the same if he buys a brand. Branding may also be said to give a *sense of security*, e.g. a wholesaler may have a large business with a manufacturer, who may suddenly sell direct to retailers. If the wholesaler has his own brand, he is secure.

Today, the growing tendency to ask for a brand makes it difficult for a new manufacturer to enter a market; existing manufacturers therefore have a monopoly.

(*d*) *Effective advertising*

Some principles of effective advertising are:

(i) *Selection of correct media.* Money spent will be wasted if a product is advertised in inappropriate media. For example, a new animal food would be advertised in magazines devoted to animals and not in general magazines.

(ii) *Sufficient concentration.* The weight of advertising must be sufficient to impress the public. For example, it may be better to advertise locally for a long period, rather than nationally for a short time.

(iii) *Repetition.* It is important to observe continuity of style and phrases when varying media are used; this makes impressions more permanent.

(iv) *Timing.* A time must be chosen when the public are more receptive to the advertisements.

(*e*) *Example of a timetable for an advertising campaign*

In this illustration, assume a manufacturer has produced a small amount of a new product which he intends to market.

(i) The product is taken to an *advertising agency*, which will test it for quality, etc., and to see that there are no harmful effects no matter how the product is misused. It is better to do this before the public or the government find out; e.g. inflammable material should not be used in the product.

(ii) *Samples* may then be distributed in certain areas to find out the comments of people using them (test-marketing). These tests will show the advantages and disadvantages of the product and will suggest the lines upon which eventual advertising will be based.

(iii) If the product is *worth promoting*, the market research department will then find out the market for the product, the best method of advertising, etc.

(iv) Whether a *national or local campaign* should be instituted must be decided upon. It may be policy to try in one area first. Before a national campaign is tried, the manufacturer must be sure he is able to produce sufficient quantities to meet national sales.

(v) The agency then *plans the campaign*; all staff are used, e.g. artists, photographers, copywriters, etc.

(vi) The *interest of the retailers*, who will sell the product, should be obtained, in order to obtain their help in promoting sales. They could receive discounts, special leaflets, and display material.

(vii) *Following up the progress* of the campaign is essential.

(f) Public relations (P.R.)

The function of P.R. is to promote public understanding and acceptance of a company, its products and services. The purpose is to ensure that the 'image' or impression which the public carry of the company is a favourable one, so that ultimately there will be greater sales of the products of the company.

The Institute of Public Relations defined P.R. as: '*a planned and sustained effort to establish and maintain mutual understanding between an organization and its public.*'

P.R. is a function of management, it is more than just press relations, and the P.R. officer is often responsible to the board of directors.

P.R. uses a variety of methods and, if reliable and interesting information is given to the press on a new product, or method of working, good, free publicity may materialize.

A company may set up its own P.R. department or utilize the P.R. department of an advertising agency, or engage an outside P.R. agency.

The qualities needed in a Public Relations Officer. The qualities needed include:

(i) Integrity, discretion and ability to make the right contacts.
(ii) A sense of timing and good journalistic ability.
(iii) Good knowledge of media, e.g. television, exhibitions, press.

Duties of a Public Relations Officer. The duties of a P.R.O. may comprise:

(i) Providing information, e.g. on new models of cars; dealing with all enquiries on matters affecting the firm, e.g. intention to raise prices.

(ii) Dealing with all relations with press and other advertising organizations, other than normal advertising matters.

(iii) Organization of visits abroad and exhibitions.

(iv) Responsibility for house journal, i.e. internal company magazine.

(g) *Concept of life-cycle in marketing*

New products are introduced after being developed; they grow, reach maturity and then eventually decline. The duration of such phases varies with different types of products; goods affected by fashion have short life-cycles.

A correct knowledge of the phase the product is at is helpful, and often vital, in planning accurately for the future. Questions to be answered are:

Which products are now in decline?

When should new products be introduced?

The diagram in Fig. 25 shows the life-cycle of a product.

Often, after the first stages of decline in sales, a manufacturer tries to make his product more attractive, or introduce a new product. It is then usually *too late* and customers may be lost to competitors.

Ideally, a knowledge of consumer attitudes is needed; improvements and new products should be available before Stage 3 ends. In the growth and maturity stages, new uses, or new products must be found for the product, e.g. model changes in cars.

Promotion and distribution strategies are related to a product's position in the cycle. A well-balanced product programme should balance a certain number of products in each stage of the life-cycle.

In Fig. 25, below, the dotted line shows when a new product is required

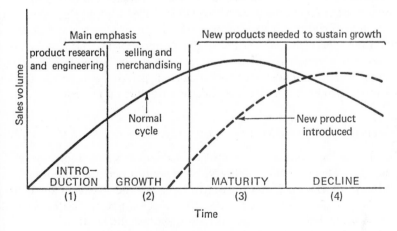

Fig. 25. Life-cycle of a product.

to maintain or increase a firm's share of the market. In most cases the life-cycle is quite long (e.g. the Volkswagen small car).

3. Packaging

The packaging of goods has become extremely important—partly because of the rôle it is thought to play in attracting the consumer—and there have been revolutionary changes in styles and materials. In addition, containers have been improved functionally and the often conflicting needs of the packer, distributor and consumer have to be met. Packaging can be regarded as the vehicle from which a product is to be sold and it must therefore protect and attract. Packaging is part of the 'marketing mix' and involves production, protection, transportation, distribution, advertising, merchandising and the selling of the product.

(a) Use of outside specialist firms

These give a comprehensive service to a manufacturer and account for a large part of the total amount spent on packaging. A manufacturer must consider the additional cost of transport to and from the packaging company and must be certain of a reliable delivery service. These specialist firms provide experience and have the capital equipment which a manufacturer must have himself if he does not avail himself of their services.

(b) A firm's own packaging department

Such a department may be under the control of a committee, consisting of persons drawn from various departments. The trend, though, is towards specialization under one person (sometimes called a packaging manager). This department may come under marketing or production and depends upon the type of business activity. For example, if the business is food, drugs or cosmetics, it will be more market research-orientated and the section will come under the marketing manager. If packaging is for an industrial product, it may come under the production manager.

(c) Factors to be considered in packaging

Briefly, packages must be designed on a drawing board, tools obtained, packages tested for compatibility with the product under conditions of use and sale. Blocks for graphics have to be made and machines for filling, erecting and closing obtained. Research and development must be planned and co-ordinated, use of colour carefully selected and controlled, together with the careful checking of the quality of components. Information is needed on all aspects of the product. Attention should be paid to the following:

(i) Special protection in packing, shelf-life, uses of product, conditions of use, type of user, type of market.

(ii) Predicted volume, special processing needed, e.g. vacuum packing, channels of distribution, needs of storage, e.g. for shipping, method of handling.

(iii) Promotional needs, e.g. consumer articles may be attached to the package of a good as a gift, as part of sales promotion.

(iv) Legal requirements, e.g. Trade Descriptions Act, 1968.

(d) New developments

New materials must be tested and examined continuously and the entire life of a package should be simulated. Containers will have to be more durable as more automated warehouses are built.

(i) *Aerosols*. More uses are being found for aerosols and these are an example of how packaging can add convenience to a product.

(ii) *Transparent film*. This is now in greater use, especially for shrink wrapping of food (articles are overwrapped in a tight transparent film). This helps to sell the products as they are easy to see and open, they also save packing and material costs.

(iii) *Pre-packing*. This is useful, especially for fruit and vegetables, which must be graded and prepared, washed, dried, trimmed, sliced and pre-cooled. Supermarkets and self-service stores make good use of this method.

4. Merchandising

This term is used to mean assisting the retailer with publicity at the point of display, to help him maximize his sales. This involves instructing him in the best use of shelf space, the provision of display material and advice on its use.

Merchandising, by means of improved packing and display, has been a notable feature in the sales of many products, e.g. drinks, where cans are becoming acceptable for beer, etc.

Pre-packaging is greatly increasing, especially in the greengrocery business.

It is worth noting that manufacturers of branded consumer goods obtain many orders from the head office of supermarkets and large retail groups, so the job of the manufacturer's traveller now, when calling on retail groups, is mainly to advise on displays and on merchandising problems.

E. SALES MANAGEMENT

Unless a manager has his own retail outlets, he needs sales representatives who will mainly be responsible for disposing of the company's production.

1. Sales administration

This assists the representatives and co-operates with those responsible for marketing policy and production programmes, in order that intelligent forecasting and accurate budgetary control be applied. The sales force must be used efficiently. This depends upon a number of factors and includes initial selection and training in co-operation with the personnel officer, good organization and accurate reporting of results, satisfactory salaries and conditions of employment.

A good administrator should possess the following qualities:

(*a*) Ability to control salesmen and assess performance, set targets and keep enthusiasm high.

(*b*) Knowledge of modern techniques is needed, so that they can be used in relevant cases. In addition, he must possess flair and imagination.

2. Selection and training of salesmen

General selection and training techniques are dealt with in chapter 8. A brief programme for a training scheme might include:

(*a*) Basic principles of salesmanship, e.g. approach, courtesy, self-control, closing techniques.

(*b*) Product knowledge—characteristics of the product, materials used in manufacture and assembly, possible defects through misuse.

(*c*) Procedures of company—company policy, routines for orders, complaints, reports, etc.

3. Planning of territories

The size of the outdoor staff depends upon many factors, particularly the method of sales (i.e. to wholesalers or retailers, or consumers). Geographical size of territory usually depends upon the physical nature of the product or service. For example:

(*a*) The sale of office equipment in London may need one representative per square mile. In East Anglia, only one representative may be needed and a large part of his time will be spent in travelling.

(*b*) A person selling specialized products to industry needs less area than one who sells staple products to dealers.

(*c*) If a product is sold to wholesalers first, the territory will be larger and fewer representatives will be needed than if sold direct to retailers.

(*d*) Competition and habits of buyers must be noted.

(*e*) The final allocation must give the salesman a territory which produces sufficient orders to give him a satisfactory remuneration and standard of living.

4. Quota setting

Sales forecasting and budgetary procedures were dealt with in chapter 2. Brief mention is made here of the setting of quotas.

A sales forecast is normally prepared and allocated to territories on the basis of the potential of the territory—this becomes the salesman's target for a period (e.g. a year). It is preferable to break this down into monthly quotas, noting any seasonal trends. A comparison of actual sales with this standard can easily be made. If quotas are adhered to, production can continue in an orderly manner; they can also be used as a basis for competition among sales staff and a basis for bonus payments.

5. Remuneration of sales representatives

Incentives must be given to obtain best results: they must be fair and reasonably easy to attain. The rewards of speciality salesmen may be higher than those to salesmen of staple goods, as they constantly have to break new ground and have few repeat orders. The speciality salesman's personal efforts are more responsible for sales than those of a salesman of staple goods who has the benefit of a secure market. Any of the following methods, or combination of methods, of remuneration may be used.

(*a*) *Salary*

This method may be used where seasonal fluctuations occur. It also applies where the product is well known and established. The salesman's function is mainly to maintain personal contact with customers and collect orders. The salesman has security, but no incentive, especially where selling is against competition of other travellers.

(*b*) *Commission*

This method is often used when a company is being built up; there is no financial risk to the employer, but there is little direct control over sales staff. The security of the salesman is small and he therefore should receive guarantees, e.g. he should receive commission on *all* orders from his territory whether he collected them or not.

(*c*) *Salary and commission*

Under this system the salary gives the salesman security while the commission acts as an incentive. A change in commission on various lines can be a useful method of pushing poor selling lines.

The more often after-sales service, or investigating, is needed, the more should be the element of salary.

(*d*) *Bonuses and special incentives*

These can be used for special efforts, for example, to sell excess stocks at the end of the season, or they may be given to a group which achieves more than their sales quota. It is worth noting that, if made annually, the reward is too far removed from the actual effort to give much incentive value.

6. Organization of sales office

Office practices are dealt with in chapter 9. Only the special points relating to the sales office are noted here.

The situation of the sales office will vary according to the needs of the business. There are advantages in having it near the factory but, as excellent communication systems are available, e.g. teleprinter, it is not so necessary. Customer accessibility, or a central position for control of salesmen may be more important.

(*a*) *Duties of office manager*

The manager in charge of the sales office usually has responsibility for order control, statistics, correspondence and records. An efficient sales office makes the salesman's job much easier. The manager must have a good knowledge of systems and must be able to prepare reports and statistics for control purposes.

(*b*) *Correspondence and reports*

Correspondence with customers and salesmen. All enquiries must be dealt with promptly. The use of standard forms for quotations and orders is essential. Complaints from customers must be especially noted and dealt with by a senior in the office. Enquiries from customers must be sent direct to the salesmen concerned, in addition to all quotations and letters sent to customers.

Salesmen's reports. These must be designed to secure economy of time in preparing them as well as to give sufficient information for control. The nature of the business will determine the particular form of report:

(i) Unit reports, separate for each call made, are needed by speciality companies. The contents may show—person seen, position held, goods discussed, special problems, stage of negotiations reached, etc.

(ii) Omnibus reports are daily reports which show orders taken, orders analysed into customers called upon, etc. They are often used for staple goods.

(c) *Statistics and salesmen's records*

Basic personal information will be in the hands of the personnel office, but the following records are most useful to the sales office manager.

Personal record card, showing monthly totals of salary, commission, expenses, etc.

Monthly records of sales analysed over lines, cumulatively, giving comparison over years.

Other statistical records will show a customer index, often kept on a visible card or strip index, either arranged alphabetically under towns, or under each salesman's area of duty, giving: name of firm, chief buyer, credit rating, discounts given, normal order, special preferences, etc. Records of old customers should be kept and also of prospective customers. Statistics are kept of the market, shares of company and competitors, tenders submitted and results, costs of distribution, condition of salesmen's cars, etc.

(d) *Control of credit*

This is an important function of sales management. The degree of control varies widely, but procedures must be laid down and observed. The following factors must be considered:

(i) What procedures must be followed to find the security of new customers?

(ii) What amount of initial orders must pass before a check is completed?

(iii) How long can credit be extended; what discounts are to be allowed?

A *credit rating* can be given to each account. The initial rating can be made by the salesman, but the final rating is the responsibility of the credit manager. This is based upon salesmen's reports, trade references and special enquiries from trade protection societies.

The following is an example of the use of modern methods in aiding some problems of sales management.

To obtain the greatest efficiency the following questions must be answered in the affirmative:

Are salesmen distributed properly around the country?
Do they know, or are they going on calls in, the 'best' order?

By the use of a computer, programmed to take account of the variable factors, these points can be answered.

International Computers Ltd, for example, offers such a service for a reasonable fee. It has already been mentioned how these new techniques can aid warehouse location and loading of vehicles. Now an answer to the above questions must take into account all the variable characteristics in a salesman's journey. A basic computer program must cover the following characteristics:

(i) Maximum daily distance, maximum time, noting average possible speed, distance and time per call.

(ii) Maximum number of visits, order of calls to be made, i.e. first or last, or morning or afternoon.

The procedure is as follows:

(i) Examine all outlets in the country and find the total amount of 'face to face' selling.

(ii) Are the prospects evenly scattered or grouped in certain localities?

(iii) Certain basic facts must be noted, e.g. most firms have a London representative.

(iv) The numerous possible conclusions are then fed to the computer.

Each case is different and the computer arrives at the 'optimum' result in terms of numbers of men, territories defined and sequence of calls.

A knowledge of National Grid References is needed and details are given to the computer. Allowances are to be made for natural barriers, e.g. rivers and mountains; common sense is essential.

Most vehicle routing and fleet-planning problems can all be catered for by programming a computer to find good routes in a very short time and a saving in vehicles of between 5 per cent and 30 per cent may be possible. It is also possible to compare the routes produced for a given load schedule, using a *simulated* fleet, with those used by the actual fleet and thereby a more effective fleet structure can be evolved.

F. PRICING THEORY

A brief revision of elementary economic concepts must first be made. Briefly, economic theory states that price is determined by the interaction of supply and demand. Cost being the main ingredient of supply and price the main ingredient of demand; they work together and continually adjust to each other.

A firm, it is said, should charge such a price and produce such an output as will enable it to equate marginal cost and marginal revenue. *Marginal cost* represents the change in total cost when another unit of output is produced; *marginal revenue* is the revenue obtained from selling this marginal unit of output. When a firm equates marginal cost and marginal revenue, the highest profit is obtained, as the difference between total cost and total revenue is at its greatest. This principle provides a key to the understanding of the factors that determine maximization of profits.

The two extreme economic conditions of perfect competition and pure monopoly do not really exist, and business is conducted in the intermediary conditions of imperfect or monopolistic competition.

In practice, business men rarely consciously set prices in this manner, for the following reasons:

(*a*) Information available is usually limited; e.g. details of price elasticity of demand (needed to get marginal revenue), cannot be easily obtained.

(*b*) Price elasticity is hardly ever constant for any length of time, so if prices were changed by applying the marginal principle, the numerous changes needed would not be practicable to operate.

(*c*) It is not easy for firms to attempt to equate costs and revenue of marginal units of output, especially if marginal units are very large, e.g. shipbuilding industry.

To survive or expand, firms must charge a price covering total costs of production in the long run and produce a normal or reasonable return on capital. The use of break-even analysis can be briefly mentioned here: for a more detailed consideration, see Fig. 18 in chapter 5.

This simple diagram shows that an output of more than 100,000 units is needed in order to make a profit. Sales below 100,000 units result in a loss. The greatest distance between sales and total cost curves shows the optimum sales or optimum output position.

Costing processes

These often form the basis for price setting. If one considers a firm engaged upon a long production run, first of all production and output capacity is estimated and fixed costs are calculated, to which are added overhead costs. The allocation of overhead costs to each separate commodity usually entails the use of a number of *arbitrary accounting assumptions*. To the total of production costs is added a margin to cover a 'fair' return on capital. This margin or 'mark up' varies widely; often the normal or conventional mark up for an industry is adopted.

This 'cost plus' system of pricing is usually inflexible in face of demand changes, but is favoured as it is very simple to operate. In the short run, there may be good reasons for keeping prices stable, but profits would tend to be higher if larger 'mark ups' were added when demand was expanding and vice versa.

Pricing decisions

There is no simple formula for management when making pricing decisions, because of the following interacting factors:

(a) The economic framework

The economic framework, e.g. imperfect or monopolistic competition, in which the firm operates is an important factor.

(b) Customer demand

A knowledge of the elasticity of demand for a product is required in order to find the volume of goods that can be sold in a given period of time and within a given price schedule; bearing in mind that consumer responses to prices may be affected by considerations other than economic.

(c) Competitors

Any price decision must anticipate action by competitors, which it can be said sets an *upper limit* on price. A price below market price will produce only a temporary increase in sales. Competitors may then reduce their prices and this may lead to a price-war. Some firms have composite price policies; depending upon the prices of competitors. For example, 10 per cent below prices of nearest competitors, as long as selling price is not below total manufacturing costs.

(d) Costs

Numerous cost concepts are used, e.g. marginal cost, and these usually set a *lower* limit on pricing. The effect of volume on costs and profits should be noted. Many companies find that their average costs per unit fall as volume is increased. Often unit costs do not decline as rapidly as the necessary reduction in prices and, in order to get additional sales volume, profit per unit diminishes. Total profit, therefore, depends upon sales volume, as well as cost per unit.

(e) Objectives of company

If a company, for example, wished to become a quality leader, this policy would be reflected in pricing policy. If product differentiation were present in the market, the company would probably decide to charge a comparable price with its competitors' products and build up sales by superior quality. Other firms may offer other services; free delivery, for example.

In most cases, therefore, the actual choice depends upon consumer reaction, as to how much they will pay for superior quality, how long differentiation exists and how much unit costs would fall if volume, rather than a high price, is sought.

(f) *Legal restraints*

The possibility of government action must be considered; e.g. on monopolies; bearing in mind that the definition of a monopoly used by the Monopolies Commission is any firm producing over one-third of the total output of a good in the country. In addition, the possibility of nationalization and the operation of the price-maintenance laws must be considered (see also page 185).

Price discrimination

Price discrimination can be used to obtain more revenue. Markets exist for every grade of prices and consumers spend their money in accordance with their scale of preferences. If markets can be divided into sections, it may be possible to charge a different price in each market, the object being to increase total revenue from any given level of production. This is done when the marginal revenue in each market is the same. This will happen only if production is in the hands of a monopolist or group of firms acting in this way and if the price elasticity of demand in each section is different. It must, of course, either be impossible to transfer goods from one section of the market to another, or the cost of transporting the goods between the markets must exceed the difference in price between the two markets.

Example of price discrimination

Tea may be sold for a high price in a branded pack, or sold loose, with no label, at a lower price.

Many other factors can be considered in pricing theory and these can be studied in the more detailed books mentioned in the bibliography at the end of the chapter.

G. EXPORT MARKETING

Successive governments have stressed the necessity for expanding exports and the need for small firms as well as medium-sized firms to enter the export field. Sixty per cent of British exports are at present achieved by only 300 companies. The potential is therefore enormous.

Objections to exporting usually follow these lines:

(*a*) Too much effort is needed to find out how to sell abroad.

(*b*) Risks are too great, especially if the home market is safe and produces a good return on capital.

(*c*) Lack of expert knowledge in packaging, transport, insurance, etc.

(*d*) Exports may rely on one or two overseas markets which may be cut off by changes in legislation, e.g. licensing laws or quotas.

The marketing of goods across national boundaries, often called global marketing, can bring many problems to the marketing manager. A list of organizations that can assist is briefly mentioned on pp. 186–7.

Two common mistakes made by companies who are successful in domestic-orientated business who consider exporting are:

(*a*) They consider long-range planning on a *regional* rather than an individual country basis (i.e. Europe, rather than France). This means that they tend to ignore the subtle differences which may be significant between the political and social environment of each country.

(*b*) Accurate knowledge of local trends can be vital to the success of the venture, for example the United States Department of Commerce have specified 27 non-tariff barriers which exist in overseas trade, which include special labels, packaging, safety standards.

To solve these problems the formation of a subsidiary company for selling a product is one answer. Other ways are to buy an existing company, to acquire shares in one, start a completely new company, or consider some form of joint venture with a local firm.

A brief consideration of the major points to consider will include:

(*a*) total population of country, wealth (gross domestic product per head of population);

(*b*) demographic structure, rate of inflation;

(*c*) assessment of risk and finance needed, availability of loan capital and stability of local currency;

(*d*) taxes, government incentives to exporters, regulations on foreign investment and transfer of profits to main country;

(*e*) data regarding local markets (state of local industry and competitors, nature of protection given to home industry);

(*f*) existing and potential market growth;

(*g*) availability of raw materials, storage facilities, climate;

(*h*) legal constraints (pollution, patent laws), cost of labour;

(*i*) political constraints, possibility of nationalization and assessment of stability of government;

(*j*) labour availability, trade union organization.

Advantages of global marketing

(1) Larger volume of production—this may justify investment in more mechanized methods of production and would increase efficiency.

(2) Greater opportunities to counter falling orders from one area, by increases from other areas.

(3) Increasing marketing knowledge from contact with a wider range of markets and competitors.

(4) Opportunities to gain experience of design, development and production of goods and services which are not needed in home country.

(5) Company is better placed to compete with foreign enterprises in home market.

Penetration pricing. A company may set price levels that will only be profitable at specified high sales levels. In this case low initial prices are set to keep out competition and when volume expands and the company leads the market, prices can then be raised.

Skimming price strategy. This is a method which starts with high prices (as can be asked for a new invention or technology). Then when demand increases, and competitors start to enter, price is lowered. A large part of the initial investment can then be recovered before any real competitors emerge.

Diversionary pricing. This occurs where one product is sold cheaply so that an associated product which has a high profit margin is automatically sold. For example, low-cost photocopying machines are sold with high-priced photocopy paper. In this case there is often one company who takes over as price-leader and others follow its lead. The outcome could lead to a price war with the winner carrying losses on some product lines by making sufficient profit from the rest.

A marketing approach to pricing considers the ability to give the customer *value*. Companies should evaluate what areas are their strength. Is it their:

(*a*) unique knowledge (such as a technological breakthrough)?

(*b*) unique marketing techniques or service to customers?

(*c*) effective research and development?

(*d*) effective control of manufacture and distribution channels?

(*e*) protection by patents?

1. First steps in exporting

Assuming a manufacturer has a good product which he feels would sell abroad, he should:

(*a*) Pick a market, preferably not one which is experiencing economic difficulties, or where home competition is strong, or where political overtones exist.

(*b*) The regional officer of the Department of Trade and Industry and the British Overseas Trade Board should then be notified, and given full descriptions and samples of goods.

(*c*) The British Overseas Trade Board (formerly British Export Board) will contact its representative in the market (Commercial Officer of the Diplomatic Service), and obtain a market report, which will say what competition exists, noting any special local regulations and if prospects seem reasonable.

(*d*) Further information may be obtained from banks, chambers of commerce and trade associations. Each country has its own peculiarities and customs. Research is essential to see if the design, packing, and colour satisfy local requirements and the price charged leaves sufficient profit. The Export Marketing Research Scheme (introduced by the Department of Trade and Industry) provides exporters with consultancy advice on planning marketing research.

(*e*) Extra costs may include:

(i) Costs of packing and transport to docks, shipping agent's charges, marine and freight insurance and overseas delivery charges.

(ii) Costs of setting up an export department.

(iii) Customs duties, port dues, agent's commission.

(iv) Insurance of credit risk.

2. Organizations which assist exporting firms

The organizations which can give help to an exporting firm include:

(*a*) *Department of Trade and Industry*

The regional offices each have an export officer to deal with enquiries. Their services include:

(i) Provision of basic market information and suggested promising markets, and advice on market research through the Export Marketing Research Scheme.

(ii) Giving information about tariffs, licensing and special duties regulations, local customs and methods of business.

(iii) Helping the firm to solve problems of how to exploit the chosen market.

(iv) Providing status information on potential business contacts.

(v) Guaranteeing credit given to foreign firms. Suppliers of capital goods and contractors for large projects have to offer, in most cases, credit over a number of years. The *Export Credits Guarantee Department* of the

Department of Trade and Industry will, for orders of £25,000 or more, involving credit of at least two years, *offer guarantees* to the commercial banks, which can provide exporters with finance at a reasonable rate of interest.

There is also a risk that payment for goods exported may not be made by a foreign buyer. Normal insurance companies do not insure for such a risk, but the Export Credits Guarantee Department has a scheme whereby it will provide complete cover for most risks up to 85–90 per cent of the value of the goods concerned, for a period of up to fifty years.

(b) British Overseas Trade Board

This body gives directions for the development of export activities and operates an Overseas Visitors' Bureau, which organizes and funds the visits of overseas buyers to Britain.

(c) Confederation of British Industries

This has a permanent staff overseas who carry out similar work to the Department of Trade and Industry. A special feature is where they can arrange for the small new entrant to the export market to obtain help from a larger, well-established company in the export field who, without charge, makes its services available and gives the small firm the benefit of its experience.

3. Methods of exporting

A manufacturer can sell to:

(a) A buying agent

Buying agents are based in this country and may also be known as confirming or indent homes. They act as commission agents for overseas buyers, by whom they are remunerated by commission, and from whom they receive their orders, specifying the goods they wish the agent to purchase on their behalf. The agent obtains quotations, places orders in the principal's name and arranges shipping.

(b) Export merchant houses

Export merchant houses based in this country may be employed. They buy goods on their own account and sell them overseas in markets in which they have specialized knowledge and where they have warehousing and selling facilities.

(c) An export agent

A manufacturer may employ an export agent based in this country. The agent will sell goods abroad and may act for a number of manufacturers of non-competitive lines. The agency carries out research and promotes sales overseas and can provide a complete service to a manufacturer.

(d) Import merchants

Import merchants, based overseas, purchase at a large discount and make their profit on the resale. They may be given exclusive rights to handle a manufacturer's products in a country or area.

(e) A branch or subsidiary company

A manufacturer may employ a branch or subsidiary company of the importing company.

(f) A commission agent

Such an agent, based in the importing country, may be given sole selling rights. This is a very popular method, but careful selection is essential in obtaining an agent and in drawing up the agency agreement.

(g) Direct to overseas buyer

This method may be used for large capital projects, e.g. nuclear reactors.

All detailed arrangements in *(d)* to *(g)* above must be done by the firm's own exporting department, unless a firm of forwarding agents is used. These agents can take over when the goods leave the factory and arrange for all transport and documentation to the destination.

REVIEW QUESTIONS

A and B. Marketing Organization and Administration and Organization of the Home Trade

(1) Outline a Schedule of Responsibilities for a marketing manager.

(2) Consider the position of the wholesaler in modern marketing and outline any new trends.

(3) Examine the effect of Resale Price Maintenance before and after the 1964 Act.

(4) What are the advantages and disadvantages of trading stamps?

C. Distribution

(1) What factors should be considered in selecting a channel of distribution?

(2) What are the main factors to consider in choosing the site, design and layout of a warehouse?

(3) How can operational research improve aspects of distribution procedure?

D. Market Research, Advertising and Publicity

(1) Differentiate carefully between consumer and distributor research.

(2) What other types of research are there in distribution?

(3) What are the principal forms of advertising?

(4) What forms of special buying incentives are there?

(5) Consider the principles of effective advertising.

(6) Draw up a timetable for an advertising campaign.

(7) Show how packaging has an important part to play in marketing.

E. Sales Management

(1) What methods are there of remunerating salesmen?

(2) Consider the types of records and statistics which would be of use to a sales office manager.

(3) Suggest a method to control credit.

(4) Describe a method of vehicle routing with the help of a computer.

F. Pricing Theory

(1) Show how prices are formed in economic theory and how in practice the theory is modified.

(2) What are the factors that must be considered when making pricing decisions?

G. Export Marketing

(1) What steps should a manufacturer take in considering exporting for the first time?

(2) Name and briefly describe the work of organizations that can help the exporter.

(3) What are the various methods of exporting?

REVIEW PROBLEMS

Marketing and Sales Management

(1) The chairman of a company which manufactures a proprietary brand of firelighters asks you to report on:

(*a*) A method of operating a national campaign whereby members of the public are allowed to make postal purchases of motoring rugs at two-thirds of the normal retail selling price on the condition that the top flaps from three firelighter cartons shall be attached to the remittance for each rug.

(*b*) The possible benefits to the company of conducting such a campaign.

(2) Explain the connexion between branding and advertising and state why it is necessary to spend large sums in advertising goods that are already well known by their brand name. Does the consumer pay for the advertising and does he really benefit from it?

(3) A small retail trader is considering whether to join other retailers and wholesalers in a voluntary organization which will purchase goods from manufacturers and distribute them to participating members of the organization. Outline the advantages that could accrue to the retail traders as a result of joining this organization.

(4) The board of a raincoat manufacturing company, with capital employed of about £250,000 has discussed the possibility of increasing the company sales by entering the export field. You are required to advise the board about the information necessary to a decision on whether to export or not and to state the sources from which advisory information for exporters may be obtained.

(5) List the factors which affect long-range *planning for marketing*. Long-range planning requires the backing of senior management and their willingness to organize properly for such planning. Describe the characteristics of a climate propitious for long-range planning.

(6) Specialization in particular products is frequently one of the ingredients in a successful business.

(*a*) What are the reasons for this?

(*b*) What constraints does this impose on managers?

(*c*) What are the problems that may arise out of a salesman's request to undertake a special order for a non-standard product and how should a manager deal with those problems?

(7) What are the points to be observed when designing and marketing products which are intended mainly for export?

(8) The sales staff of a company is bringing in a steadily decreasing flow

of orders. As sales manager, what investigations would you make and what action would you take to remedy the situation?

(9) Set out in sequence the steps to be taken to develop a product from its first concept to the time when it is ready to be put on the production line.

(10) For what activities is the marketing director of a group of companies likely to be responsible?

What specialist services may he utilize?

How may he 'keep his finger on the pulse' of the business?

(11) What factors would you take into consideration when setting the price of a new product?

(12) You are asked to examine a system for the despatch and delivery of goods to customers. What aspects would you consider to be important to ensure an efficient and economic service?

(13) Explain the function of a public relations officer and compare his work with that of an advertising manager.

(14) Give examples of statistical information which may be required by a sales manager. Each example should include a brief outline of how it would assist his decisions on sales strategy.

(15) What does the marketing function of management comprise? Illustrate your answer with a chart which shows the organization of the marketing division of a manufacturing company which sells its products direct to the retailer.

(16) Comment briefly on each of the major elements normally included in the term 'marketing mix.'

(17) Explain fully how pricing policies are likely to be determined in a company manufacturing and marketing specialized components. How may the management accountant contribute to pricing decisions?

BIBLIOGRAPHY

Marketing

Ansoff, H. I., *Corporate Strategy* (London, Pelican 1969).

Baker, M. J., *Marketing: An Introductory Text* (London, Macmillan, 1971).

Biddlecombe, P., *Financial Advertising and Public Relations* (London, Business Books, 1971).

Department of Trade and Industry, publications to aid exporters.

Britt, S. H. and Lucas, D. B., *Measuring Advertising Effectiveness* (New York, McGraw-Hill, 1963).

Buskirk, R. H. and Stanton, W. J., *Management of the Sales Force* (Illinois, Irwin, 1964).

Chisnell, P. M., *Marketing—A Behavioural Analysis* (New York, McGraw-Hill, 1975).

Chisnell, P. M., *Marketing Research: Analysis and Measurement* (New York, McGraw-Hill, 1973).

Deverell, C. S., *Marketing Management for Europe* (London, Butterworths, 1969).

Henry, H., *Motivation Research* (London, Crosby Lockwood, 1958).

Kotler, P., *Marketing Management: Analysis, Planning and Control* (New Jersey, Prentice-Hall, 1967).

Longman, K. A., *Advertising* (New York, Harcourt Brace, 1971).

Lowe, D., *The Transport Manager's Handbook* (London, Kogan Page, 1970).

Philpott, W. J., *Retail Business Administration* (London, Pitman, 1963).

Rodger, L. W., *Marketing in a Competitive Economy* (London, Hutchinson, 1965).

Schwartz, G., *Science in Marketing* (London, Wiley, 1965).

Seibert, J. and Wills, G. (eds.), *Marketing Research: Selected Readings* (London, Penguin, 1970).

Smallbone, D. W., *The Practice of Marketing* (London, Staples, 1965).

Wentworth, F. (ed.), *Physical Distribution Management* (London, Gower Press, 1974).

7 Production

Production can simply be defined as the activity of transforming raw materials or components into finished products. Production management is the process of the effective planning and control of the operations of that section of an enterprise devoted to transforming materials into finished products.

Industries vary a great deal and even within an industry firms vary in organization and methods of work. Terminology also has not been standardized to a large extent, but there are basic principles which can be *used* and *adapted* to the varying types of production.

In this chapter, a great deal of detail will of necessity be omitted, but the reader is referred to more specialized books at the end of the chapter. The terminology used is generally accepted but there are some areas where authorities differ; here an attempt has been made to indicate the nature of these other terms and meanings.

Research is made into the market to see if there is a demand for a new product. Further research is needed to give information for the design of a prototype or model. Designers then produce a specification for a product which is developed and this prototype is carefully tested. Sample products are made and these may be given to consumers for their use and they are asked to inform the company of the advantages and particularly the disadvantages they have noticed. Only then, when the disadvantages have been considered and rectified, does actual full-scale manufacture take place.

A. TYPES OF PRODUCTION

Before production commences, forecasting and planning are needed and the actual procedure adopted depends upon a number of items, e.g. whether a standard range of goods is required or whether designing is to follow special orders from customers.

Production policy therefore must be known and then the processes of manufacture, machine requirements, factory layout, storage and handling systems, skills required in workmen and their method of training can be determined. This policy is largely determined by the nature of the work being carried out. Factors to consider are the following.

193

1. Amount of repetition

This is a dominating factor and has three reasonably definite stages:

(a) *Job production (or unit production)*

This occurs when a customer requires a single product made to his specifications, e.g. a ship or a suit. Demand can be only broadly forecasted and generally production schedules can be prepared only when the customer's order arrives. There is no production for stock and there are only limited stocks of materials kept. There must be a wider variety of machines and equipment available to do all types of work and labour must have varied skills; this may not be too easy to achieve.

In practice, a firm specializing in job production may be able to produce more of a particular article and the organization may be similar to that of small batch production.

(b) *Batch production*

This occurs where a quantity of products or components are made at the same time. There is repetition, but not continuous production. Production often is for stock, but if a batch is required to fulfil a special order the items are usually completed in one run. Small batches are virtually unit production and the choice of an economic batch size is very important. The numerous factors determining this size are considered in various formulae.

(c) *Flow production*

This occurs where there is a continuous production of products of a more or less identical nature. There is very little waiting between the execution of one operation and another and each machine is continually used for one product and these are often specialized single-purpose machines. There can also be greater expenditure on equipment because of the high rate of production. It is vital that maintenance be planned to prevent breakdowns, as the breakdown of one machine can stop the production line.

There should be reliability of machines and in the supply of raw material. There must of course be a continuous demand for the products and the work must be arranged so that the best use is made of machinery.

The newer forms of flow production are automated, whereby the product is automatically transferred from one machine to another.

N.B. The term 'mass production' should be avoided as it simply means a large quantity of production, and this can be achieved *without* using the flow technique.

2. The range of products

This will vary greatly from job production on the one hand to flow production on the other. Some firms are widely diversified and produce a large mixture of products.

3. Quality

The material used must be appropriate and strict observance of uniformity of quality can mean high purchase and inspection costs.

Workmanship can vary and if permitted tolerances are finely set it could mean greater accuracy is achieved than is necessary: this increases cost and is therefore wasteful.

B. FACTORY LOCATION AND LAYOUT

The following are among the many factors to be considered.

1. Selection of site

The selection of a site may be dependent upon:

(a) Availability of land

Land of the right nature and price must be available. There must be provision for expansion. In this connexion there are government aids, e.g. in Development Areas, which provide facilities for easy land purchase, and give other benefits.

(b) Availability of labour

The availability of labour of the right type is a strong locational factor.

(c) Availability of raw material

This is closely linked up with transport *facilities*, with regard to obtaining the raw material and later in disposing of the product. Nearness to sea, river, road or rail is usually important and essential; for example, the disposal of waste from electricity power stations usually necessitates a site near a river or the sea.

(d) Climate

For some industries climate may be a very important consideration in the choice of a site.

(e) Local regulations or bye-laws

These may be an important consideration as they may place restrictions on the industry.

(f) Social facilities

Availability of cultural and recreational activities, for example, and the suitability of housing accommodation may be important.

2. Selection of type of building

Brief consideration will be paid here to some factors, particularly to the height of the building and to the use of single or multi-storey construction.

(a) Single-storey buildings

Single-storey buildings can make better use of natural lighting. Heavy machinery can be placed with fewer restrictions compared with multi-storey buildings. Transport and movement of materials is quicker and easier and there is a lower cost of building and maintenance.

(b) Multi-storey buildings

These buildings make better use of scarce land. Gravity can be used for moving materials and there is economy of cabling and heating.

There are of course many other factors to be considered by the architect, e.g. position of workshops, canteen, offices, etc. Whatever type of building is considered, Factory Act regulations must be noted, especially regarding heating, lighting, ventilation and safety. The Offices, Shops and Railway Premises Act of 1963 must be noted also, and will be considered in more detail in the section on Office Management.

3. Layout

There are two main types of layout which can be adopted:

(a) Product layout

Where machines are laid out in accordance with sequences of operations to be carried out on the product, material should move from stores through the factory to distribution areas with a minimum of movement. Design changes will greatly increase the costs of production as plant layout and re-tooling are very costly, for example, in the car industry.

(*b*) *Process layout*

With this layout machines are grouped in sections, which depend upon the type of operation performed, e.g. welding. These specialized sections are more suitable for job and batch production and are adaptable, but involve greater materials handling.

C. PRODUCTION ORGANIZATION

Organization varies widely between firms and industries. This is partly accounted for by the varying sizes and the nature of goods produced and the manufacturing processes involved. The chart of an organization shown in Fig. 26 will be used as a guide to consider each department in turn and briefly describe the nature of work carried out therein.

In smaller concerns one person may be in charge of the technical and administration sections and many other variations may occur.

The technical activity is headed by a technical manager and comprises the following sections.

1. Research and development

The nature of this activity varies from industry to industry and from the different sizes and type of firm. Research can be considered to consist of the following types.

(*a*) *Pure or fundamental research*

This is concerned with obtaining new scientific principles such as the basic properties of a new element.

(*b*) *Applied research*

This involves creating a practical proposition from an idea. The knowledge obtained by basic research is used to solve industrial problems. It involves improving existing methods, organization, processes or equipment, or reducing the cost of products, or finding new uses for existing products or by-products.

It will have been noted from Fig. 25 on p. 173 that innovation is essential in order to arrest the decline of profits which will eventually occur if existing products are not altered or changed.

Development involves the design and engineering work necessary to enable a project to reach production stage. It involves models, prototypes and pilot plants. Development is therefore associated with research and with design and there is really no specific division between these three activities.

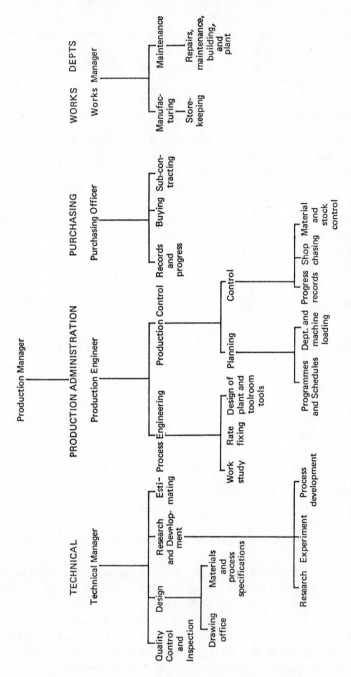

Fig. 26. Organization chart for a medium-sized factory.

A survey by the Confederation of British Industry showed that firms with the highest rate of internal research per 100 employees had a rate of growth of total net assets half as high again as those with the lowest expenditure on research.

The *stages of research* follow these lines:

(*a*) The *initial concept* is formed; this is the ideas stage.

(*b*) A *feasibility study* then takes place, whereby problems are defined, terms of reference drawn up and the possible sales are estimated and consideration is given to the economic justification of the project.

(*c*) The actual project is then *agreed upon* or rejected.

(*d*) If accepted, *a prototype* is developed, or pilot plant built.

(*e*) A *full-scale model* is then constructed with full co-operation between research and the production staff who will have responsibility for its commercial operation.

There are of course many problems, for example, the project may soon be made obsolete by technical developments, or a change in taste by consumers or a competitor's new ideas; the policy of the company could also change. (The aircraft industry is a good illustration of a case where vast amounts of money were spent on research and development, the projects being later cancelled.)

It is worth noting that barely 5 per cent of inventions submitted to the National Research Development Corporation are turned into industrial products. (These exclude individuals and private firms.)

The organization of research

There are many types of research work, and in all cases the organization of a company should enable all ideas to be co-ordinated. This sometimes is done by a research committee responsible to a research director. Many companies though will not be able to afford their own research and consequently they can take one of the following courses of action:

(*a*) Employ outside *consultants*, or consult independent research organizations, e.g. Science Research Council. The Council maintains a number of specialized research establishments such as the National Physical Laboratory and the Building and Chemical Research Laboratories.

(*b*) Join *Trade Research Associations* (e.g. Machine-Tool Research Association) which are supported by firms in those industries concerned and, by combining resources, can afford to hire top quality researchers. Member firms can obtain their help, as research information is supplied to all members.

(*c*) Contract with *University or Technical College* Research Departments to undertake research for them.

(*d*) The *National Research Development Corporation* is financed by the

Department of Trade and Industry and aids ideas which it appears industry is not going to back, but which are presumed to be in the public interest. The Hovercraft is an illustration of a project it backed.

The head of a research department (R/D) may be responsible to the technical manager or direct to the production manager. In some of the more recent industries, e.g. electronics, R/D reports direct to general management.

The question, whether R/D should be represented at board level, is sometimes asked. There can be no set answer, and the same applies to any of the other activities: it all depends whether the *person* concerned can make an effective contribution to management problems of the *business*. 'Representation' as such cannot really be a criterion of appointment to the board.

There is, though, no reason why such specialists cannot be co-opted to the board to give special research advice.

The *qualities of a research worker* can be summarized: 'technical qualifications and creative and analytical ability, enthusiasm and single-mindedness of purpose, appreciation of the commercial aspects of the firm and ability to mix with people.' Some of these qualities will need to be stressed more than others, depending upon the type of research upon which engaged.

As values are different in scientific fields, a knowledge of sociology can help to manage personnel in R/D. Scientific achievement and the discovery of new knowledge and the resultant status from professional reputation is often reward in itself.

Monetary reward is of course important, and a *suitable environment* may include such factors as:

(*a*) *Opportunity* for research and appreciation of work done.

(*b*) Allowing individuals *latitude* in following their own ideas.

(*c*) Giving *incentives* to creative work, by sympathetic management action and freedom in professional dealings.

Relationships with other departments, especially with the marketing department, are necessary. Close liaison is essential and it is here that the research programme budget can help. An interchange of personnel can be most beneficial.

Financial control of research

Management must establish objectives and policies for research and then a programme is required to attain these objectives. The main restriction is money and the allocation of money can vary enormously as there are few guidelines.

The board must consider many factors, such as the future economic position of the firm and the country, the rate of obsolescence of existing products and the amount needed (at least) to replace these, whether personnel and equipment are available, whether competitors are strong and forward-looking.

The main costs are salaries, equipment provided and the upkeep of the laboratory: these are mainly fixed costs. One graduate scientist, for example, with attendant staff and services, would cost at least £7000.

Control over research expenditure can be exercised by:

(*a*) Overall financial policy.

(*b*) Actual research programme.

(*c*) Control over each individual step from initial idea to commercial exploitation.

Method suggested

(*a*) A long-term and annual plan must be drawn up and then broken down into quarter years.

(*b*) This gives a basis for manpower needs.

(*c*) This programme, which is concerned with broad allocation of resources, can first of all be divided between different types of research, e.g. basic, applied, etc.

(*d*) Within these types of research, a further breakdown into stages is made, e.g. initial ideas, feasibility, etc.

(*e*) A further breakdown of each stage of work into, for example, division of a company, or subsidiaries, improvement of materials or reduction of costs, or customers' sponsored R/D work, etc., will enable resources to be spread so that a balanced R/D programme can be built up.

(*f*) Individual projects can now be considered within this overall framework. A list of priorities and estimated man hours and total costs required are calculated and expenditure budgets prepared.

(*g*) Periodic review and analysis of actual expenditure with the budget is essential, preferably by a policy committee composed of sales, production, finance and research personnel. Projects not considered worthwhile must be cancelled.

(*h*) Future quarter's budgets can be put into a better perspective by noting the present quarter's results.

(*i*) Ratios may be used to analyse research spending and show the factors having important effects on profitability, e.g. research costs to capital investment, total sales, or new product sales, or number of employees.

Ratios must of course be analysed carefully and, if comparisons are made with other companies in the same industry, great care is needed. (See p. 124.)

2. Design

The purpose of design is more than to improve the appearance of a product: it must also satisfy the customer in its performance, durability, simplicity of operation and cheapness. A new or changed design can be costly, as it may need new tools, or new layout of works and employees may have to be retrained.

Design *policy* must be formulated in terms a designer can understand and act upon. For example, a car firm requires low cost and high performance, while incorporating as many features as possible from higher priced models.

Product selection, simplification and standardization are also closely linked in discussing design policy. Variety reduction, for example, cuts out wasteful practices, and standard components may be used instead of special ones. (This point will be discussed later in the chapter.)

Product design indicates the formulation of articles to be made so as to specify shape and dimensions, materials and parts required and the type of finish. The product is given a complete specification to enable everyone concerned to be aware of all requirements. Design can have several aspects:

(a) *Design for production*

This is to ensure component parts are made easily and economically, so that they can be assembled and transported easily and sold at an attractive price.

The designer must therefore be aware of the production processes, the alternative methods available and their cost.

(b) *Design for function*

Value in use implies quality and reliability: the product must satisfy the customer in its purpose and give a long service.

(c) *Design for appearance*

To please the eye and attract customers.

(d) *Design for distribution*

To enable easy packing, reduction of storage space and packing costs.

A designer's ideas must be merged with those of the production engineer and the marketing side, who give market research information of customers' requirements and enable decisions to be made as to whether full-scale production should be authorized. A development committee, which was mentioned before, would contain representatives from all interested departments.

Organization of the design department

A design director may be in charge of designers in a large firm. He may also have research and drawing office staff under his direction. Small firms may have one designer or give the work to a consultant.

N.B. The Council of Industrial Design offers services to manufacturers, e.g. free advice on problems of design policy and organization, and will assist in the selection of designers.

A *design and development engineer* may be appointed to be in charge of the technical department and the following job specification shows the range of his work.

Responsible to:
Production Manager.

Responsible for:
Interpretation of company trading policy regarding new product formulation and the modification of existing products.

Determination of the design and specification of the product to be manufactured.

Establishing and maintaining the necessary facilities for drawing office and research and development work.

Preparing estimates of the cost of producing a job to customer's requirements—the estimates to be sent via the marketing department to the customer.

Providing facilities and staff, under a chief inspector, for the objective inspection of manufacturing components and assemblies.

Preparation of programme for R/D projects.

Improving existing products or extending the range.

Maintaining records of progress of projects and submission of reports and statements of expenditure incurred.

Limitations: No responsibility or authority for:
Choice of product to be manufactured.
Manufacturing programmes or delivery dates.
Purchase of plant or equipment.

Special relationships:
(*a*) with *Production Manager* for the maintenance of scheme for classification and coding; review of manufacturing methods and investigation into components proving difficult to manufacture, establishing routines for inspection of parts produced by factory.

(*b*) with *Marketing Manager* for standards of finish and consideration of technical aspects of customers' requests for product improvements.

The duties are numerous and this key position calls for a person of wide knowledge. A designer must therefore identify the many factors influencing design and any solution must cover the demands of competing requirements (e.g. function, ergonomics, economics, brand presentation, aesthetics, motivation and production).

The drawing office

The drawing office is in many firms responsible for designing all products manufactured. In the case of stock items, the office has responsibility for keeping the product up to date in design and appearance. The head should therefore be fully aware of the use of the product and the methods of manufacture.

The customers' specifications are often broad in outline and the drawing office prepares detailed drawings or decides which of the standard drawings shall be used.

Organization of the drawing office

It is important that work is not duplicated and that blueprints can be found quickly. A code number is given to each *drawing*. Each *part* also has a number. If a part can be used elsewhere all that needs to be done is to state the original drawing and part number. Drawings can be classified according to product or type of part. Standard drawings of all parts in frequent use are convenient and are issued to operatives—if they are pasted on to plywood they last a long time. Old and used drawings must be *withdrawn immediately* to obviate their being used in error.

A satisfactory method in use today is to let the drawing office, rather than the work's foreman, prepare specification lists or bills of materials, and copies are sent to production and stores. The materials required will be automatically issued before a job commences. The use of master specifications for standard lines saves time. Micro-films and aperture cards (see p. 327) are useful in saving space. They are easily accessible and can be enlarged and printed when required from the original master.

3. Estimating

Particulars of the final design are given to the planner who must have guidance as to the estimated cost. If a product is to be made to customer specifications a quotation will have been given, such details of cost being supplied by the estimating section. In smaller concerns the estimator is also the planner. If a product is internally designed, the estimate can be discussed with the marketing department which may suggest a lower price and this may mean an alteration in design. The estimator has less work to do when products are more standard. The activity is usually concerned with producing costs for making or repairing equipment for other companies rather than the general public.

The prices of standard articles are easily found, but a quotation requires careful consideration of numerous factors. Data are available from past records and a good knowledge of customer needs is essential. A cost chart can be prepared, this enables future varying requirements to be readily calculated. A knowledge of limiting or special factors of the machines and equipment is needed, e.g. the size of doorways or lifting capacity of cranes. Special arrangements may then have to be made with a corresponding cost increase.

Full co-operation between departments is needed, i.e. financial, production engineering, drawing office, marketing. The final estimate involves considering material content and expected prices, labour hours and rates, overhead costs and profit margin. The use of marginal costing for estimating is advocated by many accountants and this may be appropriate in certain circumstances.

4. Standardization, simplification and specialization

We will examine each of these terms separately.

Standardization

The word is used in many ways, but a precise definition is that it is the process of obtaining agreement on:

(*a*) A standard for a product, range of products or procedure. (This may be a standard of performance, testing, method of manufacture, composition or dimensions.)

(*b*) The application of that standard.

The objects being to facilitate interchangeability between parts and reduce costs, e.g. the use of the same instruments in all ranges of cars. The design department can play a large part. There are often small differences existing between parts, and with little effort a slight change in design could mean one part only could be used in place of a number of parts.

The British Standards Institution have now issued over 5000 standards; these are based upon the best present practice and provide a suitable standard and equitable basis for tenders.

Advantages to producer

(*a*) *Reduction in variety*, offering long production runs, and lower tooling and setting up costs.

(*b*) Greater use can be made of *special purpose machines* as output is greater—this will mean lower operating costs.

(*c*) Reduction in stocks, materials, components and finished products, tools, idle time and overhead costs.

(*d*) *Quality* can be more consistent and there will be less maintenance and service costs.

(*e*) *Purchasing costs* would fall because of the smaller range of materials.

(*f*) *Training costs* would fall as training became shorter and simpler.

Advantages to consumer

(*a*) Lower prices.

(*b*) Interchangeability.

(*c*) Better supplies, service and maintenance available.

Disadvantages

The disadvantages of standardization must be noted:

(*a*) Slowness in bringing out new inventions and fewer beneficial design changes, which can have a marked effect on any sales of some products, e.g. cars.

(*b*) Customers have fewer choices of product and there is less chance of special orders being produced.

(*c*) Costs of standardization involve possible redundant stocks.

(*d*) Parts or materials may be used which are not really suitable to get maximum standardization.

The procedure to install standardization involves examining the existing or proposed range and selecting items which are similar in material, shape or purpose. Then they are examined to see if standardization is possible in initial design or existing designs and changes can then be considered by a departmental committee.

Simplification

This is the process of reducing the number of types and varieties made. In practice simplification and standardization are closely linked, as for example when considering reduction in variety it may be seen that standard components may be introduced. The problems of variety reduction vary, but the objective, to cut out *wasteful* variety, is necessary (e.g. two engine sizes were used instead of the previous five in a motor car manufacturer's). An efficient costing system can aid the identification of products absorbing an undue proportion of manufacturing resources.

Advantages

(*a*) Longer runs which allow increased batch size and may lead to more production and greater mechanization.

(*b*) Tooling and setting up times can be reduced.

(*c*) Simpler and cheaper inspection—more use can be made of specialized inspection equipment.

(*d*) Stock control and storekeeping will be cheaper, as less capital is tied up in raw materials, components and finished products.

(*e*) Fewer drawings will be needed.

(*f*) Marketing policy could be made simpler, as prices could be lower, especially as a reduction in advertising and other costs is possible.

(*g*) Administration in general will be more efficient as there will be economies in all functions. There will also be less time spent on training personnel.

The *consumer* benefits by better value, better service in delivery and repairs and product quality.

Specialization

This occurs where resources are exclusively used to make a narrow range of products. This basic economic principle (so clearly illustrated by the example of pin-making in Adam Smith's book *Wealth of Nations*, 1796) can take many forms, e.g. product or worker specialization.

The advantages are that skills are enhanced because of concentrating on a limited range of work. Costs of maintenance and stocks fall because variety is reduced and this enables a greater concentration to be made in marketing.

The *disadvantages* include the fact that too much specialization may lead to loss as technology changes rapidly. Diversification is needed and many companies today are realizing this. There is also less flexibility and too narrow an outlook.

5. Quality control (Q.C.)

Quality control is of vital importance to British industry especially as competition is intense and consumers become more discriminating. A survey showed that larger firms are more likely to have Q.C. departments. 92 per cent of firms employing over 2000 have Q.C. departments, compared with 62 per cent of firms with under 300 staff. The food and chemical industries are strongly devoted to Q.C., largely because health inspectors enforce food and drug laws.

It has been stated that Q.C. is an attitude of mind, and there is a great deal of truth in this statement. Some qualities cannot be directly measured, these are called 'attributes'; measurable qualities are called 'variables.'

Quality determines the direction or objective: control is the statistical element which measures product quality. Statistical quality control is a method of measuring deviations from standard quality by recording sample tests on charts. If limits are known, they can be easily seen. The theory of probability is applied to samples, enabling trends to be seen and corrective action to be taken, to avoid unnecessary scrap.

Quality begins and ends with marketing; once customer requirements are defined, a quick reporting process is needed, which should be maintained throughout design, specification, manufacture and inspection.

It is the primary concern of management to find and maintain the right quality which forms the basis of a product's profitability. Thousands of new cars were recently called in by manufacturers to replace one defective part—this was a costly operation.

Organization for quality

The position of the Q.C. department shows how seriously an organization regards it. In the previously mentioned survey 44 per cent of firms said the head of Q.C. was responsible to the board of directors, 25 per cent said responsible to the works manager and 11 per cent to the production manager.

The question arises, should the head of Q.C. be independent of production and free to report direct to top management, or is Q.C. a function and responsibility of production? Most authorities would prefer Q.C. to be in a position where production could not over-ride its decisions. The *purposes of quality control* organization are:

(a) To establish standards of quality.
(b) To assess conformity to them.
(c) To take corrective action.
(d) To prepare improved standards.

Controls are required for design, supplier appraisal, incoming inspection of materials, process control, research and testing. The sources of quality lie in the *decisions and actions of people in many departments*, hence there should be good internal communications and reliable feedback of information from all departments and from consumers and preferably an after-sales service.

A designer has a problem as greater quality usually means greater cost and a proper balance must be obtained. He soon comes up against financial or technical barriers, and he must try to find the *optimum quality of design.*

The most profitable quality level is achieved by a balance between cost of quality to the manufacturers and value of quality to the consumer. (See Fig. 27.)

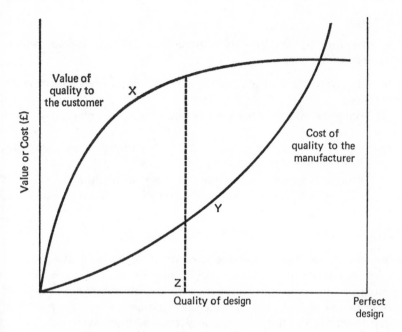

Fig. 27. Optimum quality of design. Z is point of optimum profitability, and is the greatest distance between X and Y. Above the optimum, the cost of achieving greater quality of design, more than outweighs any increase in market value.

Quality and reliability are two different but closely related aspects of the provision of a better service to customers.

A customer buys a product largely on the probability that it will continue to function satisfactorily throughout its planned working life, provided that it is used and maintained as intended. Reliability is proof of quality. In many cars there are over 600 critical components so it needs a reliability level per individual component of over 99 per cent for a high proportion of vehicles to operate satisfactorily.

The investigations of Dr J. M. Juran, the American consultant, show about 80 per cent of quality failures are *management-controllable.* Quick action is needed to secure quality and reliability and that is why any Q.R. organization must have top management backing and control.

In quality control, the taking of samples of raw materials, finished goods, etc., is known as *acceptance sampling*. Inspection of parts of a process as they are produced to detect variations is known as *process control*.

In acceptance sampling, quality levels are agreed with the supplier for sampling the materials and if rejects in a sample exceed the agreed percentage the batch is rejected.

Inspection

Any system of appraisal depends upon decisions of the inspector, who is often responsible for:

(*a*) Organizing the work of other inspectors to see that they are instructed and trained.

(*b*) Seeing that the company's policy regarding quality and standards of finish is upheld.

(*c*) Inspecting work and raw materials, recording results, notifying foremen of rejects and passing acceptable goods.

(*d*) Seeing that gauges and tools are properly maintained.

(*e*) Keeping up to date with new developments in methods of inspection.

Requirements of an inspector

Impartiality and strength of character to abide by a decision, skill in inspection and ability to decide quickly from various facts, are required of an inspector. He has to please (*a*) the works department which requires greater output at lower cost; (*b*) the sales and design departments which require high quality; thus he must be tactful and diplomatic.

The first requirement is to prevent faulty work going on to the next stage or process and preferably to stop it being made.

In some industries 100 per cent inspection is necessary, e.g. in the making of submarines. This is very costly, and often the first item produced is inspected in each batch. Reports of rejects are sent periodically to the department head and only inspectors are allowed to scrap work and arrange for re-processing or rectification of faulty work.

Centralized inspection

Under this system all work is sent to the inspection department before passing to the next operation.

The *advantages* of centralized inspection are:

(*a*) Division of labour is possible and more expensive machines may be purchased, allowing less-skilled labour to be employed.

(*b*) Work is more easily supervised.

(*c*) The shop floor is cleaner and losses from scrap, etc., more easily observed.

The *disadvantages* arise from the greater amount of handling, transport and work in process.

Floor inspection

Here inspectors go to the machine or work bench and inspect on the shop floor. This type of inspection has the following advantages:

(*a*) Less handling and delay in transfer to and from the central inspection department.

(*d*) Work in progress is reduced and faults can be remedied immediately.

(*c*) Advice can be given to the operator immediately.

6. Value engineering (V.E.) or value analysis

This is another discipline which originated in the U.S.A. and was brought to this country in the early 1950s. In 1964 full details of savings made were published and centres were set up giving instructions in this technique.

V.E. is a technique which endeavours to discover the most economical way of performing the function of each part of a manufactured product.

It is more a psychological discipline, an attitude of mind rather than a scientific formula. Management must play a large part in developing a V.E. programme and impress everyone that their co-operation is essential.

The analysis is brought right back to the *design stage*, instead of beginning with design and examining the methods used from that point forward.

Summary of method

(*a*) *Define* the function of each item or part.

(*b*) Consider *alternative* ways of performing the same function.

(*c*) Find the *cost* of these alternatives.

(*d*) If, at this stage, no alternative is significantly cheaper, either find more alternatives or abandon analysis.

(*e*) A more *detailed cost analysis* is then made of acceptable alternatives.

(*f*) *Selection* is made of the more acceptable alternatives and after careful examination, if it enables the *same function* to be performed as the original part, and if it is *less costly*, it will be approved.

It is simply a *discipline* used to examine each component in a design, logically and systematically, to see if a part, or an alternative part, can be made to perform the same function more cheaply. Conventional cost reducing techniques begin with cost and seek to reduce it. V.E. starts with the function, then considers the cost.

Place in organization

As a staff function, V.E. may form part of a quality control section or, in a few large firms, a separate function reporting to production management.

In *purchasing*, the value analyst has prime responsibility for value in material and services procured. He serves as a consultant to buyers.

A basic engineering training is usually essential plus training in value analysis. The value analyst must have a high degree of initiative and creativity, be able to sell his ideas and be *cost-conscious*.

When costs are reduced by this technique, often the quality and reliability of the product are improved, because the thinking was directed to improving the function of the part in the best possible way.

7. Production administration

This consists of process engineering, production planning and production control.

(a) Process engineering

This is a branch of production administration responsible for deciding how work is to be done, the measurement of work and the establishment of standard times and practices, the preparation and revision of process specifications and the design of tools and equipment.

The work of the head of process engineering may briefly comprise:

(i) Investigations into processes and operations to establish the correct way to carry them out, to reduce fatigue and to eliminate unnecessary operations.

(ii) Preparation of drawings for jigs and tools and inspection equipment.

(iii) Establishing standard times after collecting data and operation times.

(iv) Reporting and investigating excess costs and being aware of modern trends in manufacturing methods and machines.

(v) Maintaining company's personnel policy, training staff effectively.

Work study

This is a management tool comprising those techniques, particularly method study and work measurement, which are used in the examination of human work in all its contents and which lead systematically to the investigation of all the factors which affect the efficiency and economy of the situation being reviewed, in order to effect improvement. This definition is an extract from British Standard 3138.

The performance of a firm can be increased by either improving the processes of manufacture or by developing new and more suitable machines and equipment. This usually takes a long time for research and is called *process study*. It often requires considerable expenditure and is really part of research and development. It is linked with work study and in practice there is no clear line of demarcation between them.

Work study can bring quick improvements for the outlay of little capital expenditure.

Work study is needed because it:

(i) Leads to saving in production costs and makes more effective use of human effort.

(ii) Provides information and reveals inefficiency.

(iii) Improves conditions, methods and layout.

(iv) Ensures a steady flow of material and an equal reward for the same skill and effort.

(v) Establishes a standard rate or time for a job.

There are two techniques comprising work study, these are method study and work measurement.

Method study

This is the detailed analysis of an existing or proposed method as a basis for improvements. It is the first part of work study, and its objectives are to improve methods, or establish a correct method for job or process; this will economize in human effort and make more efficient use of men, materials and machines.

It can be applied in the office or factory and should be considered in the design stages of new jobs, as important economies can be made at this stage. The basic procedure is to:

(i) Select work to be studied.

(ii) Report relevant facts of method used.

(iii) Examine facts logically.

(iv) Develop a more effective method.

(v) Install and maintain this method as standard practice.

Recording is made easier by using cine-cameras, but basic recording techniques comprise:

(i) Process charting, which shows in a diagrammatic form the sequence of events in manufacture. Symbols are used which enable information to be set down logically and can be used to visualize the problem more easily. (See section on Organization and Methods in chapter 9.)

(ii) Flow diagrams are scale diagrams showing in detail the progress of the material or component through various departments. Multiple activity charts, motion charts and films may be used.

Work measurement

This is the application of techniques designed to establish the time for a qualified worker to carry out a specified job at a defined level of performance (British Standard definition). The unit of measurement which is common to most jobs is time. Time study is generally based upon noting the time for each element of a job. Allowances are made for personal needs, and the speed and effort of the worker and a work standard can be built up and the 'time allowed,' which is a standard, may be used as a basis for accurate costing, planning or incentive schemes. It is best suited to repetitive work.

Predetermined motion time systems (PMTS)

These systems establish times for basic human motions and are used to build up the time for a job at a defined level of performance. Operations are divided into a limited number of basic manual motions, for each of which a time has been established, this time being determined by the *nature* of the motion and the *conditions* under which it is made. The same principle can now be applied to the office as well as in the factory.

Plant and tool designers play a valuable part in designing new tools, department layouts and special machines. Tool design and making must be integrated with production programmes and this work must be closely linked with that of work study engineers in designing improvements to present methods.

Ergonomics

This is called human engineering or human factors engineering in the U.S.A., and there is a difference in *emphasis* between the terms used in the two countries.

In the past, there have been many studies of the impact of nature and environment on the capacity of men to work. Many of the new words in management describe, in a different way, approaches to subjects which have occurred in the past. Ergonomics is such a word, derived from the Greek *ergon* (work) and *nomos* (law) and has been defined as the scientific study of the relationship between man and his working environment and the application of anatomical, physiological and psychological knowledge to the problems arising therefrom.

The human machine is studied, in order to produce machines and equipment to reduce physical and mental strain. The area of activity covered by ergonomics is large and the following areas are examples.

(i) Environment in general. Studies are made of the effect of light, temperature, ventilation, noise, etc., on the health of workers, e.g. avoidance of high-pitched sounds which irritate.

(ii) In the workplace—physical problems of work are studied, including layout of equipment. Use of better-designed chairs, better positioning of hand and foot controls, and control panels.

(iii) Mental problems at work would involve studies in fatigue, fault-finding analysis, problems of age. The older workers have problems of hearing and eyesight and have a slower reaction.

(b) Production control

This is one aspect of the control function and there are many definitions of what comprises production control. No ideal system can be stated. Every enterprise is different but no matter what method of organization is adopted, production must be planned and controlled so that products are supplied in the right quantity and quality at the right time, at minimum cost.

In smaller concerns, memory and experience are relied upon to a large extent in planning and control. Larger concerns need an efficient, flexible system to plan and control the mass of information, materials and machines.

(c) Production planning

This may be said to comprise the following purposes:

(i) To transform marketing requirements into instructions to the production departments. These take the form of works orders or programmes.

(ii) To see men and materials are employed on work for which they are most suited and to keep schedules up to date, so that deviations from programmes can easily be seen.

(iii) To maintain a balance between the various manufacturing processes, to stop work 'bottlenecks' which would mean lower utilization of men and machines.

(iv) To arrange manufacturing orders in the best sequence, in economic batches.

(v) To liaise between marketing and production and to reschedule production if necessary so that delivery requirements can be fulfilled.

Simple example of routes involved

(i) When an enquiry (invitation to quote) is received, the production control section must see if the necessary labour, material and plant capacity is available. A capacity record is needed and also a record of the load on each process or group of machines.

(ii) Orders when received are broken down into operations and the time each machine will be occupied is estimated and noted on a *load record*. This record will be reduced by work completed and this loading determines whether or not orders can be accepted, or whether delivery can be on time.

(iii) From the drawings (prepared by the drawing office) *parts lists* (or specifications) can be prepared, showing material required, part numbers, numbers required and detailed descriptions.

(iv) From the parts lists, *material schedules* can be prepared; these show all material needed for the contract. Then the operation or process planning layout (or sequence schedule or route card) is prepared, showing processing sequences and the time for each process or operation, specifying *jigs and tools* required. It may also show particulars of materials, e.g. size, quantity and quality, and the particular machine and operations to be performed. The *full specification* will be shown on the top part of the document.

(v) The *scheduling* section will examine this layout chart and compile hours of work for drilling, milling, etc., breaking details into weekly quantities over the production timetable.

(vi) Target dates can now be set for the *master production schedule*. This shows *shop* load programmes enabling foremen to see required weekly output. The use of a *material delivery schedule* enables a check to be made as to whether suppliers are despatching materials on time.

When schedules have been compiled, the next stage is to authorize the production of an order, called a *works order*. This is an instruction to the foreman to manufacture a specific quantity of products. They should ideally be drawn up in advance of the time required and issued by a central authority in the production control department. Other documents need to be issued to permit the withdrawal of tools and stores. In many firms these documents may comprise material movement forms, inspection tickets and work payment tickets as well as the works orders.

The control part of production planning and control can be said to comprise progress and material control. *Progress control* implies the checking and review of all aspects of the production plan. It is the means by which the production plan is co-ordinated so as to reveal any variations. Information as to the progress of manufacture is 'fed back' to ensure a smooth production flow. Successful progress control requires speed and accuracy and a wide range of visual charting methods can be used to aid progressing.

Expediting

Expediting or the progressing of work needs a type of person who is flexible, friendly and firm in his actions and with a sound knowledge of all the company's products. Co-operation with supervisors is essential as programmes may frequently be changed and this could cause friction.

One aspect of expediting is to see that components and assemblies flow smoothly through the stages of manufacture. Another is to see information is quickly available and disseminated. The follow-up procedure is the function of the progress 'chasers' who may have a status equivalent to that of assistant foreman. They are organized in two ways:

(i) By having one progress man responsible for a section or department.
(ii) A progress man responsible for a product or group of components.

Some firms may operate both systems.

Examination of periodic lists of jobs overdue, and special checks on items having no 'margin' (i.e. on the critical path) are basic duties of the progress chaser.

Materials control

This section is responsible for ensuring that the right quantity and quality of material is available when and where required. At the same time capital must not be tied up unduly, nor must there be undue loss from deterioration and obsolescence.

A good system of materials control requires:

(i) Centralization of purchasing under a buyer.
(ii) Department co-ordination—in purchasing, inspecting, receiving, storing and issuing materials.
(iii) Simplifying and standardizing whenever possible.
(iv) Efficiency in storing in suitable accommodation, with safeguards against pilfering, deterioration, waste, etc.
(v) Planning and scheduling material requirements, and preferably control by budget.
(vi) Stocktaking procedure to be efficient.

N.B. It is pointed out later that material and stock control come under the purchasing officer in some companies.

Stores control

The position of the stores in the organization varies widely. Some companies show the stores under the purchasing officer: others prefer the section to be under the works manager. A satisfactory arrangement is for the recording of the stores to be under production control, while the physical aspect is under the works department. The details of stock should be readily available to production control so that stocks can be replenished when necessary.

Stocks are held to make production possible even though demand fluctuates. Factors aiding stock control are:

(i) Accurate coding and classifying of stores.

(ii) Perpetual inventory records and periodic physical checking of stock.

(iii) Efficient accounting procedures and a system of preventing obsolete or surplus stock.

Stores records may be ledger cards or punched cards showing minimum and maximum stock level, order or re-order level, standard order, the item's catalogue and part number, in addition to opening and closing balances, receipts and issues.

Maximum levels when set must consider price fluctuations and available capital, possible obsolescence, available storage space and whether material can be stored a long time or not, economic ordering quantity and rate of consumption and costs of insurance.

Minimum levels will be fixed after noting the purchasing time cycle. The time between placing an order and its subsequent fulfilment is called *lead* time, made up of time in placing order, time in executing order and time receiving order. Factors affecting minimum stock are:

(i) Uncertainty of demand. The greater the uncertainty, the greater the stock.

(ii) Uncertainty of lead time. If this is great, the higher the stock needs to be.

(iii) The size of the batch. The larger the batch, the less frequently will the stock fall to 'danger' level, and the smaller the minimum stock required.

(iv) The more standard the item, the more easily it will be obtainable. A special item may take longer to obtain.

Re-order levels are important and must note lead time and normal consumption.

Duties of a storekeeper

(i) Supervise and guide staff in their duties.

(ii) See records are up to date and all departments are given an efficient service.

(iii) Co-operate with planning, purchasing and inspection departments.

(iv) Receive goods from outside, check number, and arrange for inspection, reporting variances from order to purchasing section.

(v) Check stock physically at least once a year and ensure it is stored neatly and safely.

(vi) Issue stock on appropriate instructions and record accurately stock movements on documents involved, e.g. copy order, materials release note, etc.

Type of stores

Raw material stores vary with the type of industry. Component stores carry piece parts to be manufactured in the factory or purchased from outside. Raw material and component stores often go together. Finished part stores are used where the company are not using transfer machines, and finished parts have to be stored in readiness for assembly and sub-assembly. Indirect stores are, for example, the tool store, issuing tools in exchange for a tool check bearing operator's name and number.

Other tools are consumable, e.g. files. Indirect materials are stored separately, e.g. oil.

Maintenance stores keep all parts required for routine and preventive maintenance.

Arrangement of stores

The stores must be convenient for the factory. The layout should be convenient to the class of goods handled and bins, etc., should be arranged in a logical order; the following rules are important:

(i) Heavy goods should be kept near the floor.

(ii) Goods most frequently required should be easily accessible.

(iii) Goods susceptible to dampness should be kept dry and inflammable materials to be kept in fireproof containers.

(iv) Valuable or fragile goods should receive special protection.

The maximum use should be made of height, e.g. use of fork-lift trucks and pallets. Metal racks are strong and conveniently easy to erect and dismantle. Materials should flow into stores via the inspection department and then flow to works. Finished goods should move via inspection to despatch. The place and method of storage must, of course, suit the method of handling and gangways should be sufficiently wide for mechanical aids.

Centralized or departmental stores

The advantages of centralized stores are:

(i) Specialized facilities can be installed, e.g. refrigeration.

(ii) Smaller stocks can be carried, thus reducing risks of deterioration and obsolescence, reducing working capital and storage space and lowering insurance costs.

(iii) Physical stock control is easier.

(iv) Total staff may be reduced.

The disadvantages are, in effect, the advantages of departmental stores:

(i) Greater convenience to each department in having its own stores, as main stores may be far away.

(ii) Saving is made in freight and handling costs by having departmental stores. Some heavy raw materials, e.g. coal, may be easier to keep in a decentralized store.

In practice a main store for raw materials issues materials against requisitions submitted by sub-stores in each manufacturing department and replenishment is on an 'imprest system.'

Pre-production planning is a term which is sometimes used and can be considered to be a branch of production administration which includes those functions which must be carried out before production begins. It is concerned with:

(i) Product Design and Development. The needs of the customer must be known and continuous research is needed into new methods, markets and materials. The physical limitations of production capacity must be known so that orders are not accepted if they cannot be produced on time.

(ii) Production Engineering. Standard times and methods of working must be considered both for manufacturing jigs and tools and actual manufacturing operations.

(iii) Estimating. Material specifications may be built up and parts lists and operation schedules prepared so the cost can be calculated and a price fixed.

(iv) Production Planning. The other information required before production actually commences can be considered under this heading. It includes knowledge of available orders and stocks, etc., to enable an analysis of requirements of materials and components, length of time operations will take, etc. Each order can then be analysed into component factors, e.g. machine and labour hours.

Pre-production planning can be simply defined as follows: the co-ordination of information on manufacturing capacity and material availability so that control of new manufacturing requirements is facilitated. It is also concerned with the possible effect on capacity of research trends, changes in design and methods of manufacture.

8. Purchasing

The procurement of supplies for any type of enterprise is often not given the importance which the job warrants. In many cases over 50 per cent of money spent is on materials purchased and this may exceed payments for salaries and wages.

Material may be purchased at too high a price, or of the wrong quality, or too great a quantity, which may lead to obsolescence and loss of interest on capital. Too little purchased means production delays. So incorrect buying can have a marked effect upon profits.

Organization

The position of the purchasing officer or buyer varies widely. Often the total cost of materials purchased may determine whether the buyer is of equal status to the other departmental heads or is a director. He is often responsible to the works manager or another section of the production department, but no specific place can be fixed for his position.

A buyer's responsibilities vary, and in some cases he may be responsible for stores records and stores departments. In order to take advantage of specialization of skills, it may be considered that too many varied sections should not be placed under the purchasing officer. Stores records for example are often placed under the jurisdiction of the planning department and the works department may have the stores under its care. This arrangement is considered very practical as the planners need stock details, and as storekeeping is a physical job intimately connected with works, which may be dispersed, it can best be controlled by the works department.

Purchasing may be divided among buying staff according to the *types of material*: this makes full use of specialization. Another method is for a buyer to handle all purchases for a *specific section* of the business. The progress section must see all purchases are received on time and records all information in this respect. The *records* aspect deals with invoices, receipts and routine information.

A company with numerous factories may have local buyers in each factory in addition to head office buyers. Other larger companies may have a director of purchasing or supplies in charge of the function, as in Fig. 28.

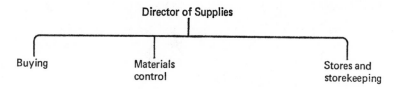

Fig. 28.

Whatever the organization structure, the company objectives on purchasing must be upheld. These may involve:

(*a*) buying materials at the lowest cost consistent with the service and quality required;

(*b*) avoiding any waste or duplication, while maintaining the lowest possible outlay on stock consistent with making the material needed for production available when required.

The use of a purchasing manual enables responsibilities to be defined and the establishment of uniform policies and procedures. This is essential where buying is decentralized.

Briefly, purchasing *policy* may be concerned with:

(*a*) Whether to buy on *contract* on a medium or long-term basis; this can be used where price variations are small. This avoids holding large stocks and such continuity of supply is very important in flow production.

(*b*) To buy when *required*; this involves limiting purchases to minimum requirements and the buyer has wide discretion. This is likely to be used for non-standard goods and results in less capital tied up in stock and hence less storage is needed. Price fluctuations are not likely to be so important, but there can be little gain if prices fall as quantities purchased are small.

The purchase of small quantities will raise unit cost, as well as increase handling and packing costs.,

(*c*) *Speculative* or *bargain* buying. As with any speculation, profits and losses could be high. Material is purchased with the hope of future price rises, thus saving money or with the expectation of re-sale at a profit later on. This latter system is used in some industries, particularly staple goods, e.g. copper. If adopted it is essential for a senior executive to control such actions.

The advantages of centralizing buying are:

(*a*) Higher degree of specialization as individuals can concentrate on a limited number of fields.

(*b*) Control is easier as records are centralized.

(*c*) Because of increased quantities, advantage can be taken of quantity discounts.

(*d*) Standardization of specifications is easier to obtain.

If stores are under purchasing control and are situated a distance away, then control can be costly and inflexible. In general, some compromise between local and centralized purchasing may be the solution. This can be done by having a manual of standard procedures, with details of local purchases being sent to head office immediately. Limits to the amounts local buyers can spend would be made. Exceptional purchases over these limits would need head office approval. Efficient two-way communication is essential.

The *work of the purchasing department*

A purchasing officer studies commodities, sources of supply, systems and procedures, inventory problems and market trends, the most effective method of delivery, whether maximum discounts are being earned, the amount and use of waste material. These are a few of the wide range of activities he may deal with. Very large companies may have a purchasing research department which has to consider world-wide supply and seasonal trends.

If we consider the responsibilities of a 'typical' purchasing officer, the work of the department can be clearly seen. The purchasing officer is responsible for:

(*a*) Material and equipment purchases while adhering to the company's purchasing policy.

(*b*) Studying all markets for prices, trends and delivery times and maintaining accurate records of sources of materials, etc.

(*c*) Developing and maintaining morale of staff, instructing, guiding and training them according to the company's personnel policy.

(*d*) Seeing the work of the department is efficiently organized, e.g.

(i) Interviewing suppliers' representatives.

(ii) Ensuring that requisitions are duly authorized before making out orders or contracts with suppliers.

(iii) Collating quotations, accepting the most desirable, and advising departments concerned of any change in prices or delivery dates.

(iv) Processing orders to see if delivery will be on time, vouching invoices when received, authorizing disposal of waste material. He must co-operate with many departments, especially the planning and progress departments, for material deliveries and quotations.

A purchasing officer

High ethical standards are needed in a purchasing officer coupled with integrity and breadth of vision. A knowledge of office methods, law and accounting and often some specialized technical knowledge are basic requirements in certain industries. Personal contact is very important, so a courteous manner is essential to cultivate the goodwill of the suppliers.

Sub-contracting

In some industries arrangements are made with other firms for the supply of components instead of the firm making them itself. It is widely used in the motor-car industry and often the components can be supplied at a lower cost than if the firm made them itself. Cost may not be the main factor, as firms may need more components than they can produce in order to meet their customers' requirements and sub-contracting is then the answer.

Reliability of quality and quantity and delivery is a problem and, if a large amount is purchased in this way, a separate section may deal with it.

9. Maintenance of plant, equipment and buildings

Poor maintenance may lead to plant failure and consequent delays in production. Companies with large capital investment must pay great attention to maintenance and it is usually a good plan to have a separate maintenance department responsible to the works manager.

The head of the section is responsible for:

(*a*) The maintenance of buildings, plant and machinery to ensure efficient working order.

(*b*) Regular periodic inspection and attention to all breakdowns and repair work.

(*c*) Maintaining discipline and the supervision and control of personnel in the department.

(*d*) Ensuring that tools and equipment are in good order and accurate records of work are kept.

The department will include many skilled trades, e.g. electricians, millwrights, carpenters and bricklayers.

Before maintenance policy plans can be drawn up the following information must be available, bearing in mind plant replacement policy:

(*a*) The relationship between the frequency and extent of inspection and plant breakdowns.

(*b*) Cost of inspection and the loss in making good the production lost through breakdowns.

Preventive maintenance

There are various types of maintenance from routine servicing to temporary stoppage of production and yearly complete overhauls.

In setting up a scheme for preventive maintenance one must:

(*a*) Prepare an inventory of plant, noting those parts of equipment most likely to wear first or break down.

(*b*) Draw up schedules, showing the location of plant and noting the frequency of inspection.

(*c*) Assess standard times for inspection. The inspection card must include maker's name, original cost, special manufacturing instructions and records of breakdowns.

It is important to keep the workers impressed with the importance of maintenance and a constant check on the cost of maintenance is essential.

The use of *mechanical fuses* is common. One part of the machine is made intentionally weak, so that if it is overworked it stops and only the weak or cheaper parts need to be replaced.

10. Production control and the computer

The amount of clerical work involved in production control is extensive. Attempts have been made to reduce the amount by ensuring a document is used for more than one purpose to reduce movement by integration and reduction of staff. Because of the large number of calculations, sorting and storage of large quantities of data and printing large amounts of information, it can be seen how the production control activities were considered eminently suitable for programming on a computer.

An introduction to the nature of computers is given in the chapter on Office Management (see p. 333). The main aim of the computer is to provide management with information so that decisions can be made. A major function of computers in production control is to supply relevant information at the time that it is required.

Examples of the way a computer can assist production control are as follows:

(i) *Stock re-ordering*—the computer is programmed to compare recorded stock balances with re-order level; if the stock balance is below this, then the files in the computer can produce the name and address of a supplier and raise an order for replenishment. A more elaborate system would analyse the demand data for an item and calculate re-order parameters.

(ii) *Capacity loading problem.* Details of operations and bills of quantities can be held on the computer file. When an order is obtained from a customer, the computer can break the product into component parts and load each manufacturing operation into its appropriate cost centre when capacity is available in accordance with a time schedule to ensure production is not delayed.

(iii) *Operation details and bills of quantities.* Details of raw materials, jigs and tools needed for the finished product and the setting up and taking down times, can be held in the memory for each manufacturing stage. The computer can then determine dates for which purchased materials should be obtained and the stages manufacturing should commence so that customers' requirements are met on the given date. It could produce a critical path analysis (see p. 137). Analyses can then be made of actual and standard operating times and produce data to show labour absenteeism and machine breakdowns.

(iv) *Works order documentation.* Complete documentation for works orders is possible. The benefits of a management information system are mentioned elsewhere in this book. Some of these benefits are obtainable especially in the integration of production control and other functions. Because the computer works so fast one can combine from customers' orders:

(*a*) an updating of the order book, and breakdown of parts needed;
(*b*) the raising of works documentation (e.g. orders raised on suppliers);
(*c*) allocation of stock items, loading capacity data and job costing data.

Other departmental activities which could be integrated include invoicing, progressing, stock valuation, standard costing and variance analysis, planned maintenance schedules and analyses of sales representatives' performances.

Advantages of computer assisted production control

(*a*) Reduced clerical costs.
(*b*) Minimization of work in progress and setting-up times, etc.
(*c*) Maximum machine utilization.
(*d*) Reduction in stocks.
(*e*) Reduction of delivery times to customers.

Disadvantages

(*a*) Cost of installation of computer and data processing personnel outweighs financial savings in clerical staff.
(*b*) The greater amount of information from the computer may need *more* persons to analyse data.

It may be difficult to compare the extra cost of the computer system with the benefit of better control and utilization of men, machines and material. Such systems are expensive, but the use of standard programmes can reduce this. It will probably take a long time to convince management that the computer can play an effective part in production control and help to overcome the inadequacies of most manual production control systems.

D. MATERIALS HANDLING

In some basic industries materials handling represents 85 per cent of all production costs: in others about 15 per cent. It is therefore obvious that by effective materials handling a marked reduction in costs is possible. The problem is often the limitation of older buildings and the lack of proper planning which makes the use of newer equipment very difficult.

If only warehousing operations are involved, it is easier to modernize, but in complex manufacturing areas integrated handling can be used only if plans are made well before building commences. The more materials handling can be eliminated and the more there is processing 'on the move' the more efficient will industry become. Co-ordinated flow lines are needed from raw materials through receiving, processing, warehousing and shipping to primary centres of distribution.

Reduction in costs is possible by the use of handling equipment and the elimination of unnecessary handling and improved layout. Accidents are reduced and work in progress kept at a minimum.

In general, there are three classes of handling equipment:

(*a*) For moving materials over a line of travel between two *fixed* points. This can be done by the use of conveyor belts, gravity or power rollers and overhead trolleys and cranes.

(*b*) For *vertical* movement in multi-storeyed buildings—elevators, hoists and spiral gravity chutes and conveyors can be used.

(*c*) For movement *between* points not in a fixed line—tractors with trucks, e.g. stillage and fork-lift trucks, can be used.

A *fork-lift truck* is a vehicle with two arms or forks which can be positioned under crates, etc. The forks move up or down the column in front of the truck, thereby raising or lowering the crates and stacking them to the desired height.

The *pallet* is a form of fork-lift truck which lifts its load only a few inches off the ground in order to transport it. The platform or pallet usually remains under the goods from the collection point to delivery point. This conception of a *unit* load is becoming standard practice. Containers can be very large and, as the goods remain intact for the whole journey, handling costs are greatly reduced, as well as costs of pilfering and packing.

Automatic pallet loaders can take as many as ten different packages from production lines, sort and stock them in any desired sequence and forward the loaded pallet by conveyor to the next stage, without human effort.

Standardization is essential, both in pallet sizes and in the loading and heights of lorry-floors; but there is still a long way to go in this field. Materials handling is so highly regarded in the U.S.A. that some companies have a director of materials handling.

E. AUTOMATION

This word is often used to refer to systems not completely automatic. In essence there must be completely automatic transfer between machines and automatic control and recordings. It is best applied in flow production, e.g. flour milling, chemical industry. It is, of course, limited by the extent of the market and cannot be universally adopted.

By a combination of punched cards and electronic and magnetic trips, machine tools are automatically controlled and thus work can be automatically transferred to the next stage.

Automation is the operation of individual automatic machines or groups of machines integrated by transfer mechanisms. New advances in closed-loop systems which sense what is happening enable errors to be automatically corrected.

The oldest form of automation is found in machine tools that perform certain operations automatically. Later the addition of a computer enabled impulses from the computer, instructed by magnetic tape, to operate the machine.

As there was a limit to the amount of work which could be done in the one place, transfer to another machine by transfer mechanism was the next stage.

Feedback of information can operate adjustments automatically when errors are sensed—this is automatic control, i.e. where corrections are made with no human intervention.

Effects on organization

(*a*) Better managers and a higher ratio of managers to operating personnel are needed. Management training is more essential especially in social leadership.

(*b*) Need for shift working.

(*c*) New trades introduced, especially the maintenance of complex machines.

(*d*) Increased dependence on machines makes it difficult to operate financial incentive schemes.

(*e*) Smaller labour force and need for redeployment and retraining.

(*f*) Better working conditions.

(*g*) Increasing capital costs, especially fixed costs.

(*h*) More standardization.

(*i*) More leisure time, which raises a big problem of how it will be spent.

Automated warehousing

Stocks are required to absorb variations in supply and demand, and to ensure even flow through productive and distributive systems. Storage, including labour, lighting and handling and accounting, only add to the price paid by consumer and can account for an extra 25–50 per cent on original price.

The use of automatic machinery, integrated with data processing by computer, which maintains stock records and accounts, can give the following advantages:

(*a*) Similar items need not be stored together, since finding and selecting are not done by human labour.

(*b*) Gangways for automatic machines are narrow and stocks can be stored higher. As people are not involved, warehouse temperature can be reduced and lighting is needed only for maintenance inspections.

(*c*) There is a maximum use of space because a whole rack is not allocated to an item in small demand.

(*d*) Damage by carelessness is reduced and accuracy of order picking and stock records greatly improved.

(*e*) Issue of advice notes and invoices and reminders is made speedily and encourages quick payment. Accurate calculations of stock are made by computer.

Example of automated warehousing

Goods are checked on arrival and placed on a pallet. Relevant information on punched cards or tape is processed by stock controller and pallet is placed by fork-lift truck on the platform of the automatic warehousing machine. The punched card or tape is fed to the computer, and by pressing a button the pallet is transported and stored automatically, usually on special racks. Mechanical handling is controlled pneumatically by contacts of photo-electric cells which feed information to the computer. Goods are stored in the most suitable space according to the computer program and documents and pay cheques prepared for the supplier. Goods are *withdrawn* by placing the punched card or tape in the computer. The machine retrieves the pallet and discharges it at the delivery point and stock records are amended immediately and the customer advised.

REVIEW QUESTIONS

Production

(1) What factors must be considered in the determination of production policy?

(2) What problems may arise in the consideration of a suitable site for a factory?

(3) Distinguish between research and development.

(4) What are the main stages in a research project?

(5) What facilities for assistance in research exist outside the firm?

(6) What principles should determine how much a firm spends on research and development and how can such expenditure be allocated and controlled?

(7) What are the objects of product design and who are interested in it?

(8) Outline the Schedule of Responsibility for a design and development engineer.

(9) Distinguish between standardization, simplification and specialization.

(10) What are the purposes of quality control?

(11) Consider the need for inspection and list the qualities required in an inspector.

(12) What are the advantages and disadvantages of centralized and floor inspection?

(13) Define value engineering and describe how it is applied.

(14) What is covered by the term production administration?

(15) Explain the need for work study.

(16) What is meant by ergonomics and how can its study increase output?

(17) Definitions of production control vary; explain what you consider is meant by the term.

(18) What is meant by production planning?

(19) Briefly list the requirements of a good system of material control.

(20) What are the duties of a storekeeper?

(21) Examine the reasons for having centralized or departmental stores.

(22) What is covered by the term pre-production planning?

(23) What should be the position of the purchasing section in an organization?

(24) Outline a schedule of responsibility for a purchasing officer.

(25) What is meant by preventive maintenance?

(26) Explain the importance of materials handling in a manufacturing organization.

(27) Define automation and give an illustration of its use.

REVIEW PROBLEMS

Production

(1) Assume that you are a quality control manager in a large-scale multiple retail business and that you are required to investigate the quality procedure of a large supplier of frozen foods as a preliminary to your company placing a contract for supplies. How would you conduct a survey to ascertain the effectiveness of the quality control in force?

(2) There is always the possibility of error in product design. The product may appear correct from one point of view and yet be quite wrong from another. List the possible areas and sources of error, illustrating fully to show your understanding and indicating how such errors can be detected.

(3) The internal transport and materials handling costs in a light engineering concern are believed to be unduly high. Suggest how they might be reduced, and indicate in what directions advantages may be gained thereby.

(4) Detail the long- and short-term benefits and difficulties brought about by automation in an industry with which you are familiar.

(5) Set out the details which an estimator would require in order to build up a quotation.

How would his approach differ if he were:

(*a*) quoting for a special product for one customer; and
(*b*) preparing a selling price for a mass produced item?

(6) What is meant by batch production?

State the factors which must be taken into consideration to ensure that batches are set at an economic level.

(7) What is meant by a product specification and what is its purpose in relation to production, purchasing and selling?

(8) (*a*) Discuss and distinguish between:

(i) stock recording procedures; and
(ii) stock control systems.

(*b*) How far should the attention of management be directed to the movement of stock and its rates of change rather than to the quantities of stock in hand?

(*c*) Explain how an analysis of stock value and movement can aid control.

(9) State the causes of losses and waste in a materials store. Consider what action should be taken to eliminate them.

(10) Describe a procedure for the control of a tool store. To what extent is the inspection function linked with the tool store?

(11) Describe the stages of a time study exercise in a production department. To what extent is consultation with the operatives necessary?

(12) Why is it essential that all buying must be controlled by the purchasing officer?

Give three sources of information from which the buyer can obtain details of requirements on which to base an order.

BIBLIOGRAPHY

Production

Bailey, P. and Farmer, D., *Managing Materials in Industry* (London, Gower Press, 1974).

Baily, P. H. J., *Purchasing and Supply Management* (London, Chapman & Hall, 1971).

Battersby, A., *A Guide to Stock Control* (London, Pitman, 1970).

Buck, C. H., *Problems of Product Design and Development* (Oxford, Pergamon, 1963).

Buffa, E. S., *Modern Production Management* (London, Wiley, 2nd edition, 1965).

Burbridge, J. L., *The Principles of Production Control* (London, Macdonald & Evans, 1962).

Burns, T. and Stalker, G. M., *The Management of Innovation* (London, Tavistock, 1961).

Cowan, A. F., *Quality Control for the Manager* (Oxford, Pergamon, 1964).

England, W. B. and Lewis, H. T., *Procurement* (Illinois, Irwin, 1962).

Gedye, G. R., *Scientific Method in Production Management* (Oxford University Press, 1965).

Lockyer, K. G., *Factory Management* (London, Pitman, 2nd edition, 1969).

Miles, L. D., *Techniques of Value Analysis and Engineering* (New York, McGraw-Hill, 1961).

Murrell, K. F. H., *Ergonomics: Man in his Working Environment* (London, Chapman & Hall, 1965).

Oughton, F., *Value Analysis and Value Engineering* (London, Pitman, 1969).

Smith, C. S., *Quality and Reliability* (London, Pitman, 1970).

Tooley, D. F., *Production Control Systems and Records* (London, Gower Press, 1974).

8 Personnel Management

Personnel management is that part of the process of management that is concerned with the maintenance of human relationships and ensuring the physical well-being of employees so that they give the maximum contribution to efficient working. It is obviously closely related to the management process as a whole and each functional manager and supervisor must apply the principles effectively. Departmental managers, by effective leadership, should ensure personnel policy is adhered to and department activities are successfully carried out. It is essential that every manager and supervisor be aware of the principles of personnel management and a close link with the personnel department should be maintained.

Personnel managers have to advise the managing director on the formulation of personnel policy and see that procedures to carry it out are effected. It is a servicing section to other managers and the department has *functional* responsibility for personnel matters.

A logical approach to the consideration of this function is to look first of all at the problem of overall company organization and manpower planning. Then the operations necessary to implement the plan, that is, recruitment and selection, training and development, and wage and salary administration. Other aspects of personnel management include industrial relations and the law of employment, welfare and safety, and other employee services.

Personnel management is intimately involved with the environment in general and certain trends are noticeable. Government intervention is growing and many new Acts have affected personnel management, e.g. Employment Protection Act. Trade unions are increasing in importance and the government's prices and incomes policy is of vital concern.

New terms and techniques are appearing, for example, manpower planning and management by objectives. Manpower planning should not, though, be regarded as a *new* technique as it embraces existing techniques, i.e. work study, job evaluation, and description performance rating, etc. Whatever new ideas appear, the criterion should be the more efficient utilization of labour.

Figure 29 shows the main functions of a large personnel department.

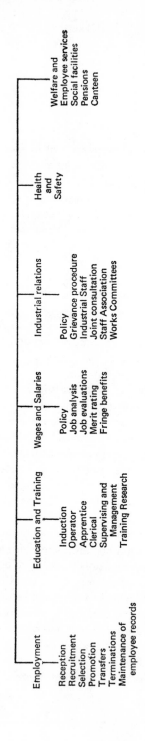

Employment	Education and Training	Wages and Salaries	Industrial relations	Health and Safety	Welfare and Employee services
Reception	Induction	Policy	Policy		Social facilities
Recruitment	Operator	Job analysis	Grievance procedure		Pensions
Selection	Apprentice	Job evaluations	Industrial Staff		Canteen
Promotion	Clerical	Merit rating	Joint consultation		
Transfers	Supervising and	Fringe benefits	Staff Association		
Terminations	Management		Works Committees		
Maintenance of	Training Research				
employee records					

Fig. 29. Functions of a personnel department. The above could be used as an organization chart for a large company. The Personnel Manager in charge of the six sections may serve on the Board and his job would be to interpret and maintain the company policy and advise on the attitude to adopt in trade union negotiations.

A. POSITION IN ORGANIZATION

The personnel manager is a specialist to whom the general manager has entrusted the responsibility for certain work. He may be responsible to the general manager directly or he may report to other functional heads. In smaller concerns the personnel and office manager may be the same person. Whatever the size of the organization, someone must perform the function of a personnel manager and titles vary greatly; he may be called labour relations or welfare officer.

His responsibility and status vary with the type of organization and he is often shown on organization charts on a level with other functional managers, e.g. marketing manager. This does not necessarily mean equality of salary and status. He usually has direct access to the chief executive and is responsible to him.

There may be personnel assistants in the branches of some companies who are responsible to the personnel manager for training and other personnel activities in the local branches, but otherwise they are directly responsible to the line manager. The personnel manager exercises *line* authority over the specialized activities which come under his direct jurisdiction, e.g. canteen, education, welfare.

The *qualities* required in a personnel manager vary with the extent of his work. Basic qualities required are a background knowledge of economics and industry and living conditions, an understanding of men and women and knowledge of social and psychological problems—good judge of human nature, friendly, firm, patient and impartial.

Summarized schedule of responsibility for Personnel Manager

Responsible to: managing director.

Responsible for:

(1) Assisting and advising managing director on personnel policy and ensuring policy is made known to staff and is effectively carried out.

(2) Developing and maintaining procedures in conjunction with other departmental heads for recruitment and training.

(3) Determining and maintaining good relations with trade unions and other bodies concerned with employment and working conditions.

(4) Ensuring adequate safety precautions and welfare services including canteen and health services.

(5) Assisting employees with personal problems, maintaining records and statistics of employment.

Special duties

(1) Advising and assisting managing director on personnel policy formulation and the development of training schemes for supervisory staff.

(2) Representing the company in all negotiations with trade unions and trade associations and maintaining interests in new ideas in personnel management.

Limitations

No right to engage or dismiss staff or determine rates of pay, without referring to relevant senior executive or managing director.

B. PERSONNEL POLICY

The co-operation of workers must be obtained if the business is to run smoothly. The workers must have confidence in the firm and this may not be easy when technical advances produce a fear of unemployment and unrest.

Policy must be determined by the board and must be clearly defined, and those employees who have to administer the policy should be given an opportunity to contribute. This may be done in joint consultative committees. In order to have a good policy, a knowledge of those factors an employee regards as important is essential. This involves a knowledge of the industrial application of sociological and psychological theory, and the forces generated should be known and controlled in order to ensure effective collaboration of individuals and groups so that company and individual goals can be reached. 'Harmony of objectives' must be the goal.

Social scientists are being enrolled in industry to examine sociological problems. A recent approach is to examine the organizational environment, the objectives and methods of management, and the forms of company structure. It may be that these conditions limit what the individual can achieve. *Personnel policies*, therefore, are concerned with providing an effective organizational structure, manning it with appropriate personnel and securing optimum working conditions; the object being to create and maintain a level of morale which evokes the full contribution of all employees in ensuring that the company operates at maximum efficiency.

The following factors may be regarded as important and necessary in a personnel policy:

(a) Remuneration

This must be at least the market rate for the job and give the employee a reasonable standard of living.

(*b*) *Security*

This is vital to the average worker; it is not so important to the young, or where there is full employment, but stability of employment is essential and there must be guarantees against unfair dismissal.

(*c*) *Opportunity*

If this is not available, a worker may look elsewhere. Vacancies should therefore be filled within a firm whenever possible or practicable. This does emphasize the need for good education and training policies so that existing staff can be trained to fill vacancies.

(*d*) *Status*

In chapter 1 it was stated that the Hawthorne experiments showed that a person's feeling that he 'counted' or 'mattered' and that he was a respected member of a group can influence output and lead to the retention of workers.

(*e*) *Justice*

This can be simply defined as confidence in being treated fairly. The security of the worker must not be threatened and specific rules regarding punishment, judgement and appeals procedure must be invoked. These should include guarantees of confidential access to the personnel manager.

(*f*) *Democracy*

In a capitalist structure it may not be easy to invoke the idea that a man has the right to a voice in the *way* he is governed, and by *whom* he is governed. Attempts along these lines are the formation of joint consultative committees and the establishment of procedures for regular consultation between managers and employees.

(*g*) *General*

To assist employees in developing social, educational and recreational amenities and to maintain policies without discrimination between employees.

C. MANPOWER PLANNING

Manpower planning seeks to maintain and improve an organization's ability to achieve corporate objectives by developing strategies which are designed to increase the present and future contributions of manpower.

There is great difficulty in forecasting future demand because of the *changes* in the following areas:

Technological—changes in materials, technical systems and methods of power.

Economic—marketing, capital formation.

Social—population trends, social mobility and education.

Political—industrial legislation (wages and salaries, monetary policy, training, redundancy).

Advantages of manpower planning

(*a*) The right number of staff is recruited at each level in the hierarchy.

(*b*) Staffing requirements can be better balanced and movement of staff made easier.

(*c*) Areas of high labour turnover are highlighted.

(*d*) Implications of changes in recruitment, promotion and succession plans are foreseeable.

Limitations of manpower planning

(*a*) Detailed records are needed plus expensive clerical staff.

(*b*) Problems of forecasting changes, especially technological and government policy areas.

(*c*) Forecasts can be uncertain even for a few years ahead.

The traditional attitude to manpower is that it is a *cost*; there is greater consideration now towards the idea that it is an *investment*. Therefore the best use of this investment should be made so as to ensure that manpower achieves personal satisfaction and the company achieves a maximum return on the 'costs' it represents. (See p. 350 for consideration of accounting for human assets.)

It is important to stress the problem of uncertainty today; changes can occur in the following more detailed analysis.

(*a*) Production and sales targets and new products.

(*b*) Plans for diversifying, expanding or contracting production.

(*c*) Centralization or other organizational change.

(*d*) Technological changes, e.g. mechanization, improved methods, new management techniques.

(*e*) Changes in hours of work, holidays, negotiations with trade unions and collective agreements.

(*f*) National policies regarding taxation and redundancy.

(*g*) Changes within company, e.g. retirements, age structure, promotions.

A company must be able to recruit and retain manpower of the type and calibre it requires for efficient operation. Change is a dominant factor today. Processes, products, systems and methods change quickly. The rôle of the computer is increasing and there is at present a shortage of systems analysts and programmers, and this will continue for a number of years. New techniques, e.g. operational research, influence the organization structure of companies and alter the pattern of manning. Some jobs need increased skills, others need less. Thus a high standard of planning is needed. The rewards to a company are high as a great reduction in costs is possible; reduction in one area in particular, labour turnover, can save a great deal of money.

Stages of manpower planning

(*a*) The *existing situation* is examined to see if the existing organizational and manning effectiveness can be improved. Procedure involved will include job analysis and grading, performance and potential appraisals.

(*b*) *Planning* to assess and determine future *objectives* for all parts of the business.

(*c*) *Organization* is then planned, breaking down the *objectives* into posts capable of being filled. The method of organization can greatly aid co-ordination of activities.

(*d*) *Precise requirements* for all types of manpower are then identified.

(*e*) *Planning the supply* involves noting present stock and its potential and determining the basis for additional requirements. Organization charts can be projected to the future, noting possible promotion candidates and people earmarked for certain jobs.

(*f*) *Career requirements* of individuals must be noted. The payment of salaries commensurate with worth is an essential part of wages and salary administration.

It was stated in chapter 1 that organization should be designed to attain the objectives of the company. Functional objectives are set and organization planned to attain them. Each department must be staffed so that the available skills and abilities are equated with tasks to be done.

Manpower forecasting

First of all, existing manpower strength and work volume are analysed and detailed forecasts made of future work volume and probable changes in methods used are considered. The future work volume is then related to past ratios to give a forecast. This is called ratio-trend forecasting.

Another method is called *theoretical requirements forecasting* and involves assessing and defining the type and volume of activity needed to attain desired results. Specific objectives are given to management.

Existing manpower and work volume are compared with forecasted future work volume and manpower, noting any probable changes in methods. So, for each category of staff, there is a statement of present and future positions, and this enables manpower requirements to be calculated.

Personal records must be adequate and kept up to date. Record cards containing relevant facts must be easily available: some firms have the details on punched cards or tape and these can be used for numerous analyses.

Information on record cards may include these details:

(*a*) Identification—name, date of birth and service, nationality, reference number, home address and next of kin.

(*b*) Education—schools, universities, technical or professional training.

(*c*) Experience—employment history and details of current job including details of remuneration.

(*d*) Potential—assessments, a note of career development and training, assignments planned and completed.

(*e*) General—leisure interests, armed forces, medical history.

Employment inventories are useful, and analysis into male and female job categories, part- and full-time is needed. The pattern of *ages* should be noted as it may be that many are retiring shortly or many are ready for promotion. Thus the problems which may arise can be dealt with if known in time. Turnover can be analysed into reasons for leaving, length of service, age group and type. The cost of turnover is great.

An ordinary *clerical* job involves these costs—advertising, management time on interviewing, temporary help or overtime paid during staff shortage, reduced output during training time and trainee's time. This could easily add up to £500 per job vacant. A reduction in job turnover from 10 per cent to 5 per cent in a firm is an enormous saving.

International Business Machines Ltd have a five-year forward plan, broken down into about fifteen main occupational groups, showing numbers to be recruited to replace predicted staff turnover and to meet the company's growth plans, which are based upon market research and product development forecasts. The key is a very detailed job classification, which is expressed in a four-digit code for computer processing.

D. RECRUITMENT

The position of the economy of a country has a marked effect upon the employment of personnel and hence upon recruitment and selection. Economic uncertainty may cause people to remain in their present job, and discourage them from moving elsewhere, particularly when finance from building societies and banks is difficult to obtain. Persons with wives and children may be less disposed to move and movement will mainly be among younger persons. Growth industries may therefore find it difficult to obtain the experienced persons required.

Use of selection or appointment consultants

The aim of management development is to get the right man, with the right equipment in the right place at the right time.

The use of consultants to recruit and select supervisory or management positions is becoming increasingly common because:

(*a*) Advances in science, technology and specialization are making it difficult to obtain the right man. Small to medium firms may not have a properly equipped personnel department scientifically to test and select persons.

(*b*) The cost of selection is great.

(*c*) Consultants are impartial in their assessment of applicants.

(*d*) Candidates may not wish to disclose their identity, unless they are reasonably certain of being considered and consultants will not disclose candidates' names until they have been short-listed.

Method adopted by consultants

(*a*) They *visit* the firm and appraise job requirements and talk over the qualifications, etc., the employer wants.

(*b*) A job *specification* is then drawn up in detail, plus additional information, e.g. location, living conditions available, place in organization.

(*c*) An *advertisement* is then drawn up and the employer asked to approve. Applicants receive the firm's own application form and a copy of the job specification. Applications are sifted and some selected for interview.

(*d*) Members of an *interview panel* are chosen because of their special knowledge of the type of position. A short list is prepared and only then are identities disclosed and references taken up.

(*e*) A *short list* is sent to the employer, with reports of interviewers and their recommendations.

(*f*) *Final interviews* are conducted by the employer who makes the choice.

Consultants deal in a wide range of appointments, although some do specialize. The fees are high and generally no appointments are considered for positions carrying salaries under £4000.

The *disadvantages* are that some consultants do not know the requirements of certain jobs and may have little experience in a particular field.

Some consultants have adopted an American approach whereby a list of ideal men for a job is drawn up; these men are then asked to join the new firm. This is called 'head hunting' and is not favoured by most consultants and certainly not by industry, although it has been used much more widely in recent years.

Main sources of recruitment

In their recruitment of staff, firms may look to the following:

(*a*) *Employee recommendations*

These have the advantage that applicants will know a lot about the firm when they arrive and employees may have more interest in their work if allowed to recommend workers. They may not, of course, be good judges.

(*b*) *Manpower Services Commission* (*Employment Services Agency*)

This is used for the recruitment of manual workers and clerical staff. There is also a Professional and Executive Register which keeps records of people seeking jobs. When a vacancy is known, suitable candidates are informed. About 50,000 people are on the register at any one time, and people are placed in positions with salaries of £3000 and above. There are no fees charged, unlike the Graduates' Appointments Register.

(*c*) *Private employment bureaus*

These charge fees for every employee supplied.

(*d*) *Advertisements*

Situations vacant may be advertised in newspapers and journals. The correct journal must be chosen.

(*e*) *Staff notice board*

This should always be used even if there are no likely responses.

(*f*) *Professional organizations*

These usually keep registers of vacancies.

(*g*) *Universities, technical colleges and schools*

Advertising is perhaps the most popular method of recruitment, but many firms do not make full use of advertising. Firms should bear in mind the following points when planning advertisements:

(*a*) *Salary* or the salary range should preferably be stated, but it is often omitted, also the duties and responsibilities of the job and nature of the organization should be given.

(*b*) It is preferable to state the *name of the company* in most cases and the part of the country where the job is situated.

(*c*) *Prospects* should be mentioned, but not exaggerated.

(*d*) *Box numbers* should preferably not be used as it is too impersonal and the applicant may not wish certain firms to know he is applying for jobs. An applicant can overcome this problem by stipulating those firms he does not wish to see his application.

A poor advertisement may raise doubts about a company's stability and efficiency. As there is usually a large volume of advertising, the right phrasing and the correct choice of media are essential. Factual information is needed and too 'brash' or startling an advertisement may have the opposite effect to that desired. This may be all right for some sales advertisements, but a carefully-worded, neatly set out advertisement, stressing the main features, is an economical way of obtaining staff.

Application forms

These need not be sent for unskilled work as they can be filled in on the interview day. Form filling can be used as a selection device, as a person's expressions on paper are a guide to his ability. A standard form makes it easier for the candidate to reply, rather than devise his own plan, and such forms are easier to evaluate.

Details usually shown on the form comprise most of the details shown on the record card on p. 240. In addition, office information is shown, e.g. remarks after acceptance of position, date commenced, department, salary, receipt of National Insurance card and income tax card.

Job descriptions (or Job analysis or specification)

These are statements of facts describing the work performed, the responsibilities involved, the skill and training required, the conditions under which the job is done, relationships with other jobs and personal requirements of the job.

The three terms above have different meanings. Job analysis records the facts, i.e. all the elements involved in performing a job; job description outlines the facts compiled from the job analysis, concisely identifying and describing the contents of a job; and job specification refers to the personal characteristics required to do a job, e.g. skill, experience, special aptitudes.

The statements of facts of a job guide management in the selection, promotion, or transfer of employees and aid the establishment of comparative wage scales and are used for training schemes.

A job description would show the following.

Job factors

Job factors include:

(*a*) Title of job and department and job code number.

(*b*) Job summary—showing in a few paragraphs the major functions and tools, machinery and special equipment used.

(*c*) Job content—lists the sequence of operations that constitute the job, noting main levels of difficulty.

(*d*) Statement showing relation of job to other closely associated jobs.

(*e*) Training required, working hours and peculiar conditions of employment, e.g. very hot or humid.

Employee factors

These include sex and age and physical characteristics required, e.g. size or strength. Mental abilities and emotional qualifications needed; cultural requirements, e.g. speech. Experience and skill needed.

In the United States a *Dictionary of Occupational Titles* shows over 30,000 descriptions which aid the use of standard job titles.

Summary of procedure for recruitment and selection of staff

(*a*) A *staff requisition* form is required to be completed by the head of the department where the vacancy arises, noting full details of the vacancy, e.g. job title, date of commencement. This can be checked against the company's establishment by the personnel department who would arrange to insert the advertisement.

(*b*) *Advertisement* is placed. It is important to word the advertisement correctly so applicants who are not really suitable do not apply. A vaguely worded advertisement will bring in more unsuitable applications. The media used for advertising should be checked periodically to ensure it is effective.

(*c*) *Short list* drawn up and interviews arranged.

(*d*) *References* can be taken up before the interviews and used to determine the final selection at the interviews.

(*e*) *Interviews* themselves can take many forms. They may be structured using standard procedures and techniques, e.g. five- or seven-point plan.

(*f*) *Tests* for specific skills are usually left to the time of the interview. Professional qualifications claimed should be checked.

(*g*) *Medical* examination may be essential and appointments are often made conditional upon passing. The Health and Safety at Work Act, 1974 regulations may mean more consideration needs to be given to this aspect, as employing persons should consider every possible area of uncertainty, and any person who has suffered from an illness which may re-occur should be examined.

(*h*) *Unsuccessful candidates* are informed of the decision.

(*i*) *Successful* candidates are informed and company records updated.

It is important to note that under the Health and Safety at Work Act, the employer's liability is greater and he must take steps which are 'reasonably practical' to safeguard the health of staff.

E. SELECTION AND ENGAGEMENT

Selection

When the short list of candidates for interview is drawn up a time-table should be prepared allocating specific periods for each interview so that there is sufficient time to interview each person properly.

The objects of interviews are:

(*a*) To assess personality of applicants.

(*b*) To obtain further details on certain matters.

(*c*) To agree terms of employment.

(*d*) To provide candidates with more information about the job.

The reception of candidates is very important as their first impression of the company is obtained at the interview. The following points should be observed:

(*a*) The *waiting room* should be comfortable and the room where the interviews are held should be private and preferably the candidate should not be facing strong light.

(*b*) It is essential to *put candidates at ease* and questions at first should be so directed.

(*c*) *Methodical assessment* is aided by having a check list of questions or the use of a rating schedule as suggested by the National Institute of Industrial Psychology's *Seven Point Plan*. This sets out each quality to be assessed, e.g. attainments, general intelligence, special aptitudes, disposition, interests and aims, health and circumstances. It is of course true that individuals cannot readily be divided into neat categories and that judgement is still essential, but a systematic approach is preferable.

Many interviews consist of a panel of persons who question the candidates *individually*. The panel usually comprises the manager of the department concerned and other interested parties; often the personnel manager is in the chair.

Group interviews are those whereby candidates are brought together and observed simultaneously by assessors, who give the group a problem to discuss, which is in the form of a committee exercise. This method can show personal reactions, e.g. those who are tactful, persuasive, or domineering. The Civil Service use this method, but it is considered that the method is probably better used for internal promotions for certain supervisory posts, as candidates may not wish their applications to be known, nor wish to meet applicants who may know them. One variant of the panel interview is where the candidate is asked to go from one interviewer to another: these interviewers meet later to compare appraisals.

Testing supplements direct personal contacts at interviews. The test creates a situation in which the applicant reacts; such reactions being regarded as samples of his behaviour in the work for which he is applying. The following tests may be given:

(*a*) Achievement tests, which sample and measure the applicant's accomplishments and developed abilities.

(*b*) Aptitude tests measure a person's capacity and potential. One form is an intelligence test designed to measure the ability to remember or reason.

(*c*) Interest tests use selected questions or items to identify areas of interest of special concern to the applicant.

(*d*) Personality tests try to find dominant qualities of a personality, the combination of aptitude, interests, mood and temperament.

Appraisal of test results is vitally important, as tests can be misused and misinterpreted. These points are noteworthy:

(*a*) Tests should be regarded as a supplement to, rather than a substitute for, other selection techniques.

(*b*) Most tests emphasize what a candidate can do, rather than what he will do, and are useful in picking out potential failures.

(*c*) A test should be *valid*, in that it can be shown to serve the purpose for which it was intended.

A most interesting checklist of the costs involved in personnel by the Manpower Society is shown in the table below.

MANPOWER COSTS CHECKLIST

Origin of costs: a checklist of headings under which costs can arise

1   *Remuneration*
1.1 Salary costs
1.1a Basic pay
1.1b Bonus payments

1.1c Overtime

1.1d Supplementary payments, e.g. shift pay, dirt pay, etc.

1.1e Merit awards

1.1f Temporary replacements for holidays, sickness, etc.

1.2 Direct fringe benefits

1.2a Car

1.2b Pension fund contributions

1.2c Luncheon vouchers/subsidized meals

1.2d Educational support for children of employees

1.2e Subscriptions to professional bodies

1.2f Subsidized housing including loans at preferential rates, special mortgages

1.2g Subsidized travel via loans to buy cars, etc.

1.2h Season ticket loans

1.2i Share ownership schemes

1.2j Location/assignment weighting

1.2k Holidays: statutory, personal days, sabbatical, other discretionary, paid vacation

1.3 Statutory costs

1.3a National Insurance contributions

1.3b Graduated pension contributions

1.3c Training board contributions (offset by grants, see section 3)

1.3d Employers' liability

1.3e Other statutory levies

2.   *Recruitment costs*—applicable to avoidable and unavoidable turnover as well as to new jobs

2.1 Pre-recruitment

2.1a Preparation or review of specifications for both the job to be done and the person to be recruited

2.1b Briefing of personnel officer (and advertising staff) with line manager

2.1c Preparation of recruitment programme

2.2 Search

2.2a All indirect promotional/advertising effort directed at furthering recruitment

2.2b All direct promotional/advertising effort directed at furthering recruitment including job advertising, stationery, postage, documentation of recruitment records and related administration costs

2.2c Head hunting costs

2.3 Candidate evaluation

2.3a Interviewing including travelling, hospitality and the university/college round

2.3b Bought-in selection costs: briefing, advertising, preliminary selection, complete selection

2.3c Selection tests either bought or created and including costs of subsequent administration

2.4 Induction

2.4a Inducement to move

2.4b Medical examination prior to establishment procedure

2.4c Orientation

3   *Training costs*—offset by grants

3.1 Induction period

3.2 Remuneration of trainee and trainer

3.3 Expenses of trainee and trainer, including travel and subsistence

3.4 Books and materials used

3.5 Machines and buildings used in continuous training

3.6 Bought-out training—school, college, government training centre fees

3.7 Development and maintenance of training programmes, including cost of staff in training departments when not actually engaged in direct training

3.8 Reports, appraisal costs of those people other than the trainee and trainer, e.g. counselling reviews

3.9 Training for retirement

3.10 Assimilation costs—the costs incurred of employing a person after induction but before he/she is fully proficient

3.11 Higher material wastage until trainee is fully experienced

3.12 Loss of possible production from trainer whilst he/she is engaged in training

4   *Re-location costs*—temporary and permanent

4.1 Hotel charges—long term

4.2 Hotel charges—short term

4.3 Direct disturbance allowance

4.4 Costs of disturbance, e.g. legal fees, removal costs

4.5 Premiums paid with regard to housing price differentials or house purchase assistance

4.6 Temporary travel subsidy

4.7 Travelling expenses

4.8 Ex gratia re-equipment costs incurred in moving house

5   *Leaving costs*

5.1 Loss of production between loss and recruitment

5.2 Statutory redundancy payments (less rebates)

5.3 Ex-gratia payments

5.4 Retirement payments (other than pensions)

5.5 Liquidation of direct fringe benefits—could be plus or minus costs (Note: leaving may give rise to Recruitment and Training Costs, and sections 2, 3 and 5 should be considered together when considering cost of voluntary turnover)

6 *Support costs*
6.1 House magazine
6.2 Social club
6.3 Subsidy for other social activities
6.4 Medical welfare schemes
6.5 Canteens
6.6 Safety facilities
6.7 Long-service awards
6.8 Suggestion schemes
6.9 Music-while-you-work
6.10 Security service
6.11 Schemes for preferential purchase of goods, including costs in purchasing department
6.12 Insurance premiums
6.13 Library and information services
6.14 Use of firm's resources for private ends (whether acknowledged or illicit)
6.15 General travel and entertaining expenses not specifically allocatable to a project
6.16 General background training not specifically allocatable to the job being done
6.17 Prestige accommodation
6.18 Car park costs
6.19 Death benefits
6.20 Rehabilitation/convalescent homes
6.21 Holiday homes

7 *Personnel administration*
7.1 Organized manpower records—these could be in more than one location in a company with decentralized company activities
These records include:
7.1a Personal record cards
7.1b Personal files
7.1c Salary administration records
7.1d Job specifications
7.1e Manpower planning record
7.2 Salary review costs
7.3 Maintenance of industrial relations, including consultative committees
7.4 Manpower research project costs
(The checklist has been drawn up by the Manpower Society.)

Engagement

The formal offer of the appointment is made and acknowledged. The offer states certain main terms and conditions. Sometimes a handbook is sent with all conditions of work, etc., explained carefully.

A formal contract may be prepared for senior staff. Such a contract usually states:

(*a*) Period of engagement, place of employment, capacity.

(*b*) Hours, salary, increments payable, illness arrangements, expenses and other benefits.

(*c*) Whether inventions belong to employer, provision for arbitration in disputes.

Salesmen may have additional points in their contracts:

(*a*) Calculation of salary, e.g. commission on sales plus expenses.

(*b*) Agreement to work exclusively for employer.

(*c*) Whether to charge commission on bad debts.

(*d*) Not to compete within a certain radius after termination of contract, nor to solicit employer's customers.

A medical examination may be regarded as essential in some jobs. It ensures a person is physically suited for the job and safeguards the firm from the engagement of anyone who suffers from infectious diseases and strictly forms part of selection procedures.

Equal Pay Act, 1970

The Equal Pay Act, 1970 seeks to eliminate discrimination between men and women as regards pay and other terms and conditions of employment. It aims to do this by:

(*a*) Establishing the right of the individual woman to equal treatment when employed on work of the same or similar nature to men, or have been given an equal value by job evaluation.

(*b*) By providing for the National Arbitration Board to remove discrimination in collective agreements, statutory wages orders and employers' pay structures, where they contain provisions for men or women only, and which have been referred to the Court.

Any disagreement with an employer can be referred to an Industrial Tribunal for a decision.

Contracts of Employment Act, 1972

This Act requires an employer to give an employee *written particulars of his terms of employment* and also a period of notice related to his length of service. The following is a summary of the main points of the Act.

(1) Within thirteen weeks of commencing an employment, an employer must give the employee written particulars stating the parties, date of commencement, remuneration and intervals of payment, the terms and conditions relating to hours of work, holidays and holiday pay, pensions, sick pay, the length of notice the employee is obliged to give and entitled to receive to terminate his employment.

(2) The Act applies to all employees, whether their contract is in writing, oral or implied.

(3) The obligation does not apply to temporary, seasonal or part-time workers.

(4) The minimum period of notice that must be given by an employer is stated.

The written statement should not be confused with the contract of employment and it is not required if all the particulars specified are included in a written contract.

There is no compulsion to give a reference for a former employee but, if one is given, care is needed in the phrasing or there may be a case for defamation of character.

Employment Protection Act, 1975

For a number of years there have been slow improvements in industrial relations. Some companies have satisfactorily negotiated new terms and conditions of employment and discussed ways of coping with redundancies, etc., and practical solutions have been worked out between unions and management which give the most benefit and cause the least hardship to the company and its workers. This does not apply to all industries and the Act was brought in to draw together the widely differing conditions in companies so that workers will be provided with *new rights and greater job security*. The Act sets up and extends existing machinery to help to promote better industrial relations and encourage the extension of collective bargaining.

The Act affects *everyone* who is an employer. Certain groups of *employees* are excluded from some parts of the Act.

For a brief summary of the Act see p. 252.

The Employment Protection Act has greatly affected personnel practice. Three of the principal statutes dealing with rights of individual employment have been substantially changed: the Trade Union and Labour Relations Act, the Redundancy Payments Act and the Contracts of Employment Act.

The parts of the Act providing for disclosure of information, handling redundancies and extension of terms and conditions and provision of trade union recognition, allow trade unions to bring actions against employers in certain circumstances.

Many features of the 1975 Employment Protection Act are being practised in other parts of the world and the provisions extend the 1972 Contracts of Employment Act in the following ways:

(*a*) The written statement will have to *include the title of the job* which the employee is engaged to do.

(*b*) It will have to include a *reference to any previous* employment which can be counted as continuous with the current employment and the date on which that employment began.

(*c*) It will have to *specify any disciplinary rules* which are applicable to the employee, or refer the employee to a document which specifies them and to which he has reasonable access.

(*d*) *Specify a person* to whom the employee can apply if he is dissatisfied with *any disciplinary action* or decision taken against him, and indicate the manner in which an application should be made.

F. INDUCTION AND TRAINING

Arrangements should be made for new employees to be introduced to the firm and to the job. A new employee must be shown where his place is in the organization. This service varies greatly among organizations, but a systematic course of induction should cover:

(*a*) Brief history of company, products, place in industry, present organization, names of department heads and the work of various departments.

(*b*) The rules of working and safety and health regulations.

(*c*) Personnel policy regarding discipline, education and training and promotion, holidays, method of computation, and date of payment of salaries and wages.

(*d*) Introduction to the new employee's own department and a detailed summary given of department's work.

Some form of training is needed for all employees. It may give a wider general knowledge of new techniques or a broader outlook, but can be most beneficial to employee and employer.

An effective training programme can:

(*a*) Improve efficiency and morale.

(*b*) Introduce new techniques.

(*c*) Provide for succession, enabling qualified replacements to be available.

(*d*) Raise the standard of unskilled personnel, thus helping overcome labour shortages.

(*e*) Develop supervisors and decrease the amount of supervision needed.

(*f*) Lead to a reduction in scrap rates and improve machine utilization.

Before discussing methods of training, the concept of the *learning curve* can be considered. The curve seeks to present in diagrammatic form the progress of an individual. It ascends quickly, showing increasing proficiency, then levels out later. There are various plateaux in the curve, where a person is consolidating and developing his knowledge. Where a group of persons is being trained, the group may set 'norms' which may stop individuals from moving ahead, and therefore it is important to ensure that the group norms are the same as the objectives of the trainer, so that individuals can progress.

Many companies do not regard training as a professional activity, and in many cases training officers are not themselves trained. Many courses are held and employees sent to colleges without any serious thought being given to the *real training needs* of a company.

After identifying the development needs of the individual the choice of course must be made. Some firms have noted the waste of money on external training. Course objectives are often ill defined: these should be determined together with the staff's qualifications and experience. Course literature is more attractive than informative and the training officer needs objective advice on courses. A system of reporting back after each course is essential. The report should go to the training officer as well as to the departmental head. In addition, individuals must be given an *opportunity to use* the knowledge gained.

De La Rue have an index scheme based upon a standard reporting system for all managers who attend courses outside the company. Part of the system requires courses to be graded against five headings, e.g. achievement of objective; lecturing efficiency; supporting paperwork; level or standard of other delegates and administration efficiency.

This is briefly the input data. Output data consist of written assessments of establishments and courses. Other large firms have joined the scheme, e.g. Albright and Wilson, and Guest Keen & Nettlefolds.

Training needs must be assessed to determine:

(*a*) The jobs for which planned training is required.

(*b*) The number of people who need to be trained annually for these jobs.

(*c*) The standards of training required. When the skills and knowledge required have been noted, a training programme is needed. An essential part of the programme is the need to train instructional staff and design a method of controlling progress. These programmes should be of course periodically evaluated. The training officer, therefore, advises management on training policy, basing his advice on training needs. He analyses jobs to identify skills; he plans programmes and follows them up. He must be familiar with the Industrial Training Act, and the assessment of training needs and job analysis; he must know how to plan programmes and evaluate cost of training; also he must keep abreast with methods of training, including *programmed learning*. A *linear* programme, for example, presents information in very small steps, each step being followed by a question and on the next frame the correct answer appears. If an incorrect answer is given, a person may have to return to the previous frame. In a *branching* programme, each frame contains more information and questions are of the multiple choice type; each question and answer contains a branch of further information. If a correct answer is given, a person moves to the next frame; if incorrect, he is given information of a remedial nature.

Training can be considered as the creation of learning opportunities. The required needs of managers and supervisors can be said to consist of:

(*a*) Knowledge—Basic knowledge for the job; this usually comes from education early in his work, or before employment. Reading assignments, seminar discussions aid the post experience manager, especially drawing examples from the working environment. A senior colleague could act as tutor, or programmed learning could be used to teach specific techniques.

(*b*) Skill and experience—These are related closely to the job content. Preparation for new jobs can be made by giving a person assignments, case studies, decision-making exercises and management games to simulate real conditions. Group projects and rôle playing can supplement planned work experience to enable a person to increase his effectiveness.

(*c*) Attitude—The development and conditioning of attitudes and patterns of behaviour depend more upon *learning experiences*. A person will, for example, benefit more by experiencing co-operation than reading about it, and a person's ability to adapt to change, co-operate with others and be more self-confident, comes partly from the work situation. The development of attitudes can be quickened by organizational development training (see p. 273). These methods, briefly, teach a group to monitor its own performance, identify and agree problems and their resolution. Other business exercises can be operated under conditions of stress to improve the effectiveness of the individual, the group and the company.

Managers learn better when they see the *relevance* of what they are learning in relation to their own jobs. In everyday work, there is no time to conceptualize. A person should be given an opportunity to try out his ideas in a situation as near as possible to real life conditions and practices. Therefore training that is relevant and provides persons or groups with an opportunity to use the ideas learnt will be preferred.

The Industrial Training Act, 1964

This Act was the first attempt to make statutory provisions for industrial training which apply throughout industry and commerce. The objects of the Act were:

(*a*) To ensure that the right numbers of people are trained to meet the needs of industry.

(*b*) To ensure that the training given to each person is appropriate to the job and of the highest quality.

(*c*) To distribute the costs of training more equitably between employers.

The 1964 Act introduced a new principle that employers had to contribute to a fund to be used for training purposes, whether or not they wanted to train staff. A number of Training Boards were set up for various industries. A *levy* was imposed upon employers in each industry and *grants* were paid by each industry training board to firms who provided training of an approved standard. Levies are usually expressed as a percentage of the payroll.

There are points for and against Training Boards:

In favour:

(*a*) They stimulated activity to train, particularly because of the system of levy grant. Training officers were in great demand and training generally showed an improvement.

(*b*) Group schemes were developed for firms with small numbers of employees and good training practices were developed.

(*c*) There were excellent results, particularly in apprentice training.

Against:

(*a*) Companies with different products were involved with more than one Board, and some overlapping of responsibilities occurred.

(*b*) The basis of the Boards were industries, and this was not so suitable for occupations which were common to a number of industries.

(*c*) Small, highly specialized industries had different training needs from large industries of a more homogeneous nature.

(*d*) The levy-grant system led to concern on the amount of money for rebate and tended to give a wrong emphasis on actual training requirements from those required.

This system was reviewed in 1972 and led to the *Employment and Training Act, 1973* which established the *Manpower Services Commission* (M.S.C.), which took over the oversight of the employment and training services which had previously been under the Department of Employment. Two other organizations, the *Employment Services Agency* (E.S.A.), dealt with employment exchanges and the Professional and Executive

Register (P.E.R.) and vocational guidance services; and the *Training Services Agency* (T.S.A.) which was responsible for co-ordinating the work of the Industrial Training Boards and other industries and for running the Training Opportunities Scheme (T.O.P.S.).

A major provision of this Act was to provide for exemption for certain firms from the system of levy-grant. Firms which were considered to be training their employees satisfactorily and certain small firms were exempted. An upper limit for levy was made of 1 per cent of the payroll.

Apprentice training

Apprentice training originated in the age of hand craftsmen where the individual craftsman taught the practical skills to the apprentice. Briefly, a systematic scheme for training apprentices involves:

(*a*) Employer taking responsibility for training and assessing the training needs annually to determine the numbers required in each category.

(*b*) The required skills and knowledge are then analysed.

(*c*) With this information a programme can be prepared for:

(i) Induction training.

(ii) Basic training in skills required.

(iii) Planned experience, to enable skills to be applied on the job. This needs detailed specifications of what should be taught and needs a good system of recording and measurement. Projects are needed to meet an apprentice's skill and progress.

(iv) Further education; to provide technical knowledge of a general nature. This can be done at a Technical College, a Polytechnic or at University.

N.B. Training Boards have set up their own centres for basic training.

Operative training

Eventually, each Training Board will publish training recommendations indicating the standard firms must observe if they wish to receive grants for operative training. The traditional method of training operatives is for them to learn by watching others. This is often inefficient as the others may do the job wrongly or they may be poor teachers. An operative training programme may include the following:

(*a*) Selection of the job to be studied.

(*b*) Analysis of *what* is done and *how* it is done.

(*c*) Recording and analysing common faults.

(*d*) Determining the elements of a job to be taught in parts and devising exercises to illustrate the parts.

(*e*) Setting target times and standards to see if speeds of experienced workers can be reached.

(*f*) Writing syllabus, training staff, preparing time-tables, designing record forms.

(*g*) Checking results frequently.

Supervisory training

Again, the nature of the work must first be analysed. From an analysis of the job, the skills and knowledge required can be determined and from this an *appraisal* of the performance of existing supervisors is needed in order to identify their training needs. Ideally, appraisal should be based upon target setting and the supervisor should preferably help to set his own targets.

Training programmes may be conducted internally or externally and may take the form of:

(*a*) Courses in skills and knowledge of a general or specific kind.

(*b*) On-the-job development, by planned project work and planned experience under immediate superior.

Internal courses can instruct upon technical subjects and company procedures. It is preferable to use participation techniques rather than lectures.

External courses are of particular use to the smaller company. They can be for the National Examination Board's Certificate in Supervisory Studies. It is important to see that such courses meet a *specific* training need and be organized in a practical manner.

The Department of Trade and Industry has encouraged firms to adopt its *Training Within Industry* (*T.W.I.*) *Scheme*—Programme for Supervisors —the object of which is to train foremen in their place of work in basic arts of job methods, job instruction, job safety, job relations, paying special attention to management of subordinates, leadership and discipline. These courses are also often used for office supervisors.

Management training and development

The main objective is to improve current performance and provide a suitably trained staff to meet present and future needs. A person's knowledge and skills have to be improved and his attitude and behaviour modified by training and development.

The volume of management training and development has increased greatly in recent years and there is a proliferation of courses available. These courses are not necessarily geared to the needs of the individual and, therefore, before courses are organized, it is vital to analyse training *needs*.

Once the true needs are known the most effective means of training can be determined. Within the framework of overall manpower needs, supervisory and management succession plans can be drawn up. The needs of each individual manager must be considered and his performance appraised and weakness remedied.

From a recent survey of 30 organizations on the system of appraisals for managers it was found that the more successful schemes showed common characteristics.

(*a*) Appraisal was a regular activity, with a continuous monitoring of performance by subordinates.

(*b*) Salary review was a separate activity from appraisal.

(*c*) The outcome of appraisal meetings was not pre-determined.

(*d*) Self-appraisal was part of a move towards self-development.

An *individual* benefits from appraisal when he understands his strengths and weaknesses as a manager and his potential for future development is indicated.

An *organization* benefits if information is obtained about total management resources available for planning and deciding on the needs of training and management development.

There are a number of reasons for performance appraisal, some of which are:

(i) to reduce any element of favouritism;

(ii) to help staff improve their present job performance and indicate possible career development;

(iii) to create a more effective organization where staff know what they are doing and the reason for it.

Further points to note on an appraisal system include:

(i) all levels of management, unions and employees should accept the scheme and understand its purpose and nature;

(ii) line managers shoulder the final responsibility of appraisal and they should be properly trained to implement the scheme;

(iii) the methods of appraisal should be uniform and the system reviewed periodically and necessary changes made;

(iv) subordinate participation in the setting of performance targets increases the commitment to, and success in, achieving them.

Problems which have arisen from such schemes are:

(i) quality of appraisal reviews is not of a high average standard, and the time scale often used (one year) may be too long;

(ii) the real reasons for the appraisal may still be unclear and persons receiving a favourable interview may lead them to expect rewards or promotion;

(iii) some managers have inadequate job descriptions of their staff and take no follow-up action after the appraisal. They are reluctant to take adequate time over appraisal and some are reluctant to discuss results with subordinates.

Other *advantages* which have been found are:

(i) people understand their jobs better because of job descriptions being required;

(ii) managers are appointed usually up to their experience and ability (not beyond, as suggested by the 'Peter Principle', see p. 99);

(iii) people are encouraged to develop themselves and take higher qualifications, and some like the opportunity to discuss their problems in performing their jobs with superiors.

(a) *A rating system for management staff*

This requires the rater to consider certain features and mark according to a scale. For example, *analytical ability* (ability to grasp essentials and make sound conclusions). A number of items are shown on a scale and one of them is to be marked, e.g. A—outstanding; B—very good; C—average; D—fair; E—poor.

This can be continued for other qualities, e.g. co-operativeness, dependability, self-expression, knowledge of job, judgement, leadership and organizing ability. The working of the five points in the above scale may differ a little for each characteristic.

(b) *Forced distribution rating scales*

These start with a distribution theoretically expected for a given group of workers on similar jobs. Using this basis, a five-point scale may be used to distribute a group of employees between the extremes of good and bad job performances, e.g. 10 per cent—outstanding; 20 per cent—good; 40 per cent—satisfactory; 20 per cent—fair; 10 per cent—unsatisfactory. The assessor is asked to rate the group so that ratings are distributed in the above percentages.

(c) *Graphic rating scales*

These permit the rater to mark performance at some point on a line from 'excellent' to 'poor' on separate factors, or an overall judgement.

For example, *leadership*—the ratings range from *not acceptable*, poor leader and negative personality, on the one hand, to a fifth rating of *outstanding leader*, good judgement, accepted without question.

(d) Ranking systems

People are compared with *each other* and listed in order of merit and placed in a simple grouping. Few of these schemes are linked with performance and the appraisals are subjective.

Management by objectives

This is a different approach, and has been described briefly on p. 38. It uses a *performance-based* approach using, wherever possible, objective standards of measurement. The basis of the system is that every manager is given a clear idea of the results expected. A detailed job description and targets required are agreed *with the superior*. Appraisal is made by comparing results with targets.

Fundamentally, management achieves objectives through people. If therefore the objectives of people could be linked with those of management a *harmony of objectives* would result to benefit all.

Management by objectives was an idea expounded by Drucker in the 1950s, it had a participative connotation and required many managers to change their basic dispositions or 'style of management.'

It is based on the assumption that managers will be more effective and will be more committed to objectives if they are themselves involved in establishing them.

It also presupposes that they work in an organization that encourages self-control and self-development.

McGregor and Hertzberg adopt the approach of the need first to change management style or attitudes and behaviour, and then other changes may occur. More details of how to change management style will be mentioned later.

M.B.O. is not yet practised on a very wide scale, although it has been widely talked and written about. Larger companies, as may be expected, use it to a greater extent than small companies. A main feature of the idea is the recognition of the importance of company strategy, especially the function of marketing.

Key results areas for individual managers must reflect the overall strategy, which is reflected in the marketing programme. The main points in the approach have been described on p. 38.

Advantages

(1) The need to clarify objectives is stressed and suggestions for improvement are obtained from all management levels.

(2) Each manager has a clear idea of the important areas of his work and standards required.

(3) The performance of staff can be assessed and their needs for improvement highlighted.

(4) Greater participation may improve morale.

(5) Managers have to plan to achieve *results* which are a means to achieving growth and profits.

Disadvantages

(1) It takes a few years to be effective.

(2) Too much paperwork and difficulty in measuring key operations.

(3) Achieving objectives may be at the expense of organizational goals, e.g. cost reduction programmes have been achieved by deferring maintenance. Sacrificing everything to meet goals may lead to poor managerial judgement.

(4) Some companies tend always to *raise* targets; if these are too high staff become frustrated.

(5) Appraisals are sometimes made on personality traits rather than on performance.

(6) Some companies have geared their salary administration to appraisal by results (easy targets may be set to allow a promotion).

(7) It is not easy to set measurable objectives for staff groups who only exist to help the 'line' achieve its ends.

(8) Review and counselling of managers may be ineffective.

(9) Some employees do not want to be held responsible and goals forced upon them may lead to ill-feeling.

(10) Some of those giving appraisals were not properly trained, they were not motivated to make the system work and tended to treat it in a mechanical manner.

Another development of this approach is discussed by W. J. Reddin in *Effective M.B.O.* (1971, Management Publications Ltd). He seeks to refine M.B.O. concepts by new interpretations stressing *achievement* and output results rather than 'input behaviour.' Planning is emphasized, so is the need for relevant correct information providing checks against standards.

Characteristics of effective appraisal

(*a*) Constructive attitudes by superior, and the outcome not predetermined.

(*b*) Participation in discussion and decision of the subordinate should be of a high level.

(*c*) Mutual approach to solving problems.

(*d*) Opportunity for self-appraisal encouraged, so manager can be encouraged to develop himself.

(*e*) Appraisal must be a regular activity (perhaps once a year is too long). A year is used to reflect the needs of the organization (e.g. end of budget cycle), rather than to suit the needs of individuals or work groups.

(*f*) Salary review must be separated. Schemes that try to deal with salary grading have most discussions on this aspect rather than objective appraisal of performance.

The establishment of company objectives was discussed in chapter 1 and these objectives must be known before divisional or sectional goals can be clarified. They should be known by each person so that he understands how his own goals relate to the broader objectives of the business. The objectives should, of course, be periodically redefined.

(*a*) J. W. Humble in his booklet *Improving Management Performance* advocates stating for each manager the *key results* he should achieve; these key result areas are important areas of objectives.

(*b*) Within these areas, a *performance standard* must be set; these standards may be quantitative, e.g. units produced in a week, or qualltative. In any case, they need to be prepared for all subordinates and agreed with them by superiors.

(*c*) The organization structure must provide for freedom to perform them, as badly designed structures mitigate performance. There may, for example, be no clear line of authority, or badly arranged divisional or functional organization.

(*d*) Control information should be in a convenient form, and sufficiently frequent, so that managers can take quick corrective action.

(*e*) Then follows a *review of performance* of managers. The superior analyses how far the key results have been achieved and this formal review enables any gaps to be filled by guidance and training.

(*f*) At the same time the *potential* of a manager is considered, to assess whether for example he is ready for promotion now, or should he be given more varied work.

(*g*) The final stage involves *frank discussions* between manager and subordinate.

N.B. This review stands or falls on the ability of the appraisers, the way they appraise and how specific are the discussions. There is a great tendency to generalize and, if little attention is paid by the management to appraisal reports, then managers will pay little attention to appraisal.

Figure 30, which is reproduced by kind permission of Urwick, Orr and Partners, shows in a brief form, how to *improve management performance.*

Management training

Once the real needs are known, training can begin. The training should develop knowledge, skills and attitudes, through various methods of instruction, demonstration and experience. The following methods are adopted:

(a) *Job rotation*

This can be instituted within a department, within a company, or within another company. The purpose is to improve a manager's understanding of jobs other than his own and provide a specific experience which will equip him for promotion. It is, of course, easier to arrange for lower levels of management. Short periods in different departments was at one time widely used for induction training of university graduates, but it was never fully satisfactory and led to a high labour turnover. As the period was so short, it did not enable the trainee to feel a sense of responsibility as he was not answerable for the results of his decisions.

(b) *Projects and assignments*

A good assignment should involve investigations into a number of departments and can reveal a person's capabilities. Superiors should be interested and carefully examine findings. Assignments given to a group of managers will give good experience in team-working. This approach is adopted on management courses, where members are split into syndicates to work on a problem, and here the problems of other departments become known to all.

(c) *Junior board*

This is a group of young men from different functions, appointed by top management for a limited period. Terms of reference are laid down by the senior board and problems given to them are of a general nature, e.g. problems of staff and public relations. The junior board will investigate and submit recommendations to the senior board. Group assessment is possible and it provides a good experience in general management.

(d) *Personal assistant*

The *assistant to a manager* is a staff rôle and he speaks only in the name of his superior and helps him in his work.

An *assistant manager* has a line rôle, as he shares some responsibility with his superior. The position is often the centre of controversy as reporting relationships become uncertain.

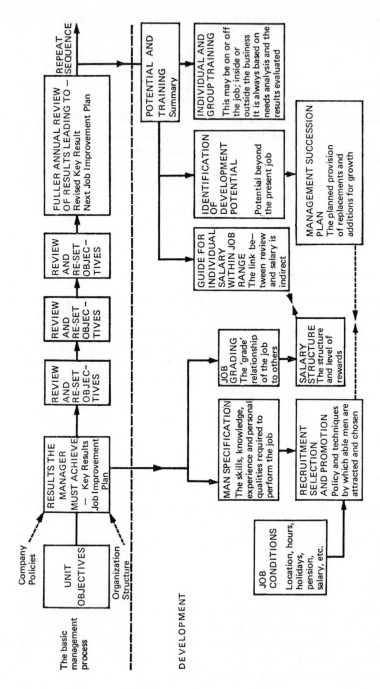

Fig. 30. Improving management performance (Reproduced by permission of Urwick, Orr and Partners Ltd.)

(e) *Formal management courses*

These cannot teach anyone to manage, but can accelerate management development, if combined with the right experience. New management tools are occurring frequently and formal courses are efficient and economical. They can modify and widen perspectives and this is needed by functional managers who aspire to general management.

Management courses are often not effective because:

(*a*) They accept too wide a spectrum of members (e.g. graduate trainee and senior executive). This can limit discussions.

(*b*) They do not allow interaction and participation between course members themselves and the tutors.

(*c*) The background knowledge and experience of tutors are not credible.

(*d*) The concepts and ideas on the course are not able to be put into practice or are not related to work situations.

(*e*) The place of the course and its surroundings may not be conducive to free speaking. Reports made while a person is on a course can inhibit the contribution from that member.

Training needs must be noted carefully. Training is required to make persons behave differently or more efficiently, for example, to improve *performance* of operators or to improve *attitudes* of salesmen. Needs can arise from variations between existing and desired performance which may be due, for example, to present manpower lacking in potential or knowledge to do jobs effectively. Training needs also arise from the recognition of a person's potential for a higher position and the preparation of the person for the position.

A most important factor should be considered. Assuming all the relevant points have been noted, for example, the job has been defined and its function stated, the levels of authority and responsibility determined and the training need; the *attitude* of the person who is to be trained should be considered carefully. One cannot *impose* training, the person to be trained should be motivated or persuaded to be enthusiastic and the *benefits* to the individual should be made clear to him. Course members usually pose themselves these questions:

Will I be able, after training, to: earn more, make my job easier or more interesting, earn promotion and improve my status?

Will I be reported upon? Why have I been chosen? What are the administrative arrangements (food and accommodation)?

Will I be shown up on the course because it is too demanding? Will I be able to practise the new ideas shown to me?

Therefore clear guidelines should be given, showing *how* the course learning can be applied to the work situation. Persons should be selected carefully for training and their individual training needs analysed, and false hopes should not be aroused. There must be effective briefing and de-briefing on return from the course and action programmes prepared within a stated period.

Training programmes should therefore be systematically *planned* and *supported* by relevant personnel policies which are based upon the objectives of the company, and should be periodically *reviewed*.

Management training and development can never be fully effective unless the manager himself recognizes a *need*.

This can be simply illustrated as follows by showing various needs and the methods by which they can be effected.

Need	*Method*
(*a*) Agree what you expect from me	Key results areas and statement of objectives.
(*b*) Give me an opportunity to perform	Job improvement plan and organizational planning.
(*c*) Let me know how I am getting on	Control information and performance review.
(*d*) Give me guidance when I need it	Management development methods and potential review.
(*e*) Reward me according to my contribution	Salary structure and succession plan.

An excellent analysis can be found in *Improving Manager Performance* by John Humble.

Figure 31 shows in a diagrammatic form how various methods of training can increase managerial effectiveness.

(*f*) Internal courses

These courses may meet some training needs. Many management courses are residential and companies set up Staff Colleges where courses are held which are concerned with outlook and attitudes; the different atmosphere aids work.

Management training techniques

The main techniques used are shown in the table on pp. 269–71.

Group dynamics can be considered further. Another name is sensitivity training or T. Groups.

Students are put in groups, which may be *structured*, i.e. with a set idea and a brief plan, or *unstructured*, with no plan at all. Discussion ensues and students are encouraged to observe the stresses and strains that occur between members, how these shift as the group takes on new tasks and as

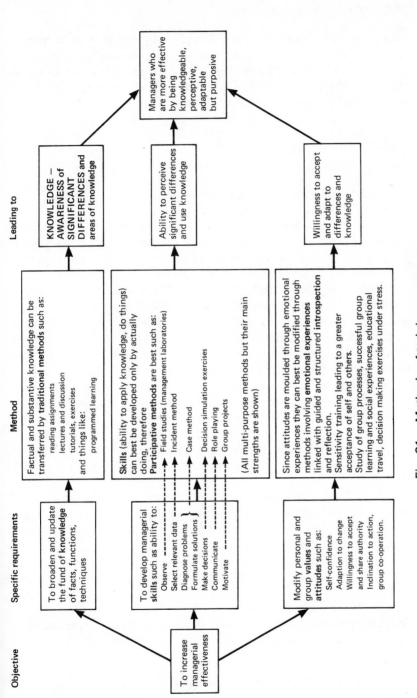

Fig. 31. Methods of training managers.

individuals assume different rôles. There is no *agenda*, goal or formal authority and frustrations, conflicts and collaboration abound. By observing this, group members begin to observe the dynamics of group behaviour. Again, skilled instructors are needed, as it is a strain on members, who should be selected carefully.

Other training techniques

The managerial grid

Grid organization development was evolved by R. R. Blake and J. S. Mouton, *The Managerial Grid* (1965, Gulf Publishing Co.). The model postulates that a manager's two main concerns, for production and people, can be shown on a matrix. Each scale from 1 to 9 expresses either a concern for people or a concern for production. Blake selects five positions (1/1, 1/9, 9/1, 9/9 and 5/5) for consideration. He suggests we accept 9/9 as the preferred management style, showing a maximum concern for people and production. Managers complete a questionnaire and place themselves on the two scales, deficiencies are highlighted the farther they are away from 9; these 'deficiencies' can be acted upon. Managers tend to accept this approach, although the idea does not have much evidence to support the link between managerial style and organizational performance.

The object of the training programme is to achieve 9/9 managers, and to achieve production through mature interpersonal relationships which are integrated with the purposes of the organization.

1–9 = Thoughtful attention to needs of people for satisfying relationships leads to a comfortable friendly organization atmosphere and work tempo.

9–1 = Efficiency in operation results from arranging conditions of work in such a way that human elements interfere to a minimum degree.

1–1 = Exertion of minimum effort to get work done is appropriate to sustain organizational membership.

5–5 = Adequate organizational performance is possible through balancing the necessity to get out work with maintaining morale of people at a satisfactory level.

9–9 = Work accomplishment is from committed people; interdependence is through a 'common stake' in organization purpose and leads to relationships of trust and respect.

The 3-D organizational effectiveness programme

This training programme, advocated by W. J. Reddin, is based on his grid model of managerial behaviour which extends Blake's grid and adds

Method	What it is	What it will achieve	Points to watch
Lecture	A talk given without much, if any, participation in the form of questions or discussion on the part of the trainees.	Suitable for large audiences where participation of the trainees is not possible because of numbers. The information to be put over can be exactly worked out beforehand—even to the precise word. The timing can be accurately worked out.	The lack of participation on the part of the audience means that, unless the whole of it, from beginning to end, is fully understood and assimilated, the sense will be lost.
Talk	A talk incorporating a variety of techniques, and allowing for participation by the trainees. The participation may be in the form of questions asked of trainees, their questions to the speaker, or brief periods of discussion during the currency of the session.	Suitable for putting across information to groups of not more than 20 trainees. Participation by the trainees keeps their interest and helps them to learn.	The trainees have the opportunity to participate but may not wish to do so. The communication will then be all one way and the session will be little different from a lecture.
Job (skill) instruction	A session during which a job or part of a job is learned in the following formula: 1. The trainee is told how to do the job. 2. The trainee is shown how to do the job. 3. The trainee does the job under supervision.	Suitable for putting across skills. The job is broken down into small stages which are practised. The whole skill is thus built up in easily understood stages. This gives the trainees confidence and helps them to learn.	The skill to be acquired may best be learned as a 'whole' rather than as parts.
	Each of these parts may be a complete session in itself: (a) talk (b) demonstration (c) practice.	More suitable when the skill to be learned is one which depends on a lot of knowledge first being learned. Many clerical skills are of this sort.	It is difficult for trainees to absorb large chunks of information and then to be shown what to do at some length before they get the opportunity to put the learning into practice.
Discussion	Knowledge, ideas and opinions on a particular subject are freely exchanged among the trainees and the instructor.	Suitable where the application of information is a matter of opinion. Also when attitudes need to be induced or changed. Trainees are more likely to change attitudes after discussion than they would if they were told during a talk that their attitude should be changed. Also suitable as a means of obtaining feedback to the instructor about the way in which trainees may apply the knowledge learned.	The trainees may stray from the subject matter or fail to discuss it usefully. The whole session may be blurred and woolly. Trainees may become entrenched about their attitudes rather than be prepared to change them.

Method	What it is	What it will achieve	Points to watch
Rôle-play	Trainees are asked to enact, in the training situation, the rôle they will be called upon to play in their job of work. Used mainly for the practice of dealing with face to face situations (i.e. where people come together in the work situation).	Suitable where the subject is one where a near-to-life practice in the training situation is helpful to the trainees. The trainees can practise and receive expert advice or criticism and opinions of their colleagues in a 'protected' training situation. This gives confidence as well as offering guidelines. The trainees get the feel of the real life situation.	Trainees may be embarrassed and their confidence sapped rather than built up. It can also be regarded as 'a bit of a lark' and not taken seriously.
Case study	A history of some event or set of circumstances, with the relevant details, is examined by the trainees. Case-studies fall into two broad categories: 1. Those in which the trainees diagnose the causes of a particular problem. 2. Those in which the trainees set out to solve a particular problem.	Suitable where a cool look at the problem or set of circumstances, free from the pressures of the actual event, is beneficial. It provides opportunities for exchange of ideas and consideration of possible solutions to problems the trainees will face in the work situation.	Trainees may get the wrong impression of the real work situation. They may fail to realize that decisions taken in the training situations are different from those which have to be made on the spot in a live situation.
Exercise	Trainees are asked to undertake a particular task, leading to a required result, following lines laid down by the trainers. It is usually a practice or a test of knowledge put over prior to the exercise. Exercises may be used to discover trainees' existing knowledge or ideas before further information or new ideas are introduced. Exercises may be posed for individuals or for groups.	Suitable for any situation where the trainees need to practise following a particular pattern or formula to reach a required objective. The trainees are to some extent 'on their own'. This is a highly active form of learning. Exercises are frequently used instead of formal tests to find out how much the trainee has assimilated. There is a lot of scope in this method for the imaginative trainer.	The exercise must be realistic and the expected result reasonably attainable by all trainees or the trainees will lose confidence and experience frustration.
Project	Similar to an exercise but giving the trainee much greater opportunity for the display of initiative and creative ideas. The particular task is laid down by the trainer but the lines to be followed to achieve the objectives are left to the trainee to decide. Like exercises, projects may be set for either individuals or groups.	Suitable where initiative and creativity need stimulating or testing. Projects provide feedback on a range of personal qualities of trainees as well as their range of knowledge and attitude to the job. Like exercises, projects may be used instead of formal tests. Again there is a lot of scope for the imaginative trainer.	It is essential that the project is undertaken with the trainee's full interest and co-operation. It must also be seen by the trainee to be directly relevant to his needs. If the trainee fails, or feels he has failed, in the project there will be severe loss of confidence on his part and possible antagonism towards the trainer. Trainees are often hypersensitive to criticism of project work.

Method	What it is	What it will achieve	Points to watch
In-tray	Trainees are given a series of files, papers and letters similar to those they will be required to deal with at the place of work (i.e. the typical content of a desk worker's in-tray). Trainees take action on each piece of work. The results are marked or compared one with another.	Suitable for giving trainee desk workers a clear understanding of the real life problems and their solutions. The simulation of the real situation aids the transfer of learning from the training to the work situation. A valuable way of obtaining feedback on the trainees' progress. Also useful for developing attitudes towards the work, e.g. priorities, customers' complaints, superiors, etc.	It is important that the contents of the in-tray are realistic. The aim should be to provide trainees with a typical in-tray. The marking or comparison of results must be done in a way which will not sap the confidence of the weaker trainee.
Business and management games	Trainees are presented with information about a company—financial position, products, markets, etc. They are given different management rôles to perform. One group may be concerned with sales, another with production and so on. These groups then 'run' the company. Decisions are made and actions are taken. The probable result of these decisions in terms of profitability is then calculated.	Suitable for giving trainee managers practice in dealing with management problems. The simulation of the real-life situation not only aids the transfer of learning but is necessary because a trainee manager applying only broad theoretical knowledge to the work situation could cause major problems. Also a valuable way of assessing the potential and performance of trainees. It helps considerably in developing many aspects of a manager's rôle.	The main difficulty is in assessing the probable results of the decisions made. Sometimes a computer is used for this purpose. The trainees may reject the whole of the learning if they feel the assessment of the probable outcome of their decisions is unrealistic. There is also a risk that the trainees may not take the training situation seriously.
Group dynamics	Trainees are put into situations in which: 1. the behaviour of each individual in the group is subject to examination and comment by the other trainees, 2. the behaviour of the group (or groups) as a whole is examined. (The trainer is a psychologist, sociologist or a person who has himself received special training.)	A vivid way for the trainee to learn of the effect of his behaviour on other people and the effect of their behaviour upon him. It increases knowledge of how and why people at work behave as they do. It increases skill at working with other people and of getting work done through other people. A valuable way of learning the skill of communication.	Difficulties can arise if what the trainee learns about himself is distasteful to him. Trainees may 'opt out' if they feel put off by the searching examination of motives. It is important that problems arising within the group are resolved before the group breaks up.

a third dimension 'effectiveness' to 'tasks orientation' and 'relationships orientation'.

Again a test is completed to show each manager his own style. This is a flexible training programme which consists of nine stages and can be tailored to meet the needs of individual companies.

A final look at research on the nature of the relationship between management and supervisory style and the performance and satisfaction of co-operating individuals, must include the work of R. Likert, *The Human Organization* (1967, McGraw-Hill).

He put forward four recognizable Systems of Management.

System 1: Exploitive—authoritative.
   This is a bureaucratic, hierarchical structure with rigid authoritarian control.
System 2: Benevolent—authoritative; results are achieved by a system of rewards plus some delegation.
System 3: Consultative—achieving a measure of employee involvement while reserving policy making for the top.
System 4: Participative—group; communications move freely up and down, management provides adequate rewards and full use is made of group involvement to set high performance goals.

The ideal—System 4; he considers is more beneficial. The organization has mutual trust and supportive relationships between employees and managers. He claims that managements tending to System 4 have higher output and better industrial relations.

The approaches to management of McGregor, Blake and Likert appear similar. The needs and talents of workers and managers can be satisfied and utilized more effectively if the environment is suitable. Each one classifies a style of management, Blake, 9/9; Likert, System 4; McGregor, Theory Y. To the extent that managers do not reach these ideal positions, training is needed to change attitudes and behaviour towards them.

Job satisfaction

Research into job satisfaction usually involves dealing with matters of a subjective nature and this means results are difficult to evaluate. One element of importance is that workers in a successful undertaking which is publicly prominent derive satisfaction from their work. A worker's attitude to his work depends a lot on the informal social organization in the undertaking. The experiments of Elton Mayo were considered in chapter 1 and those of Hertzberg in chapter 4; research by Miss Joan Woodward in her book *Industrial Organization: Theory and Practice*, points to several general conclusions about the effect of relations with workers and of different types of *work organization*.

She found that relations with workers on batch production work and flow production (motor-car industry) tend to be less good than those on unit (craftwork) or continuous process work (chemicals). On individual production work variety provides interest and workers have some control over quality. On continuous process work there tends to be a high ratio of managers to operatives who work in smaller groups and thus closer relations develop. In batch or flow production work, workgroups may be large and difficult for supervisors to control closely; there is little opportunity to control quality and the worker is under continued pressure, as productivity usually depends upon speed of working.

It may also be true that *opportunities for promotion* may influence the degree of satisfaction a worker will have in his job. If educational attainments are going to be essential for promotion, opportunities for study may be essential to retain good worker relations.

Organizational development

Behavioural scientists have recently learned how to help organizations to cope with a changing internal and external environment. Research into industrial psychology has changed to the examination of *organizational* psychology, with emphasis on groups and relations between groups. The emphasis was on *individual* training and development, but it appeared that a broader outlook was needed to look at the complete *organization*, concentrating on organizational group and interpersonal processes, and develop plans to improve the whole system.

Organizational development (O.D.) can be considered as an approach to the introduction of planned change, concentrating on the *process* of change, rather than the content. It involves a number of behavioural science techniques which are designed to build a more effective organization. The concept aims to help the organization gain an insight into its own processes. The emphasis is in creating a more flexible open-minded organization, which is more receptive to change and where people can recognize the *need* for change and implement action themselves.

The increasing need for change led to the development of O.D.; created by changes in:

(a) technology and labour skills;
(b) attitudes of employees;
(c) size of organization;
(d) need to improve performance.

Traditional training methods did not appear to be adequate to cope with the need to bring about changes in social system behaviour. Ideas from social psychology of attitude change, group dynamics techniques, 'change agent' skill, counselling, are all part of O.D.

The reason why conventional training methods did not appear to produce satisfactory long-term benefits may be because:

(*a*) Persons who have been on training courses are often disillusioned as their newly-acquired skills have little chance of being used when they return to work.

(*b*) The attitude of senior managers to training is often on a short-term basis; they look for certain results soon after the course and tend to lose interest if they are not forthcoming.

An 'agent of change' is needed to act as a catalyst. He may be from inside or outside the organization. The aim is to help the company solve its own problems and the focus is on organizational, group and inter-personal *processes* (process consultancy).

Many aspects of the organization are examined and activities are largely group based. Members are encouraged to speak more openly about problems and inter-group activities are encouraged.

Interacting factors which govern the behaviour of organizations are clearly set out by H. J. Leavitt in *A Handbook of Organizations* (1965, Rand McNally).

Figure 32 below summarizes the points involved.

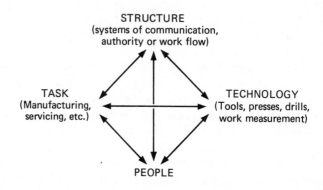

Fig. 32.

The above factors are all inter-dependent as a change in one, for example *technology* (introduction of a computer), will influence *tasks* (nature of work changes, i.e. output is greater and quicker); organization *structure* (fewer staff needed); *people* (by their accepting or not accepting the need for a computer).

It is often the case that there is too much rigidity in the organization and this does not enable creative ideas to be introduced. Some methods used to overcome this are:

(*a*) *Diversification*—Companies with too narrow a product base buy interests in other industries.

(*b*) *Decentralization*—parent company has overall control, but units are given authority to make major decisions and the unit managers are held accountable for results to the parent company.

(*c*) *Venture groups*—group is given resources to develop a new idea, which may have come from a group member.

One major problem is that usually people do not like to change. Change is a threat to routine and their rôle in the organization. It is also true that many persons do *not* know what their rôle is, and in recent years attempts have been made to clarify individual rôles or objectives (key results areas) by management by objectives. M.B.O. involves the management of organizational change. (See p. 260 and note the stereotyped attitude to M.B.O. by some companies.) The *task* can be boring, because of specialization; remedies include job rotation, job enlargement and enrichment (see p. 284). Only in job enrichment does an operative get the chance to discuss with management ways of re-organizing the work.

Advantages of organizational development

(*a*) Concentrates on team work rather than on individual development; this may raise morale and efficiency.

(*b*) Helps employees to face changes themselves in an ever-changing environment.

Disadvantages

(*a*) Difficult to convince staff of the *need* to change.

(*b*) May be costly to implement.

(*c*) Needs continual support by top management and their *conviction* of the need for change.

Suggested stages of the process of O.D. are:

(*a*) The 'change agent' and senior executives *discuss* the *aims* of the programme and the ideas behind it, bearing in mind future needs.

(*b*) The *main problems* and objectives are set out clearly.

(*c*) An '*audit*' *of the organization* is effected, e.g. state of morale, existing relationships between persons (this can be done by interview, questionnaire, etc.).

(*d*) Targets for *improvement* can then be set and agreed.

(*e*) A *check on effect* of plans is needed to ensure that the new methods are maintained.

Experience has shown that managers would be more effective if they:

(*a*) did not rely *too much* on their experience;

(*b*) adopted a more flexible rôle in discussions;

(*c*) encouraged the definition of problems in many varied ways;

(*d*) helped others to methodically talk through points involved;

(*e*) are skilled in questioning persons and working *with* them in making decisions;

(*f*) have a management 'style' conducive to change.

It can be seen that the work of a manager in a changing environment is more complex; there are various pressures he has to integrate, e.g. from colleagues, subordinates, superiors, in addition to external agents, such as suppliers, customers and government, who form around him certain *boundaries* which produce relationships he has to manage to ensure his territory remains intact. It is therefore important to examine briefly the preferred 'styles' of managers who have to implement changes and consider the need for good 'integrators.'

Paul R. Laurence and Jay W. Lorsch pointed out in the December 1967 issue of the *Harvard Business Review* the difficulties that managers have in reconciling the need for specialization with the need for integration of effort. Inter-departmental conflicts need to be resolved and decisions made more quickly and smoothly. So in order to co-ordinate and integrate more effectively the person appointed should have certain attributes and adopt suitable behaviour characteristics in the resolution of conflict. Preferred styles were found to be from managers who:

(*a*) prefer to take initiative and are confident and persuasive;

(*b*) seek status and are forceful and effective in communication;

(*c*) have wide scope and breadth of personal interests and social poise;

(*d*) are enthusiastic and imaginative and spontaneous, adventurous, humorous, flexible and assertive.

This is an area where research into the effectiveness of O.D. is sparse but will become increasingly more important, perhaps to the extent that the status of the *integrative function* will reach senior management, or at least departmental level. Organizations in a dynamic environment wishing to achieve a competitive advantage must pay special attention to the planning and integration of jobs and to the selection and development of persons to fill them.

G. PROMOTION AND TRANSFER

1. Promotion

A policy for promotion is needed and its contents may be:

(*a*) All promotions to be made, as far as possible, within the firm.

(*b*) The main basis of promotion to be merit and ability. Seniority (often the number of years' service) to be considered but not to form the sole reason for promotion.

(*c*) Opportunities given to all employees to reach the highest grades.

(*d*) Vacancies be advertised and be kept open to all employees.

(*e*) Accurate personnel records must be kept and these must include job grading and merit ratings and other relevant details.

2. Transfers

These occur from one department or job to another or both and may solve a number of problems. Clear records are essential to obtain knowledge of the new job's requirements and the qualities needed for it. The employee himself, or his department head, may have requested the transfer. Care and tact are needed in these situations.

H. WAGE AND SALARY ADMINISTRATION

Remuneration policy and methods cannot be considered in isolation from the country's economic policies. Wages may account for up to 80 per cent of total costs in some industries and about 10 per cent in certain process industries.

The objects of a policy of remuneration are:

(*a*) To attract and retain sufficient staff of the required calibre to meet the firm's objectives.

(*b*) To provide incentives for better staff work.

(*c*) To have a policy which is logical and consistent, easily understandable and flexible.

After objectives, policies and priorities have been determined, the methods of remuneration to be used to achieve them should be considered, i.e. job evaluation, merit rating, incentive schemes and fringe benefits.

Job evaluation

It is not easy to produce an acceptable system of wage structure today, especially as inflation is increasing and social values are changing. The difficulty is in finding a base or pattern of stability for wage bargaining. A job evaluation plan may be agreed only to find that what was deemed a fair differential between grades is now no longer supported—as social values have changed.

In the search to find a stable pattern, each yearly wage bargaining round has been associated with a 'normal' increase, which it is hoped will be sufficient until the next round of bargaining. Job evaluation systems also try to give a position of stability, but this is affected by inflation.

Schemes to establish a systematic means of relating rates of pay to jobs are collectively known as *job evaluation*, which is intended to arrive at a rate for a job (usually through negotiation) irrespective of the attributes of individual workers who are employed on the job. The British Institute of Management defines job evaluation as 'the process of analysing and assessing the content of jobs, in order to place them in an acceptable rank order, which can then be used for a remuneration system.'

There is an increasing interest in job evaluation, because in addition to providing a measure of uniformity, a flexible pay structure can deal with changes in job content and complexity and the more there is company and plant bargaining, rather than national bargaining, the easier it is to incorporate job evaluation into agreements. The Equal Pay Act, 1970 implies the need to use job evaluation to ensure that jobs are ranked in a fair and equal manner.

Although the scope of job evaluation is unlimited in principle, its application has been rather restricted to groups of relatively homogeneous jobs in a company, e.g. manual or clerical.

A summary of the main points in the application of this technique will include:

(1) Deciding *who* shall carry out the work.

(2) *Training* the persons (usually a committee).

(3) *Selecting key* jobs (benchmarks) to represent a range of levels and functions.

(4) *Analysing* jobs, writing job descriptions and specifications for them and deciding on *job elements*, or factors, which provide main headings for job assessment.

(5) Agreeing *importance* (or weight) of these factors and analysing all other jobs, then comparing them to produce a ranking order.

(6) Noting *levels of payment*, nationally and locally, then deciding on number of job grades and the rate of payment for each grade.

(7) Agreeing structure, implementing and reviewing its application periodically.

A job *description* provides information on which each job can be rated or evaluated. The measures of value can then be translated into wages and salary rates. Evaluation gives one job a rating as compared with a rating for another job.

Workers' representatives frequently participate in job evaluation, which may be done by a committee representing management and workers. Once jobs have been described, one of the four main systems of job evaluation may be used:

(a) Ranking systems

These assign measurable points values to jobs and establish a number of pay classes and determine the relative position of jobs. They often include a few broad qualities which are characteristic of all jobs to varying degrees, each job being treated as a whole and not broken down into factors. They are simple to operate and best suited to small organizations where the ranking committee will know all the jobs.

(b) Job classification

For each main class of job, a specification is prepared, noting the work and responsibility that will be included. Salary ranges may be allocated to each class and sub-class. All jobs are fitted into these classes. This method also is suited to small units.

(c) Points systems

A manual sets out the elements or factors upon which each job is to be rated and provides yardsticks by which each factor is to be valued. Job elements are described and *weighted*, and each job is given a total points value by adding up the factor points. The factors are usually:

(i) Skill—comprising education, experience, initiative, dexterity and integrity.

(ii) Effort—physical, mental or visual demand.

(iii) Responsibility—for equipment or process, material or product, safety or the welfare of others.

(iv) Job conditions—working conditions, monotony and unavoidable hazards.

Against each of these factors will be a maximum points rating; each factor will be assessed for every individual and his points total noted. Then, depending upon the points number, a job classification will be allotted, e.g. A—up to 100 points; B—up to 150; C—up to 200. If for example a person had 140 points he would be in class B. A wage structure could then be determined from the above simple illustration by allowing a rate per hour for class A of sixty pence; class B of seventy pence; class C of eighty pence.

(d) Factor comparison

This is more involved and not easy to explain to employees, but resembles the points system as each job is analysed into factors considered common to all types of jobs. These factors are usually—mental and physical effort, skill, responsibility and working conditions. A survey is made of the wage structure, from which a number of *key jobs* are selected, representing various wage levels. An analysis is then made to determine the proportion of total wage paid for each factor. Scales are prepared for each factor, against which all the other jobs under review may be compared factor by factor; these jobs can then be placed in their relative positions of importance on the scales.

(e) HAY-MSL guide chart method

This is derived from the previous basic methods and is based upon a points system where points are awarded to significant elements of a job. The importance of jobs relative to others is measured and this is determined mainly by the *purpose* of the organization. Guide charts are produced which represent the structure of the organization and cover areas headed: problem-solving, accountability and know-how. *All* staff are included and jobs can be compared logically and effectively. Comparisons between salaries paid in other companies are included.

Know-how—is the amount of skill and knowledge and experience needed to do a job (including knowing how to work with people).

Problem-solving—the amount of discretion or judgement needed and the type and frequency of problems and the necessity for the holder to develop new ideas.

Accountability—assessment of the degree of impact the job has on the department or the company, the area affected by the job and whether it affected large or small amounts of money and the extent to which the job holders were responsible for large or small areas of work. Salary is paid according to performance (100 per cent is satisfactory).

Advantages of job evaluation

Job evaluation has the following advantages:

(*a*) It provides a systematic procedure, describing and placing a value on a job.

(*b*) Job descriptions can be employed in recruitment and selection.

(*c*) Men are paid for work performed, and the satisfaction derived can lead to higher morale and better co-operation.

(*d*) Unions can play a part in deciding between levels of pay.

Disadvantages

The disadvantages are:

(a) No allowance is made for differences displayed in the performance of a job. (Merit awards can be used.)

(*b*) Pay rates are also affected by market conditions, i.e. supply of, and demand for, labour.

(*c*) Assessment may be inaccurate and, if the number of grades is small, jobs of a different character may have to be put in the same grade.

Merit rating

A person's ability can be assessed and a payment for merit may be given. It is a subjective assessment, usually made by department heads. They decide ratings by one of a number of systems. These could be alphabetical, i.e. A.B.C.D., or descriptive, e.g. very good, good, average, below average, or on a percentage rating. Some of the factors to consider are timekeeping, quantity and quality of work, initiative, co-operativeness, dependability. Points can again be awarded for each factor out of a maximum number. It is a system often applied to salaried staff.

Some qualities obviously are difficult to determine, but it may be better to use this method for promotion candidates rather than use it to select people at their first interviews.

Wages and incentives

In most incentive payment schemes, performance above a level taken as standard for job evaluation will receive a reward. The form of reward is usually cash. There are three main groups:

(*a*) Merit rating.

(*b*) Payment by results—the incentive here is linked purely with output, at a given level of quality.

(*c*) Overall schemes, whereby the reward is more remote from the direct output of the individual or group, but is linked with the firm's output or profit or overall economy.

As many schemes are based upon subjective assessment by supervisors, they are opposed by trade unions as inequitable. About 35 per cent of industrial workers receive payment based on output. Schemes based on output are obviously inappropriate when the operator cannot control the level of output or where measurement is difficult. Such schemes may comprise payments which are:

(*a*) Proportionate to output—i.e. straight piece work.

(*b*) Proportionately less than output, e.g. Halsey, Rowan, Bedaux schemes, where workers 'share' the benefits of higher output with the employer.

(*c*) Proportionately more than output, i.e. a high piece rate or accelerated bonus scheme, which is progressively proportionate—these can be used where the main consideration is maximum utilization of expensive capital equipment.

(*d*) Variable in relation to output, e.g. Taylor, Merrick, Gantt, Emerson schemes, where reward has a different ratio at different levels of output.

High day or measured day rate

A number of progressive firms have been abandoning piece-work systems as no longer appropriate to their circumstances and have introduced such systems as measured day work, under which an employee is paid a time rate, plus a bonus, which is conditional on his maintaining a pre-determined level of output. The standard required is high and if the level of performance is not maintained, a lower payment is made or transfer, training, or dismissal ensues. There is also a *contractual* measured day rate, where the employee is allowed to determine his own rate of working and must maintain it consistently. Such systems have advantages in the control of production as output is predictable, but must be used in appropriate circumstances, i.e. they would not be used if there were much slack time.

Overall, or collective bonus schemes

These have arrangements whereby the employee receives a bonus or periodic payment, e.g. weekly or annually, based upon a *number* of factors, such as reduction in labour costs, or total costs per unit or increase in total profit, or output. They are said to be economical to install and operate and encourage co-operation and improve the employee's interest in the business. They are of course very remote from the actual work and the bonus may be too small a part of the total wage to be significant and the employee cannot calculate in advance what he is to receive.

Examples of these schemes are the *Scanlon plan*, which starts by fixing a *ratio* between total manpower costs and total sales value of goods produced. A reduction in this ratio, therefore, is a saving, and the amount of the saving is distributed. The *Rucker plan* is based upon a formula relating payroll costs to *sales value added* by the manufacturer. Both are common in the U.S.A. but are little practised in Great Britain.

Incentives for indirect workers

The following schemes are used to give indirect workers, i.e. non-production workers (supervisors and managers), some incentive. Payment may be by:

(*a*) Bonus based on profits of company, e.g. if a 12 per cent dividend is paid on shares, then the bonus is 12 per cent on salaries.

(*b*) Issue of shares in company or an option to subscribe in the future.

(*c*) Bonus given on output of department for which responsible.

Fringe benefits

There are two main types of fringe benefit, direct and indirect. *Direct* benefits may comprise profit sharing, co-partnership, sick pay and pension schemes; payments are generally made in cash. *Indirect* benefits are aimed at improving morale and increasing the stability of employment. Examples are free luncheon vouchers, sports or welfare amenities, provision of car or a mileage allowance, telephone, purchases at a discount, education for children, sports, canteen, social facilities. Today, the provision of fringe benefits is increasingly recognized as being part of total remuneration but this was not always the case. They were originally provided on ethical and moral grounds to assist needy employees.

The question often arises, whether to give cash or fringe benefits. Many executive fringe benefits are quite high and one reason is that a firm can give its employees more this way than a cash payment which cannot avoid being taxed.

Staff status

Most manual workers are not able to share fringe benefits as they are confined to staff (usually monthly-paid workers). There is now a tendency to provide staff status for manual workers. A major responsibility for raising the status and security of workers must rest with management. Any raising of standards costs money and must be paid for by higher productivity. The granting of staff status has been put into effect by a few progressive firms. Certain of the workers, who may be the longest serving, or at a certain level of responsibility, are rewarded by staff benefits, e.g. longer holidays, annual salary and special sick pay schemes. Salary can be difficult to determine especially if the worker was used to piece-work rates and overtime.

Job restructuring

Two basic dimensions of job restructuring are:

(*a*) *Enlargement of jobs*—by the addition of one or more related tasks. This term is used to describe changes to increase the *variety* of tasks of persons. The aim being to help problems of fatigue, low morale and apathy which occur because of the need for specialization. Workers are given more varied tasks and given increased scope for initiative and skill. A person who produces a 'whole' unit should, in theory, increase output and lead to greater job satisfaction.

Advantages

(i) Reduction in operator fatigue and relief from boredom where work is specialized and repetitive.

(ii) Operator can exercise more control over his working speed and use a wider range of skills.

Disadvantages

(i) Although personal satisfaction is increased it may not produce a more technically efficient product. Reductions in output and quality have been noted in a number of cases.

(ii) More time and cost in training is involved.

(iii) Some workers resist change and may not wish for enlargement of their jobs.

(iv) The actual system of production may not leave much scope for enlargement of jobs.

(*b*) *Enrichment of jobs*—by increasing the motivational content of jobs through the addition of different types of task, or the provision of increased worker participation and involvement. An *individual's* job has greater responsibility (*N.B.* An autonomous working group (see p. 65) is concerned with extending the responsibility for the *group*).

The idea of job enrichment leads on from the theories of McGregor and Hertzberg, who emphasized that individuals were more motivated when they were given opportunities to exercise discretion and were given more responsibility. The theories noted that a person *seeks* responsibility and will exercise discretion and aims for achievement and self-development. If he is allowed to do this he will be better motivated. So if a job is *extended* to include other duties, possibly of a higher level with more responsibility, the job is *enriched.*

Jobs can be enriched by giving a person the whole job to complete and allowing him more freedom to set targets; or re-defining a job to allow a person or team to have authority and discretion for a unit of work.

Reasons for job enrichment being installed are varied. Workers today are better educated and higher paid. People must be used more efficiently and effectively, if not, absenteeism and a high labour turnover and poorer workmanship are the result.

Advantages

(i) More workers are able to do various jobs; this can overcome the problem of absenteeism.

(ii) Teams can do their own checking and less supervisors are needed.

(iii) Reduction in labour turnover and absenteeism may occur.

Disadvantages

(i) Possible high cost of re-designing plant or re-tooling.

(ii) Unless all levels of workers and management are committed to change, it may not work. It takes a long time to change attitudes.

(iii) It is easier to introduce only if there is an *end* product.

(iv) Some persons do not want more responsibility and this must not be considered a substitute for an appropriate pay scheme.

I. TERMINATION

Termination of employment may arise from a number of causes. The Contracts of Employment Act, 1972, as amended by the Employment Protection Act, 1975, provides for minimum periods of notice and for payment of normal earnings during this period. There may be other arrangements with unions to give advance warning of notice and the allowance of time off to seek other work.

Redundancy is inevitable in a changing technological world, and a policy for redundancy is essential. Where transfer is not possible, the Redundancy Payments Act, 1965 (as amended), provides for compensatory lump-sum payments if an employee is 'dismissed' for redundancy—a term which is defined in the Act.

Disputes about redundancy payments are referred to Industrial Tribunals. The right to redundancy payments is given to employees between eighteen and sixty-five years of age, who normally work twenty-one hours or more weekly and have completed two years' continuous service with the employer.

Payments are not subject to tax and do not affect the recipient's title to unemployment pay. Generally, the employer can reclaim about two-thirds of any redundancy payment from a fund which is built up by extra contributions by employers—these are collected with National Insurance contributions. No payment is payable if employer offers suitable alternative work.

Labour turnover

This refers to the measurement of the number of employees leaving a company. From records, the labour turnover can be calculated by dividing either the total *separations* or the total *replacements* by the average number on the working force, and expressing the result as a percentage.

This figure is an indicator of the stability or otherwise of the labour force. A high turnover figure is wasteful and varies with the type of industry, sex (i.e. more women than men leave work) and age, which is one of the main reasons for leaving. Examination of the figure may pinpoint vital information; for example it may indicate poor selection techniques, poor placement or working conditions. A high turnover is costly. It involves extra costs of recruitment, engagement, training, and possibly more accidents and failure to meet orders on time. (See also Fig. 32 on p. 274.)

Employee interviews

A good personnel policy implies a guarantee against unfair dismissal. The personnel officer may call employees for interview if they have been recommended to be dismissed and examine the facts. The trade union representative or shop steward should preferably be there also.

Those employees leaving for personal reasons should also be interviewed in an 'exit interview.' Detailed records of the reasons should be kept, although the *real* reason may not be made known. An analysis of the records may spotlight weaknesses in the firm's policy or organization. Records may analyse causes under:

(*a*) Voluntary leaving—personal betterment, dissatisfaction with job, or pay conditions.

(*b*) Management action—discipline, incompetence, redundancy.

(*c*) Unavoidable—retirement, death, incapacity, marriage, leaving district, etc.

Morale or attitude surveys

These should be made regularly, e.g. at least annually, as the knowledge gained about any dissatisfaction enables early remedial action to be taken *before* employees decide to leave.

Some schemes provide measured reactions to supervision, communication, working conditions, pay, employee benefits, security status and recognition, administration, confidence in management and opportunity of development.

Answers to questions must be secret or they may be inaccurate. An example of a question is: 'The company as a place to work is—very poor, poor, fair, good, excellent.' There may also be open-ended questions, e.g. 'What do you like best about working for the company?' Questions of course must not be biased or misleading. Persons skilled in interviewing are needed and the services of the National Institute of Industrial Psychology may be utilized.

Recent legislation has greatly affected this area and dismissal is now more costly and more difficult for the employer. Termination of contracts have been restrained by public policy.

Redundancy causes problems to employees and the Personnel Department can help adjustment to the new conditions by instituting counselling services. An organized approach is needed, together with other agencies that can help, e.g. the government-sponsored Employment Services Agency. Recent legislation requires that news of impending redundancy must be given well in advance to public service agencies and trade unions.

Unfair dismissal

The concept of *unfair dismissal* and the right of an employee not to be unfairly dismissed was established by the 1971 Industrial Relations Act and later the Trade Union and Labour Relations Act, 1974. It is for the *employer* to state the reason for dismissal and he must show he acted *reasonably* and equitably in considering the act as justifying dismissal. Brief points regarding what are *prima facie* reasons for selecting persons for dismissal (assuming no discrimination) are that they must be:

(*a*) related to the *capability* or qualification of the employee for performing work of a kind which he was employed to do; or

(*b*) related to the *conduct* of the employee; or

(*c*) that the employee was redundant; or

(*d*) that the employee could not continue in work without causing either the employer or employee to contravene a legal duty or restriction.

A category of inadmissible reasons for dismissal is given in Schedule 1 to the 1974 Act and reliance on such reasons to justify dismissal would render it unfair. These reasons are connected with an employee's acting, or proposing to act on behalf of an independent trade union. Employees who are aggrieved by such dismissals can appeal to an Industrial Tribunal which may recommend re-instatement or re-engagement by the employer.

The onus of proof rests upon the employer who must give the employee a written statement of the reasons for dismissal. The right not to be unfairly dismissed does not apply to certain categories of employee (e.g. those employed in a firm with fewer than four employees). There should be no discrimination in the selection of employees for dismissal (for example, on grounds of race or sex of person).

Periods of notice have been established which must be given by either party.

These statutory provisions placed upon existing policies and practices in companies will mean that companies will have to look at all aspects in a careful and methodical manner, and develop a 'complete' policy for industrial relations.

It was shown by an Industrial Relations survey for the Donovan Commission in 1966 that disciplinary questions were among the most common issues to be considered by shop stewards and managers. Statistics have shown that since then there has been an increase in working days lost due to disciplinary issues. In view of this a few points regarding ways of minimizing problems arising from unfair dismissals will be further considered:

(*a*) Rules and procedures for discipline should be in writing and have been agreed by representatives of all parties involved. These should now be stated on Contracts of Employment Statements.

(*b*) Senior managers should be given authority to dismiss rather than the immediate supervisor, who can only suspend the employee or recommend dismissal.

(*c*) Good control and monitoring of employees should indicate poor work performance or misconduct and employees should be given warning of areas of inadequacy and asked to improve. Written warning is needed on disciplinary matters (1975 Employment Protection Act).

(*d*) Advise trade union of case and discuss before acting.

(*e*) Establish facts carefully and give employee an opportunity to state his case.

(*f*) Record of employee should be maintained carefully and referred to before taking action.

(*g*) Decisions made should be fair and appropriate to the case and consistent with previous measures.

(*h*) Reasons for decision must be made known to all and confirmed in writing, giving an opportunity to appeal.

J. EMPLOYEE SERVICES

Many undertakings have paid more attention to the improvement of the environment in which workers work and live. These are usually entitled employee services, and a number of them will be briefly mentioned.

(1) *Superannuation.* Many firms conduct pension schemes either as *separate trust funds*, where the firm's contribution (and the employee's contribution in a contributory scheme) are invested and the scheme controlled by trustees, or as *life office* schemes, where a contract is made with a life assurance office. A firm may contract out of the State graduated pension scheme if it has its own scheme which gives a pension at least equal to the maximum under the State scheme.

(2) *Catering.* This can be a very important service and plays a part in securing suitable labour. Most canteens are subsidized by the company, but its cost is allowable for purposes of taxation. The personnel manager may have to decide whether the company shall use the services of outside caterers or provide the service itself.

(3) *Sickness and benefit schemes.* Employees absent from work for certain periods may still be paid their full wage, or a proportion of the wage.

(4) *Other services.* These may include sports or recreational clubs,

assistance with housing, special provision for transport, assistance with tutorial fees and text books for those studying for professional examinations.

K. SAFETY WELFARE

The maintenance of safe working conditions and the prevention of accidents are most important. Accident prevention is the responsibility of management and this responsibility is often delegated to the personnel manager. In other firms, it may be the responsibility of the works engineer or works manager.

The Factories Act, 1961, lays down requirements concerning health, safety and welfare, and the Offices, Shops and Railway Premises Act, 1963, applies to other types of premises. A new Act is very comprehensive:

The Health and Safety at Work Act, 1974 mentions the word 'welfare,' which has never been clearly defined. The Act states: 'Employers have a duty to maintain a working environment that is safe, without risk to health and adequate as regards facilities and arrangements for welfare at work.'

Health and safety have always been part of the welfare function of personnel management, but the part played by the personnel manager has often been limited.

The objectives of the Act are:

(*a*) To secure health and safety and welfare of persons at work.

(*b*) To protect persons, other than those at work, against risks to health and safety arising out of or in connexion with the activities of persons at work.

(*c*) Controlling the keeping and use of explosives or highly inflammable or dangerous substances and preventing people from acquiring, possessing or illegally using such substances.

(*d*) Controlling the emission of noxious or offensive substances from any area.

The Robens Committee, which prepared the way for the Act, had a guiding principle—to put responsibility for preventing hazards on those who created them. The employer has therefore to run his business with regard to the health and safety of those he employs, *or* those with whom the establishment might establish some possible contact.

A breach of this *new statutory duty* could be an unlimited fine or a two-year prison sentence. The Act forces the employer to examine very carefully all aspects of the company which may cause damage to health. He must try to *ensure* employees do take care of themselves or he may be held criminally liable. (*N.B.* Employees *too* have a responsibility under the Act to co-operate.)

Safety officer

If a person is appointed to this position he may be responsible to the personnel officer or other department head. He should have good experience of industry, and knowledge of engineering principles and the Factory Acts, and have a common sense approach to problems. Qualities required include efficiency, high morale, courage, so that he can be respected, and he should be able to mix well with other people. His duties will include:

(*a*) Making routine, thorough inspections of plant and buildings, etc., preferably with the department manager concerned.

(*b*) Seeing that all safeguards are in operation, that protective gear is being worn and fire escapes are clear.

(*c*) Seeing newcomers are instructed in safety measures.

(*d*) Keeping records of accidents and their causes and taking effective action where special trends appear.

(*e*) Advising on safety implications of plant layout, working methods, etc.

Dangerous features should be pointed out and full use made of posters, films, demonstrations.

'Good housekeeping' is essential. A well laid-out plant, clearly marked, having floors free from oil and litter, is a necessity. Education in handling and transporting materials is essential.

Works safety committees

These may be formed and the terms of reference should be specific. It should be an advisory committee which meets regularly, e.g. at least monthly, to discuss action required about unsafe working conditions or methods. Members of the committee may comprise works manager, personnel manager, safety officer, department and union representatives. Chairmanship could alternate between management and workers and arrangements for retirement of members periodically would possibly ensure a flow of new ideas.

L. INDUSTRIAL RELATIONS

The field covered by industrial relations is very wide, so only a few important sections of this large topic will be briefly mentioned.

Some firms have a department of industrial relations quite separate from other aspects of personnel and its main functions may consist of:

(*a*) Prevention and settlement of trade disputes.

(*b*) Helping to form and maintain machinery of joint consultation.

(*c*) Keeping in close touch with the state of employer–employee relations.

(*d*) Advising the firm or the government on industrial relations problems.

Disputes may be settled by negotiation, conciliation, arbitration, investigation and formal enquiry. Each trade or industry's union regulations must be known by the personnel officer.

Personnel managers need to have a thorough knowledge of procedures of consultation and negotiation and the function of consultative bodies. Loss of output through industrial disputes seems to increase yearly and the proportion of strikes which occur without union support has also increased.

Whether or not the purpose of an organization is to make a profit, employers are continually under pressure to ensure that resources are fully utilized and labour costs are stabilized or reduced. Workpeople have different interests. Their main concern is to maintain and improve their standard of living. They seek improvements in wages and salaries, increased leisure, better working conditions, stability of employment, opportunities for advancement and satisfaction in their work. Although interests are not usually the same, especially when technological and industrial changes keep occurring constantly, there is one common point of interest between employers and employees, and that is to ensure continuity of production and hence employment—to keep the enterprise viable.

Trade unions

The main function of a *trade union* is to advance and protect the interests of its members. There are craft unions, industrial and general workers' unions, also those for non-manual and professional groups. Most of these are affiliated to the voluntary body called the *Trades Union Congress*, which has as its objects 'to promote the interests of all its affiliated organizations and generally to improve the social and economic conditions of the workers.' Broader issues of national policy affecting trade unions are also discussed with the Trades Union Congress and the government.

Shop stewards first came into existence as far back as 1896 when district committees of the Amalgamated Society of Engineers allowed them to be appointed. Their function was to recruit new members and see old members did not break the rules and remained members. It was not until about twenty years later that they were formally recognized by management in the engineering industry.

Management should regard the shop steward as a vital link in its chain of communication. A lot depends upon the support he receives from local and national officials. There is an increasing tendency for firms to provide *training* for shop stewards. The National Council of Labour Colleges and the Trades Union Council offer courses covering functions of trade unions, collective bargaining and negotiating procedures, incentive schemes, effective speaking and writing, etc. It is unfortunate though that after receiving this training, over half do not return to the shop floor, they enter technical colleges or become personnel managers.

Their position today varies from union to union (and their rôle and effectiveness depend upon several factors: one important factor is their personal characteristics). They are elected by union members and their duties are:

(*a*) To inspect union cards to see contributions are paid up to date.

(*b*) To act as recruiting officers.

(*c*) To see that working agreements between management and union are carried out.

(*d*) To represent their fellow workers who have grievances. They are in effect part-time union officers, but they do not normally receive payment from their union and they usually are allowed to negotiate with management during working hours with no loss of pay.

M. THE NATURE OF GOALS AND GOAL CONFLICT

Human activity systems are not easy to predict or 'model.' Human resources have an *individual* as well as a *corporate* existence, each person having certain goals and aspirations. Conflicting goals can cause problems. Some organizations have full commitment to their goal, for example, a voluntary organization. Their main problems would be to agree on the various ways of achieving the goal, and there could be some personality conflict. When we consider industrial and commercial organizations where persons are brought together for *more* than one reason, e.g. to earn a living, interest in the job itself, conflicts are more likely to arise. Not many may be interested in seeing the goals of the organization are achieved, those that may be interested are possibly more likely to be in a higher position in the organization.

It is worthwhile considering briefly the nature of individual goals— these may regard the job as an instrument to achieve: good pay, status, good domestic and social life, promotion and job satisfaction.

Even these may conflict with each other; for example, moving to another area for promotion may conflict with the desire for a settled family life in a certain area.

Within every organization there are various sub-goals of the various groups, and management attempts to manipulate these sub-goals to ensure the survival of the organization is more readily achieved. This involves co-ordinating all demands, both from inside and outside the organization (e.g. shareholders and government).

People usually work in groups and behave in a certain way within that group (a normal or accepted way). The group norm must be accepted or the person will be rejected from the group. It may happen that there is conflict between group norms, individual goals and organizational goals.

Sources of conflict

Conflict can be said to occur either on a *horizontal axis*, that is, between individual managers or between workers. Or on a *vertical axis*, between workers and managers. Conflict can exist between people in the organization and those *outside* the organization. Many of these conflicts would relate to economic aspects of pay and prices, others relate to competition for sales and markets.

The main source of conflict to be discussed here is *internal* and can be summarized under the following headings.

(a) Money

The ratio of profits to wages—a conflict between workers and managers. Or between workers themselves where a sum of money is to be shared.

(b) Job

Rates of pay are different for each job and sometimes one group 'claims' a job, possibly to safeguard their future security, or loss of earnings, if the job is given to others. This 'right' to do the job can lead to disagreement between groups on 'demarcation lines' between jobs, and frequently occurs (e.g. should a metal worker or wood-worker fit a wooden frame to an aluminium surround?).

(c) Goals

Managers are concerned with efficiency and workers with security. Managers may want newer, more efficient machinery, this may displace workers as less are needed. Conflict may occur *between* marketing and production *managers* as their policies and interests often differ.

(d) Environmental factors

Downward fluctuations in the market for a product are a threat to workers' security. Such problems may cause conflict even within a union, if the rank and file do not think their leaders are doing sufficient to secure their jobs.

(*e*) *Authority and power*

Workers are pressing for more say in decisions which affect their lives. This is vertical conflict. In addition, subordinates may resent the fact that there is always a superior above them.

(*f*) *Nature of work itself*

The socio-technical system organizes men in a particular way which often leads to a boring job, no control of the pace of work, no responsibility or group identity.

It was mentioned in the first paragraph that human activity systems were difficult to model. Some attempts have been made to produce a general theory of conflict. The rest of this section will look at some theories and suggest ways in which conflict may be prevented. More consideration of these ideas can be examined in the reading lists at the end of the chapter.

Model A—Unitary. Views the industrial enterprise as a team moving towards a common objective. The emphasis usually tends to be on profit maximization for the joint benefit of management and workers. Any conflict is seen as a weakness in interpersonal relations or leadership style. A remedy, influenced by the work of Elton Mayo, was to encourage workers to identify their aims with those of the organization, and to improve communication and adopt a more appropriate style of leadership. This model views all behaviour which is against the common objective as *irrational*. This can lead to more authoritarian ideas, that to achieve unity, one must accept the 'rational' views of management.

The approach does not consider the possible strong conflicting ideas regarding varying interests, values and goals.

Model B—Pluralist. This recognizes that there are many sources of constraint and many interested groups (e.g. shareholders, employees). There is a *plurality* of interest groups, all with various loyalties and goals which have to be *managed*. This recognizes the fact that decisions are made with many competing claims by government, employers, laws, consumers, etc. The various pressure groups set off interacting tensions that have to be held in *equilibrium*. So, by *accepting conflict* and channelling it through institutional mechanisms (e.g. collective bargaining) may help to stabilize or *balance* the various conflicts of interest. The organization adapts to pressures from within and without; conflict is not repressed, it is brought *within the system* and absorbed. Thus it is held that conflict can be controlled by evolving a set of rules and procedures, as in collective bargaining—an institutional mechanism to resolve conflict.

Model C—Class conflicts. This newer approach has not been too readily accepted by managers in industry. It strongly criticizes pluralism and disagrees that conflict can be institutionalized, as basic differences between conflicting parties are too fundamental to lend themselves to compromise. They do not regard that there is equal power representation of management and workers, and that as it is *management* that determines the terms in which any problem is defined, management, therefore, sets the boundaries of any discussion.

Methods of resolving conflict

(*a*) *Participative style of leadership*

A less authoritarian style of leadership has been shown to reduce conflicts from the workers' resentment of the power of managers. Where managers are pleasant and co-operative and acknowledge feelings of others conflict is reduced. (Theory Y approach, see p. 98.) There is also the idea to institute structural changes to *reduce* the amount of supervision a worker is subjected to and give him greater control over his own job. There is, of course, no guarantee that all workers will have higher morale and productivity, and sometimes output may fall if workers do not think an increase in productivity is in their *interest* (the goals of management and worker often differ).

(*b*) *Job design*

Some researchers stress that too much emphasis has been placed upon mechanical efficiency, division of labour and specialization (i.e. *technical* aspects), and this has led to higher labour turnover, strikes or poor work. The harmful *social* effects were ignored. So advocates of the *socio-technical* approach regard these two aspects as parts interlocking in the organization system, where a change in either can affect the whole system. (See E. L. Trist, *Organizational Choice* (1963, Tavistock.) Job enlargement and job enrichment are techniques advocated for redesigning jobs (see pp. 283–4).

(*c*) *Communications*

Any improvement here is said to be beneficial. There is, though, no guarantee that if communications are good the workers will act rationally and agree to the 'wisdom' of management—clarity cannot guarantee *acceptance*.

(*d*) *Collective bargaining*

This is an important technique or mechanism for resolving goal conflicts and may be said to have these main features:

(i) It is a joint activity where each side recognizes the right of the other to be present on equal terms.

(ii) The respective interests of those represented in collective bargaining should be identified so common interests can be noted and means found to reconcile areas of conflict.

(iii) The result is the joint regulation of the work situation by establishing a framework of rules and practice to govern relationships between the management and workforce.

The first step towards effective collective bargaining is for employers to recognize trade unions, who both agree to negotiating procedures resulting in collective agreements, which may be for a company, a unit, or the industry as a whole. The policy of the government has been to encourage and support collective bargaining and most employers negotiate with unions to agree terms and conditions of employment for 'blue collar' and 'white collar' workers. Collective agreements between unions and employers cover many issues and may relate to a whole industry, a company, or a single unit. In some industries joint negotiating bodies have been set up with formal constitutions. Other industries have more informal meetings between employers and unions. It is important that these agreements should be continually reviewed as they may soon become out of date. The pluralist approach still seems dominant, in that there seems to be an acceptance of the inevitability of conflict in industry and the need to negotiate joint solutions. Management still consider only *they* should determine some issues (e.g. hire and use of labour). Issues submitted to collective bargaining by management usually cover wage rates, hours of work, holidays, etc. The strength of the two sides determines the result. Strength depends upon:

(i) Quality of organization of unions and management.

(ii) Ratio of capital to labour; the smaller the proportion of the labour cost to total costs the more likely management may grant their demands.

(iii) Degree of skill; the more skilled workers, who can move readily to other jobs, are in a stronger bargaining position.

(iv) State of the market for products; the more a firm approaches a monopolistic position the more easily it can pass costs on to consumers by higher prices and still retain a good share of the market, then the firm may more readily accede to union demands.

(v) State of demand for products; full order books enable more concessions to be made by management; low order books may even encourage management to force a strike, which will reduce labour costs.

One final point to note in this brief summary is that there is a complex mixture of factors within and without the organization which affects the bargaining relationship and that although there is an agreement to go through grievance or disputes procedures (in a constitutional way) the *majority* of strikes in this country are *unconstitutional*, that is, in breach of procedure.

(e) *Joint consultation*

This term is used both to mean the arrangements in an *industry* as a whole for consultation between trade unions and employers' representatives, and committees set up within an *individual* firm. The industry bodies are usually permanent and are known as joint industrial councils (or Whitley Councils) and may constitute the negotiating machinery for collective bargaining. Within the firm they are known as works councils or joint production committees.

It is desirable that these committees do not concern themselves with pay rates, etc. Joint consultation provides means of:

(*a*) Regular two-way communication between management and employees.

(*b*) Keeping employees advised of the firm's policies and plans.

(*c*) Obtaining employees' suggestions and giving them a say in the provision of amenities.

(*d*) Enabling them to air their grievances regarding discipline or work rules, etc.

Like any organization, objectives must first be known. Mutual respect and confidence are needed and there should be a democratically elected committee representing all ranks, but not necessarily one person from each department. Subjects to be discussed should be clearly stated. Examples are holidays, welfare, discipline, engagement, training. There should also be good secretarial arrangements and a system for reporting back to employees.

Works councils, or joint productivity committees, pay more attention to production details, e.g. efficient use of safety precautions and supplies of materials, improvements in production and maximum use of machinery.

Committees act as a forum for *discussion*, where common problems are discussed and measures considered to improve productivity, it is not a bargaining forum. This shows the uncertainty of the situation, a pluralist and unitary approach can be seen to exist side by side. The question is, are there issues which can be put into compartments by saying—here are items of *common interest* to discuss and here are *items of conflict*? Or, should management accept that there can be conflict on *all* items, and increase the issues coming under consultation and negotiation?

(f) Productivity bargaining

The real difference between conventional methods of negotiations over union claims and productivity agreements is that, when new proposals are agreed, there is sufficient control to see they are carried out. Management offers an inducement to workers in return for increased production, the removing of demarcation lines, reductions in manning, or in overtime.

The long-term objective is to create an atmosphere in which employees will be more willing to accept new working arrangements and be more ready to co-operate in raising productivity.

(g) Informal bargaining

This usually takes place between shop stewards and foremen or first line management and can relate to issues such as overtime, speed and manning of machines. These unwritten agreements become a custom and may be regarded as a 'law.' So although the agreements satisfy people on the shop floor, this may conflict with the ideas of higher management. Shop stewards can obtain wider control through such agreements. Foremen agree, in order to ensure work flows smoothly through their section, although the agreement may conflict with *overall* company policy.

There, therefore, seems to be a case for management to consider widening the range of issues in which formal bargaining occurs (i.e. a pluralist approach). Management may lose control in the long term if it does not do this, as many inhibiting customs and practices could be cleared away under a comprehensive agreement negotiated with the unions, as in the Fawley oil refinery (1964). (A simple account of this is in T. Lupton, *Management and the Social Sciences*, pp. 70–3; 1971, Penguin.) The comment made by W. W. Daniels and N. McIntosh in *The Right to Manage* (1972, MacDonald), that those in subordinate positions have shown an increasing demand to be able to influence their own lives and if these strong social values, formed *outside* the organization, cannot be accommodated *within*, management may lose effective control.

MAIN FEATURES OF EMPLOYMENT PROTECTION ACT, 1975

Collective bargaining

One purpose of the Act is to encourage the extension of collective bargaining. A procedure is laid down whereby unions can apply for recognition and the disclosure of information for collective bargaining where employers do not do this.

Institutions

The Advisory, Conciliation and Arbitration Service (A.C.A.S.) is set up on a statutory basis. It offers industrial relations advice, provides a conciliation service and may arrange for arbitration. It can conduct enquiries into industrial matters and publish its findings. A.C.A.S. will also publish (subject to Parliamentary approval) codes of practice on industrial relations which will replace the current Code of Industrial Relations Practice. The Central Arbitration Committee (C.A.C.) is set up. A.C.A.S. may refer disputes to C.A.C. for arbitration if the parties concerned agree. C.A.C. has powers in connexion with trade union recognition and disclosure of information, as explained below. It will also take over existing functions of the Industrial Arbitration Board in connexion with, for example, equal pay.

A certification officer is to be appointed, responsible for certifying the independence of trade unions. This officer also takes over functions of the Registrar of Friendly Societies for trade unions and employers' associations, and maintains the lists of trade unions and employers' associations provided for in Section 8 of the Trade Union and Labour Relations Act, 1974.

A new Employment Appeal Tribunal is established. It hears appeals from the decisions of industrial tribunals (which now go to the High Court) on points of law. It will also hear appeals from the decisions of the certification officer.

Recognition of trade unions

The Act sets out new procedures for examining questions of recognition of trade unions by employers. If an employer refuses to recognize a trade union which has a certificate of independence, the union can ask A.C.A.S. to examine the matter. A.C.A.S. will consult all interested parties, including of course the employer. It will try to settle the issue by conciliation, but if that fails it may make a recommendation for recognition. If the employer fails to comply with that recommendation, the union may complain to C.A.C. which can if necessary make an enforceable award of terms and conditions of employment for the employees concerned.

Disclosure of information

Employers are required to disclose information to the representatives of recognized, independent trade unions which it would be good industrial relation practice to disclose. The information must be requested by the union for collective bargaining purposes. There are limits set to the information which must be disclosed. For example:

(*a*) information which would be against the interests of national security;

(*b*) which would cause substantial injury to an employer's undertaking;

(*c*) which had been communicated in confidence;

(*d*) which was about an individual;

(*e*) which was relevant to legal proceedings; or

(*f*) which it would be illegal to disclose.

If C.A.C. upholds a complaint from a union that an employer has failed to disclose information which, in its opinion, should have been disclosed, it will make a declaration to that effect. If the employer continues to refuse to disclose the information C.A.C. will be able, if necessary, to make an enforceable award of terms and conditions of employment for the employees concerned.

Terms and conditions of employment

The Terms and Conditions of Employment Act, 1959 will be repealed and replaced by new provisions. These will enable a trade union or an employers' association to make a claim to A.C.A.S. that an employer is observing terms and conditions of employment which are less favourable than the recognized negotiated terms and conditions for the trade or industry. If there are no such terms and conditions, a union or an employers' association may claim that an employer is observing terms and conditions of employment less favourable than the general level in the same trade or industry in the district. A.C.A.S. may settle the claim by conciliation, but if this fails the claim can be referred to C.A.C. which may make an award.

Guarantee payments

Employees who lose pay because of short-time working or lay-offs will be entitled to guarantee payments for a limited period.

An employer who lays off a worker, or puts him on short time because he cannot provide work, must continue to pay his normal wages for a limited period. He is obliged to make this payment only if a full day's work is lost. The amount of guarantee payments will be a normal day's pay but limited to a maximum of £6 per day. Pay will be guaranteed for 5 days in any calendar quarter. Where there is no work because of action involving other employees of the same or an associated employer he will not be obliged to make guarantee payments.

The Secretary of State for Employment may make an order excluding employees from the rights to guarantee payments if a joint application is made by all the parties to a collective agreement, and if the agreement provides guaranteed pay on terms which are no less favourable to the employees concerned than those in the Act.

Wages councils

The powers of wages councils are extended by the Act. They can now fix all terms and conditions of service and are not restricted to those affecting pay and holidays. The councils can also fix the date from which new minimum pay and terms of employment shall operate.

Wages councils may also be converted into statutory joint industrial councils without independent members. This is designed as a move towards voluntary bargaining arrangements.

Medical suspension

An employee who has to be suspended from work under statutory regulations following examination by an employment medical adviser or an appointed doctor will be entitled to be paid normal wages for the time of suspension up to a maximum of 26 weeks.

Maternity

For the first time pregnant employees are protected by law (for details, see Act).

Trade union membership and activities

If an employee wishes to join an independent trade union his employer may not victimize him for wanting to do so. Equally, if he belongs to a trade union his employer may not victimize him for taking part in its activities. Nor can the employer take action against an employee to make him join a trade union that is not independent. If an employee is victimized on any of these counts he can complain to an industrial tribunal and be awarded compensation.

Insolvency

An employee whose employer becomes insolvent will not lose money owed to him by that employer. An employee owed wages or any similar payment (including guaranteed pay) may obtain the outstanding debts relating to a period of up to eight weeks, and up to a maximum of £80 a week per employee.

Itemized pay statement

Employees will be entitled to a detailed pay statement which shows their gross pay, any variable and fixed deductions and their net pay. The employer may issue a standing statement of fixed deductions, but only if any alterations are notified to the employees when they are made and it is re-issued at least once a year.

Periods of notice

Employees are entitled to longer notice of dismissal. An employee is entitled to one week's notice after *four* weeks' service, and *two* weeks after two years' service. He is entitled to an *additional* week's notice for each year of service, up to a maximum of 12 weeks after 12 years. Employees who have a contract for less than 12 weeks (e.g. seasonal workers) are not entitled to a week's notice unless they actually work for more than 12 weeks.

Redundancies

An employer planning redundancies is required to consult the appropriate trade unions about their implementation, and to take note of and reply to any representations made by them. If an employer does not consult the unions concerned they can apply to an industrial tribunal for a protective award. This would require the employer to continue to pay the employees affected by the redundancies for a specified period.

An employer is also required to notify the Secretary of State for Employment of any redundancies being planned which would affect more than 10 workers over a period of one month.

Remedies for unfair dismissal

An employee whose complaint of unfair dismissal is upheld by an industrial tribunal is entitled to ask the tribunal for an order for reinstatement or re-engagement. If the tribunal thinks this is practicable it will make such an order. If a financial award is made instead, it will consist of a basic award, usually equivalent to the employee's entitlement to a redundancy payment as well as a compensatory award to reflect the loss suffered by the employee as a result of dismissal.

Written statement of reasons for dismissal

Employees who are dismissed are entitled to a written statement of the reasons for dismissal provided they ask their employer for one.

Time off

Employees will be entitled to time off from work for the following purposes:

Trade union duties and activities

An official of a recognized, independent trade union is entitled to reasonable paid time off to carry out his official duties connected with industrial relations where they concern his employer; and for approved training related to those duties.

Employees who are members of a recognized, independent trade union will be entitled to reasonable time off in working hours to take part in that union's activities (other than industrial action). A.C.A.S. will issue a code of practice providing guidance on the circumstances in which time off for trade union duties and activities may be allowed, and what constitutes reasonable time off.

Public duties

An employee who is a Justice of the Peace or a member of certain public bodies (e.g. a local authority) will be entitled to reasonable time off to carry out the necessary duties.

Looking for work

An employee who is being made redundant is entitled to reasonable paid time off to look for work, or to arrange training for a new job.

Trade dispute disqualification

The grade or class and financing provisions of the trade dispute disqualification from unemployment benefit will be abolished. A number of people who would otherwise have been disqualified under these provisions will in future be able to obtain unemployment benefit.

Action that an employee can take

Any employee feeling that he or she has a complaint to make under any of the provisions of the Act in force at the time should first talk to his or her employer or union representative to see if the complaint can be settled without outside involvement.

If still unsatisfied, the employee should go to the nearest office of the Department of Employment for advice on how to register a complaint.

REVIEW QUESTIONS

Personnel management

(1) Outline a schedule of responsibility for a personnel manager of a medium-sized engineering company.

(2) What factors should be included in a personnel policy?

(3) What is involved in manpower planning?

(4) What are the main sources of recruitment?

(5) Outline the various stages in the procedure which might be followed by a large firm in selecting employees. Explain the reasons for each stage.

(6) Name and describe briefly two recent pieces of legislation affecting the personnel function.

(7) What matters do you suggest should be included in service agreements with executives?

(8) Indicate what you think should be included in induction training.

(9) What is meant by the term 'Management by Objectives'?

(10) What points should be considered in developing a policy for promotion of personnel?

(11) Describe two systems of job evaluation.

(12) What is meant by merit rating?

(13) Consider the types of wage incentive and suggest schemes for giving non-productive workers some incentive.

(14) What is meant by the terms (*a*) staff status, (*b*) fringe benefits?

(15) What is meant by industrial relations?

(16) What is the place and function of shop stewards?

(17) Distinguish between joint consultation and collective bargaining.

(18) What are the advantages of good employee services to the employer and employee? Give illustrations of such services.

(19) How may managers deal with the problems of redundant staff?

(20) How can organizations avoid getting involved in 'training for training's sake'?

REVIEW PROBLEMS

Personnel management

(1) You are required to prepare a report to the chairman of a holding company with five horizontally-linked subsidiary companies, in an industry of your selection, giving the draft of a practicable management development scheme for the group.

(2) You are chief financial executive of a company with a total number of employees of about 5000. The works accountant at one of the two factories of the company is due to retire in six months' time. You are responsible for appointing a replacement, either by internal promotion

or by external appointment. Outline the procedures you would follow until the actual offer of appointment is made to the successful candidate.

(3) You are the recently appointed production manager of a new factory owned by a large public company. You are requested by the chairman of the company to prepare a report advising him of:

(*a*) The main factors to be considered in the selection and training of production control staff.

(*b*) The duties and responsibilities of the staff of the production section.

(4) What are the essentials of a sound policy for the training of supervisors? How would a training scheme for senior management differ from that for supervisors?

(5) You are required to draft an advertisement for insertion in a professional journal, for the appointment of a group personnel officer. In addition you should prepare, in summary form, a schedule of the responsibilities of this officer.

(6) You are required to prepare a standard personnel practices manual for a large firm. Give the main headings for the sections of such a manual. Take any two headings and give a detailed breakdown for each. How would you obtain management and supervision acceptance of the manual? Show how any one of the recent pieces of legislation would affect your manual.

(7) Construct an executive rating scale which will indicate your view of the qualities to be considered in appraising an individual. For each trait on your scale, describe the several levels in such a way as will clearly convey a rating.

(8) Outline a management development scheme for a medium-sized company stating:

(*a*) The purpose of such a scheme.

(*b*) The techniques to be employed.

(*c*) The method of introduction to the management of the business.

State your views on appraisal interviews. Under what conditions would you expect such interviews to be effective?

(9) When administered wisely, the attitude survey can be a very useful method of unearthing communication problems at all levels of an organization and of appraising the success—or otherwise—of communication methods. List the uses of a good attitude survey and state the possible disadvantages which accrue from such an operation.

(10) 'The safety officer should be a man of qualities rather than a man of qualifications.' Discuss this statement and also outline the functions of an industrial safety officer.

(11) Within all kinds of organizations there is a definite move towards

participation at all levels and this is shown both in current legislation and in the 'mood' of management and employees.

As a manager:

(*a*) what practical action would you take to increase participation amongst your staff?

(*b*) what problems and difficulties would you have to be particularly aware of when doing this?

(12) (*a*) By what means can the cost effectiveness of recruitment policies and procedure be assessed?

(*b*) Robert Blake and Jane Mouton published their book *The Managerial Grid* in 1964 in which they described various managerial styles in terms of 'concern for people' and 'concern for production.'

Describe briefly the significant managerial styles which can be shown on the 'grid' and their implications for an organization.

(13) Job enrichment is a new approach to the problem of motivation and is concerned with the arrangement of both task and responsibilities in order to maximize work output and job satisfaction. One of the most famous examples of this approach is that of the Volvo car plant in Sweden.

If you were introducing a job enrichment programme in your department what are the major principles you would wish to consider?

Answers should be illustrated by practical examples.

(14) What is the rôle of the personnel officer in the company?

Should he, in a dispute, act independently or as a representative of management?

How may the overall performance of the personnel officer be judged?

(15) (*a*) Discuss the proposition that 'money, like prestige, if sought directly is almost never gained. It must come as a by-product of some worthwhile objective which is sought and gained for its own sake.'

(*b*) How far can this view be reconciled with executive incentive schemes?

(*c*) How can a company ensure that its managers are properly rewarded?

(16) It is currently fashionable to communicate new ideas by means of staff conferences and seminars. What considerations would you bear in mind if required to organize such an event in your firm?

(17) The consequences of a wrong choice of internal candidate for promotion are likely to be serious. What steps should the organization take to ensure as far as possible the success of its arrangements for the internal promotion of staff?

(18) Redundancy of middle managers has recently attracted considerable attention.

(*a*) For what reasons are middle managers made redundant?

(*b*) Explain why, when middle managers become redundant, many are unable to obtain appointments on at least equivalent terms.

(*c*) State the factors important for a policy for management development of the staff remaining after redundancies have taken place.

(19) It is sometimes considered easier to manage in an expanding company operating in a buoyant market within the industry, but rather more difficult when business is depressed. Why should this be so?

When may it become necessary to dismiss senior members of staff? How should this be done?

(20) In a company employing several hundred staff, salaries have been proposed by department heads subject to approval by top management. Union action now seems likely because of complaints of salary variations for jobs similar in content. What steps should be taken to overhaul the present system and establish an equitable basis for pay levels?

(21) Management selection agencies represent one method of obtaining new senior staff.

(*a*) What services does such an agency provide?

(*b*) What other methods of recruiting staff may be used?

(*c*) What are the factors which should govern the choice of method?

(22) On what bases should a firm institute a scheme for staff training and development? How may the relative success of such a scheme be judged?

BIBLIOGRAPHY

Personnel management

British Institute of Management, *Job Evaluation, a Practical Guide*, 1961.

Brown, M. and Sidney, E., *The Skills of Interviewing* (London, Tavistock, 1961).

Brown, W. B. D., *Piecework Abandoned* (London, Heinemann, 1962).

Cartwright, D. and Zander, A. (eds.), *Group Dynamics: Research and Theory* (London, Tavistock, 2nd edition, 1960).

Clegg, H. A., *The System of Industrial Relations in Great Britain* (Oxford, Blackwell, 1970).

Daniels, W. W. and McIntosh, N., *The Right to Manage* (McDonald, 1972).

Davis, L. and Taylor, J., *The Design of Jobs* (London, Penguin, 1972).

Doulton, J. and Hay, D., *Managerial and Professional Staff Grading* (London, Allen & Unwin, 1962).

Humble, J. W., *Improving Management Performance* (London, British Institute of Management, 1965).

Hyman, R., *Strikes* (Fontana, 1972).

Industrial Society, *Personnel Records, Forms and Procedures*, 1965.

Kahn, H. R., *Repercussions of Redundancy* (London, Allen & Unwin, 1964).

King-Taylor, L., *Not for Bread Alone* (London, Business Books, 1972).

McBeath, G. and Rands, D. W., *Salary Administration* (London, Business Publications, 1964).

McGregor, D., *The Human Side of Enterprise* (New York, McGraw-Hill, 1960).

Northcott, C. H., *Personnel Management* (London, Pitman, 4th edition, 1960).

Smith, P. B., *Groups within Organizations* (London, Harper and Row, 1973).

Stainer, G., *Manpower Planning* (London, Heinemann, 1971).

Tannehill, R. E., *Motivation and Management Development* (London, Butterworths, 1970).

Tannenbaum, A. S., *Social Psychology of the Work Organization* (London, Tavistock, 1967).

Turner, H. A., *Trade Union Growth, Structure and Policy* (London, Allen & Unwin, 1962).

Woodward, J., *Industrial Organization: Theory and Practice* (Oxford University Press, 1965).

Yoder, D., *Personnel Management and Industrial Relations* (London, Pitman, 5th edition, 1964).

9 Office Management

The word 'office' is not easy to define. It refers to work of a clerical nature which occurs to varying extents in every enterprise. It is convenient to refer to the office as a collection of departments carrying out clerical work.

The Offices, Shops and Railway Premises Act, 1963, Section 1, sub-section 2, defined certain terms:

(*a*) 'Office premises,' means a building or part of a building, being a building or part, the sole principal use of which is an office for office purposes.

(*b*) 'Office purposes' include the purposes of administration, clerical work, handling money and telephone and telegraph operating.

(*c*) 'Clerical work' includes writing, book-keeping, sorting papers, filing, typing, duplicating, machine calculation, drawing and editorial preparation of matter for publication.

An office can be said to comprise the following functions:

(*a*) Receiving information, i.e. sorting, distributing, filing, entering up and posting.

(*b*) Providing and arranging, i.e. re-arranging information in a certain manner for management to act upon, also indexing and collating.

(*c*) Communicating, i.e. typing, duplicating, photocopying, telephoning, teleprinting, mailing.

(*d*) Control and protection of enterprise, inspecting, checking and auditing.

A. RESPONSIBILITY FOR OFFICE WORK

The person in charge may vary widely. He may be a secretary or accountant; some departmental heads may be in charge of their own clerical staffs.

There often is a central general office with one person in charge, who is responsible for the provision of clerical services throughout the enterprise. Such a person must be a specialist in this field as it calls for special skills and, in particular, a knowledge of alternative techniques by which results may be obtained. It also involves a knowledge of the economical use of office machines and the planning and co-ordinating of office procedures.

Such a person may be called the office manager and in a large enterprise his schedule of responsibilities may be as follows.

Schedule of responsibilities for office manager

Responsible to: Chief accountant.
Responsible for:

(1) Advising and assisting departmental managers in the planning of clerical activities, including equipment, methods of work, supplies, personnel required and layout of office accommodation.

(2) Scrutinizing all clerical procedures and the forms and stationery associated therewith, and making recommendations to the departmental managers concerned.

(3) Maintaining the following general office services, including supervision of staff engaged therein:

(*a*) Opening and distribution of inwards mail, collection and despatch of outwards mail.

(*b*) Telephone, messenger and internal post services.

(*c*) Central filing room.

(*d*) Typing pool.

(*e*) Duplicating section.

(*f*) Stationery store.

(4) Maintaining the Office Manual of Procedures and Forms and approving requisitions for office equipment and supplies for all departments, and establishing with the purchase manager a satisfactory procedure for their purchase.

(5) Regularly reviewing office machinery and equipment with a view to its maintenance and replacement where necessary and reporting thereon to the chief accountant.

(6) In association with departmental managers, establishing, in relation to clerical procedures, work schedules and output controls with a view to securing efficiency and economy in the use of clerical staff and the completion of routines to time.

(7) Assisting the personnel manager in establishing satisfactory standards of welfare and grading arrangements for staff mentioned in item (1), informing him of expected vacancies in such staff and approving proposed appointments thereto.

Special responsibilities

Elimination of delays in clerical procedures in all departments, in association with managers thereof.

Limitations

No line authority over personnel other than those in item (1). No machinery or equipment costing over £200 to be ordered without sanction of chief accountant.

B. PLANNING AND ORGANIZING THE OFFICE

Basic organization principles must be applied, bearing in mind that the position of the office in the hierarchy will vary with the type of enterprise. In small firms, responsibility for the position will form a part of the duties

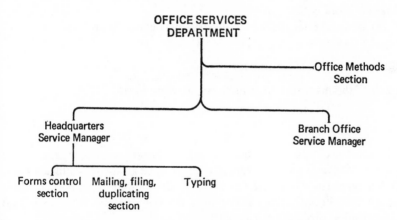

Fig. 33.   Office services department. Organization chart.

of another position, e.g. accountant. Where the volume of administration is great, e.g. banks and insurance companies, it may be a distinct section, possibly called office services department, under the direction of an administrative office manager.

The chart in Fig. 33 shows such an organization.

Centralization and decentralization

As far as *office work* is concerned, *centralization* is desirable for the following reasons:

(*a*) There is economy of staff and machinery. Flexibility is improved as staff can more easily be moved to other work. Expensive machinery may be used economically.

(*b*) Control is facilitated and standards of work can be made uniform.

(*c*) Consultation and communication are easier and personal contact is possible.

(*d*) Specialists can be employed. Where office work is confined to one building or location, it is possible to centralize the bulk of the clerical work. Where plant is in several locations more decentralization of office services may occur. In such a situation it is unlikely that accounting work will be decentralized as the more computers are used and the better the means of communication, the more accounting work can be centralized.

There are advantages of *decentralization of office work*:

(*a*) Clerical work is better done near to the practical work to which it relates, since clerks are more likely to understand the implications of documents that they handle and are more likely to spot errors and obtain answers more easily.

(*b*) Better service is given to department management.

Centralization of office services

Each of the main sections can be briefly considered:

(*a*) *Typing*

The supervisor can ensure quality and uniformity of style. Work can be distributed evenly and experienced typists can be given more difficult work. Better typewriters (electric) can be used. Centralized dictation is possible which has the advantage that typists do not need to leave desks and transcription problems are avoided.

Audio-typing pools are not too well liked by typists, one of the main reasons being the lack of the human element. The National Institute of Industrial Psychology published a report in 1966 on this problem and recommended regular breaks from work, smaller groups, freedom from noise and more effective supervision.

(*b*) *Filing*

This again may be centralized or in departments.

The main point to consider is—can a document be obtained in reasonable time? Where promptness is essential, e.g. for use on the telephone, department filing is needed.

(*c*) *Duplicating and office printing*

Duplicating machines in departments are rarely fully used. Centralization can therefore make good use of expensive specialized equipment, which may be used and maintained by skilled operators. Small machines, e.g. spirit duplicators, may conveniently be used by departments.

Selection of office site

The main points to consider are:

(*a*) There must be space for employees and equipment and also for expansion in the future.

(*b*) The need to locate office services near to manufacturing or sales departments or to customers for convenience. Also proximity to banks and transport facilities.

(*c*) Availability of labour and cost of premises (to rent or buy). The Location of Offices Bureau was set up in 1963 to provide information and help to firms which wish to leave the centre of a congested London. Outside London there are of course lower building costs, and cheaper rent, and it may be healthier for staff. On the other hand, premises away from town centres may suffer from communication problems, difficulty in obtaining specialist staff required and a possible loss of prestige.

Layout of office

After acquiring the building, the layout of departments must be studied. The following factors should be noted:

(*a*) Large open spaces are more desirable than a series of small rooms.

(*b*) As much natural light should be used as possible.

(*c*) The chief executives may be given private rooms, situated near each other for convenience of consultation. This may not be so very important when closed-circuit television becomes more widespread.

(*d*) The flow of work should be facilitated by arranging departments in accordance with the normal work flow wherever possible.

(*e*) Machines should be preferably kept out of general offices as their noise may distract.

The environment must be considered. There are statutory requirements laid down by the Offices, Shops and Railway Premises Act, 1963, which, briefly, requires the following minimum standards:

(*a*) Temperature to be over 16°C. (60·8°F.) by one hour after office opens.

(*b*) Minimum of 400 cubic feet of space per worker.

(*c*) Other rules include ventilation, lighting, washing, eating facilities, fencing of machinery, first aid and fire precautions.

Other important factors include the careful use of colour, which can influence morale and efficiency. Noise is always a problem, but acoustical cabinets enclosing machines, thick floor coverings and rubber-tipped chair legs and glass partitions help a great deal to absorb or mitigate noise.

Open offices

The traditional office building had a lot of wasted space. In open-plan offices a saving of space of about 33 per cent has been claimed, plus cheaper maintenance and cleaning because of no interior walls.

The main arguments in favour of open planning are increased flexibility of layout, economies of cost in building and running, and easier communication, administration and supervision.

A study was made in 1965 by the Pilkington Research Unit into the design and performance of office buildings. The team consisted of an architect, psychologist, geographer and physicist. They investigated open-plan offices and some of their findings were:

(*a*) Large offices have too many distractions.

(*b*) Management became involved in routine matters.

(*c*) Absence of 'status' symbols tended to lower morale of ambitious staff and the feeling emerged that they were likely to be forgotten in the mass of people around them.

(*d*) Supervisors thought *esprit de corps* and discipline were adversely affected.

Another development, the *landscaped office* or, as it is known in Great Britain, *Panoramic Office Planning* (P.O.P.), differs from open-planning in a few ways. It is said to overcome the disadvantages of open-planning. This type of office, which is being used by a number of large firms, has a high standard of equipment and furnishings. Desks are placed in a rather random fashion and the use of acoustic screens, filing cabinets and plants breaks up the floor area. Status is served by allocating more space and better furnishings to supervisory staff. Noise and distraction are reduced greatly by furnishings and careful arranging of equipment.

Within each work area, an individual can have his own personal arrangement of screens, etc., and rest periods are not fixed, but the rest area at one end of the floor can be used whenever required. This rest area provides light refreshments and comfortable seating. These facilities have not been found to be abused.

C. ORGANIZATION AND METHODS (O. AND M.)

In many companies the office manager may not have the time to review specific clerical procedures in depth. This has led to the establishment of advisory services, with a full-time staff whose object is the analysis of administrative practices. The Civil Service a number of years ago set up departments known as 'Organization and Methods.' This term is now widespread, although the work of such departments may be done in sections called clerical work study or systems and procedures. There is yet no accepted terminology in this field. The emphasis, in practice, is more on method than on organization.

O. and M. is a section of specialized staff which investigates systems in an office and tries to re-design and replace them with a more efficient or economical system.

There are advantages in such an appointment:

(*a*) Such specialist staff can give undivided attention to the work whereas this is not easy for an office manager.

(*b*) The O. and M. team can be regarded as impartial, and can therefore view work objectively.

(*c*) They can obtain and apply specialized knowledge of systems and machines.

Qualities required in an O. and M. specialist are mainly an inquiring mind and the tenacity to keep a problem in mind until it is solved. He must be original in outlook and have tact and patience and be able to express himself clearly both orally and in writing. The other requirements can be learnt, and cover:

(*a*) Background knowledge of company, its policy, products and services.

(*b*) Knowledge of organization structure.

(*c*) Knowledge of office equipment in broad outline and knowledge of where to get more detailed information.

(*d*) Basic office methods—he must know office practices for every section in which he is likely to be concerned.

(*e*) O. and M. techniques—the theory and practice of these techniques can be taught. These include methods design and form design and will be mentioned later in more detail.

It is important to remember that O. and M. is purely an advisory section and ideally should report to the senior executive responsible for offices in an enterprise. Such a person may be a financial director, secretary, accountant or office manager.

The selection of suitable assignments is important. When the section begins work, it is preferable to give it assignments which are likely to produce profitable savings. Often the section must wait until it is called in by the management to deal with problems, but it can suggest to management areas in which it can be of assistance.

Costs of the O. and M. service should be kept and one method adopted is to charge the cost for the service to the department which has received benefit.

Members of the team may come from different backgrounds, e.g. accounting, engineering. Often each member specializes in one field, e.g. office machines. O. and M. departments have been set up for different reasons and vary widely in organization, so they have varying duties and responsibilities.

O. and M. may report to the accountant, especially if the section arose from internal audit. There may not, though, be objective application of O. and M. recommendations if they affect the chief accountant's area of work, so it is deemed preferable to make the section responsible to an independent executive, often the managing director.

Method of investigation

Where the department is called in to do a project:

(*a*) The leader of the O. and M. team should talk over the job with the department head concerned and make a brief survey of the work involved, and then agree the aims and obtain 'terms of reference' for the assignment, to whom he is to report, and in what manner.

(*b*) The O. and M. staff are allocated to parts of the job.

(*c*) After the introduction of the O. and M. staff to departments and personnel involved, procedures are studied.

(*d*) Reports are collated and the team prepare a revised procedure.

(*e*) When the new procedure is ready, it is offered for criticism to colleagues and management and any revisions are then made.

(*f*) The new system must be 'sold' to the department concerned. First the outline, then the details must be placed open for criticism and comment, i.e. by the staff, and often a specimen run-through of the system is a great help.

(*g*) A detailed schedule of equipment and staff, etc., needed having been already prepared, the procedure is installed. It may be necessary to run the old and the new system together for a short while; this will enable staff to obtain experience and any problems can be sorted out.

(*h*) A few months later, the procedure should be followed up to see if everything is performing correctly.

Methods of ascertaining present procedure

The main methods used are:

(*a*) *Procedure narrative*

This is a step by step statement of the procedure showing the person's name, type of action performed, e.g. posting, sorting, and a brief description of action taken, e.g. invoice checked.

(*b*) *Methods analysis*

This is similar, but symbols are used to represent various types of operation, e.g. typing, sorting, transporting. These are noted in columns, so that by looking at these symbols a better picture of the operations can be seen, and unnecessary operations can be spotlighted.

(*c*) *Procedure or flow chart*

This shows the movement of the forms and documents between members of staff and departments. Columns are drawn vertically representing departments in an office, documents are pictured by rectangles and their movements between departments indicated by horizontal arrows. This pictorial means of analysis can be used either on its own or in conjunction with procedure narrative or method analysis sheets.

(*d*) *String diagram*

Desks and people are depicted on paper, and the flow of movement is noted by drawing lines, or by using string between pins. This method makes it easy to see if any doubling-back of documents, etc., occurs.

(*e*) *Specimen chart*

A simple form of chart can be prepared by completing actual documents used in a procedure and pasting them on a large board in their order of preparation. Coloured tapes can be used to show movement and brief notes of operations may be made. Some standard symbols used in charting are shown on p. 318.

Forms design and control

There is a mass of information in business and most of it can be recorded and communicated by putting it on paper. Most documents created for this purpose are forms, which are standard documents with descriptive matter and the use of them establishes a routine method of dealing with information.

Principles in form design

(*a*) The number of operations necessary in the use of the form should be reduced.

(*b*) The form must be easy to read and to use.

(*c*) The number of copies and the number of forms should be reduced. This can be done by designing forms to serve more than one purpose.

(*d*) The layout of the form must be such that it is related to other documents with which it will be used.

(*e*) Appearance must be attractive with entries easily made and instructions easily read. Colour should be used with care.

(*f*) The form must be large enough to contain all information required; any limits because of its use with machines must be noted, in addition to postal regulations and mailing and filing facilities.

(*g*) Instructions and identification. Titles should be concise, the form reference number and destination should be clearly visible.

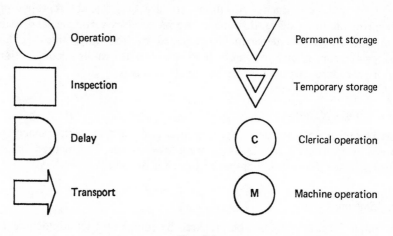

Operation

Inspection

Delay

Transport

Permanent storage

Temporary storage

C — Clerical operation

M — Machine operation

Fig. 34.

(*h*) Paper and printing. The quality of the paper should be considered. This depends upon the use of the form. If it will be handled a lot, thick paper is needed. In addition, its use on duplicators may mean the use of special paper, e.g. non-absorbent when used with hectographic duplicators. Entries may be made by pen or machine, the paper surface must be suitable for these entries.

(*i*) Spaces for entries should be adequate and in the most natural order for use. Every fifth line may be thicker for guidance and columns for ticking or inserting notes allowed for.

Forms control

This is vitally important. To initiate forms control, one person should be given the job to set up and maintain an efficient system of forms control. Steps in setting up such control may be as follows:

(*a*) Inform staff that forms control is starting and that no new forms should be released.

(*b*) All new forms to be issued by the forms office which initially needs copies of every form in existence.

(*c*) Forms should be standardized where possible and a register kept of all forms to be used in the new system.

Work measurement

It is not as simple to introduce work measurement in the office as it is in the factory. Some work is non-repetitive and an appropriate unit is not easy to establish. Standard rates of working are not easy to make as interruptions occur at varying intervals, e.g. phone calls. It may be possible to measure at least 50 per cent of the work in the office and the following methods are used:

(*a*) *Simple timing*

This involves studying a number of average clerks doing repetitive work and setting a standard, e.g. 600 lines of typing per day.

(*b*) *Recording devices*

These may be used on machines (e.g. tapometers) which register the number of key depressions or taps. Documents could be weighed. Audio-typists' work could be measured by the number of inches of dictated tape, or by pages typed.

(*c*) *Activity sampling*

This consists of random observations taken periodically and is based upon the law of statistical regularity. It enables the time spent on various activities to be noted.

(*d*) *Pre-determined motion time systems*

Gilbreth's basic divisions of the fundamental motions were the forerunners of these systems.

In these methods, elements of an operation are described according to various physical and mental factors and, by analysing a job and dividing it into its basic motions, each motion receives a time value which is obtained from a table; when these are totalled, the *standard time* is obtained.

There are more than twelve methods available for determining standard time data, but the basic techniques are essentially the same. Two of these are Master Clerical Data and Methods Time Measurement.

(e) Variable Factor Programming (V.F.P.)

This method uses a different approach. It was developed by the Wofac Corporation in America. The emphasis is on using measurement primarily as a psychological rather than a mechanical stimulus to greater productivity.

It can be applied to all forms of 'indirect' ancillary work, e.g. spares maintenance as well as the office. It is a technique for improving the work flow of indirect departments and eliminating idle time. It begins by measuring each activity the worker performs and setting a target time for each task. The total man hours needed and the manpower requirements can then be found. Work can then be programmed so that there is a smoother flow and idle time is at a minimum. Supervision is vitally important and there must be proper training for supervisors to implement the scheme, which comprises the following steps:

(i) The work content is evaluated. Each member of the department lists the work performed by him. Data are then co-ordinated and definitions standardized.

(ii) Jobs are timed by workers and averaged over about four weeks. All breaks are noted, e.g. telephone calls, and reasonable target times are set.

(iii) Work is assigned in batches to control work flow and work not completed in the time fixed is investigated. Another method of control is for employees to record the time taken against the target time. Daily and weekly reports are sent to the supervisor.

(iv) *Variable manning tables* can be drawn up, based upon target time; these give the work load in man hours and from these the number of staff required can be estimated.

It is more suitable for repetitive work, but it has been applied to drawing offices and research laboratories with reasonable success. Projects, for example, can be noted and estimated times obtained. There is a big problem in 'selling' the idea to workers and unions; if this can be done there can be large savings and greater job satisfaction.

(f) Group Capacity Assessment (G.C.A.)

This has already been adopted by a number of firms in Britain. Its purpose, like V.F.P., is to analyse labour costs and reduce them where necessary. Its origin is again in America where the accounting consultants, Arthur Young & Co., perfected the idea of measuring *groups* rather than individuals.

In a cashier's or purchasing department, measurement of the work of an individual would produce a standard for him alone; such a standard would not be appropriate for others in the section because of the variety of jobs performed in it. But if the work of small groups is measured collectively, results can be collated for *each department*.

Analysts must be carefully trained, they are then divided into teams and given a department or group to assess.

Their work has two stages:

(i) All tasks are defined and the number of times they are performed weekly determined. The rate of work on each element is then compared with that of a reasonably competent operator and a *standard time* is fixed for a group of people.

(ii) Man hours can then be calculated by multiplying the number of work units (of output) by the standard time for each type of task (i.e. each work unit). Over- or under-staffing is then apparent.

The advantages of this system are:

(i) Manpower planning can be forecast more accurately.

(ii) Jobs can be more accurately evaluated and skills better utilized, e.g. skilled personnel may be doing simple clerical tasks.

(iii) Inefficiency is spotlighted, labour costs can be reduced, and staff morale can be improved.

D. OFFICE MACHINERY AND EQUIPMENT

Media of office communications

Office services comprise specialized activities, e.g. communication, filing, mailing and duplicating, which can be usually most effectively administered when centralized.

We will consider the essential features of each type of equipment and methods used, stressing advantages and disadvantages and other considerations to be noted when considering their purchase or use.

Selecting the means of office communication needs careful attention to the following factors:

(*a*) *Speed and cost*—Will the extra cost for greater speed of delivery warrant the use of a particular medium? Does the frequency of using the medium influence the cost?

(*b*) *Secrecy*—Is this essential?

(*c*) *Responsibility*—Should responsibility for receipt be fixed by having it in written form with a copy retained?

(*d*) *Error*—Does the possibility of error or misunderstanding make it necessary to have written rather than oral communications?

A simple start to the problem of effective communications is to decide first which communications must be in writing and which may be orally transmitted. The oral grouping is then divided into urgent and not so urgent; then those frequently used and those infrequently used. Then prepare a list of media of transmitting oral communications and study each method from the viewpoint of cost, speed and effectiveness.

The same process is followed with written communications.

Communications may be written and oral and transmitted both within and without an organization.

1. Written communication

Internal communications may be between offices or departments and of the nature of special and routine reports and data, etc. The volume of communications under each heading will determine which of the following methods are used:

(*a*) Personal messenger—training and supervising may be costly.

(*b*) Conveyor systems—used where volume of work is great and the following systems may be used:

(i) Pneumatic tubes—container is sent to various centres by means of compressed air.

(ii) Conveyor belts—folders travel along motor-driven belts.

(iii) Vertical lift and chain wire conveyors.

(*c*) Electric longhand transmission—writing made by pen is converted into electric currents which actuate a receiving pen. This method is used mainly within departments of a firm.

We will now turn our attention to external written communications. Correspondence must conform to certain standards, these are easier to standardize if the work is centralized. *Centralized dictation* offers a simple way to increase office efficiency and has three main advantages:

(*a*) Executive can dictate with minimum effort and delay.

(*b*) Central pool means fewer typists than dictators.

(*c*) Smoother work flow increases typing productivity.

The main systems of making written communications will be considered.

Dictaphone systems

These may use a P.A.X. network (private automatic exchange, i.e. the internal telephone system); the P.A.B.X. network (private automatic branch exchange, i.e. G.P.O. external system), or a separate wired system.

(i) P.A.X. is generally the most economical, flexible and satisfactory when installed, as dictating points are readily available where an internal telephone exists and, by a push-button system, the dictator can have instantaneous communication.

(ii) P.A.B.X. dictation is not so satisfactory or so common as dictation may collide with external calls.

(iii) Separately wired systems entail higher installation costs but give excellent service, especially if the amount of dictation is great.

The audio-typing room may have recordings set out in a *single bank* of instruments, or in a *tandem* arrangement, where a girl has two machines. She transcribes from one, while the other receives incoming material, this arrangement allows communication between dictator and typist.

The nature of the job will help to decide the best recording medium. It could be *magnetic tape*, which gives longer playing time, while *discs* and *belts* allow a speedier location. Belts which are expendable are initially cheaper, but in the long run re-usable belts are cheaper.

Control facilities for these machines are basically similar. They are for starting, stopping, playback and correction. Most systems have provision for correction by the dictator by over-speaking and where provision is made for after-hours service this enables executives to dictate letters when working late. Other common features include intercom between dictator and transcriber, voice operated start/stop mechanism, visible and audible signals to handle urgent dictation, automatic indexing. A choice depends upon cost, suitability and balancing facilities offered.

Capital cost may be recouped in a year by the saving, on average, of a 40 per cent reduction in typing staff. Dictators must use the machines properly, otherwise there is delay and cost of re-typing.

Facsimile reproduction and transmission

An exact duplicate of anything written, drawn or typed is transmitted between two distant points. A scanner passes over the surface, the light and dark areas are converted into corresponding impulses. At the receiving end a marking device governed by these impulses 'burns' a duplicate image on specially prepared paper.

Teleprinters and telex systems

A *teleprinter* is a machine fitted with a typewriter keyboard which is connected by telegraph wire to a similar machine. Messages typed at one machine are reproduced simultaneously on the other machine. Teleprinters are rented from the G.P.O. and are used *within* the individual firm and the rental varies with the distance between the machines. Once the rental is paid, calls may be made as often as required.

Telex is a kind of teleprinter connected to a public teleprinter system, where calls can be made to any other telex subscriber in the United Kingdom or overseas. A flat rental is paid plus a charge per call depending upon length and distance. Punched cards or paper tape can be transmitted by installing tape or card converters. There will be in the future a great increase in transmission speeds (G.P.O. circuits are known as the Datel range) and a steady increase in the number of 'real-time' systems.

Real-time systems

These reduce the delays associated with entering data into the computer by connecting the communications channel directly (on-line) to the computer via control units. These real-time systems are able to process data at the instant they are transmitted from the remote point and send a reply in seconds. Early examples of this use are *airline booking systems*, where a booking clerk types a question on a console which is linked to a computer and receives a reply within seconds.

Routine paperwork can be cut immensely by such systems. In the field of insurance, a computer can assess risks, calculate premiums and print insurance certificates. Agents can type normal proposal forms on a combined policy schedule and certificate of insurance document. As the details are typed, they are transmitted simultaneously to a computer, which checks the proposal's acceptability, calculates a premium and transmits terms back to the agent's office, where they are automatically typed on the policy and certificate. Costs, though, are very high.

2. Oral communication

(*a*) *Telephone*

Except for small offices, most systems require the use of a switchboard, so that several incoming and outgoing calls may be handled simultaneously. P.A.X. and P.A.B.X. have been mentioned. The main deciding factor as to which method is used will be the ratio of internal calls to external calls at different extensions. If all extensions need outgoing facilities frequently, P.A.B.X. or P.M.B.X. (Private Manual Branch Exchange) may be used.

There are special machines which can be connected to the telephone which will answer the call and record any dictated message. These are recorded on magnetic tape and can be played back later by the person or persons interested.

(*b*) *Intercommunication* (*intercom*) *systems*

These relieve the telephone switchboard. Some permit one-way, others two-way, communications. There are two main types:

(i) Telephone type installations, independent of regular telephone service.

(ii) Electronic devices using principles of radio.

Telephone installations usually operate on a battery or transformer and calls can be sent by pressing a button to call a person in another office, where there is a similar machine which enables the conversation to be heard through a loudspeaker. Conversation may be two-way or one-way. They are direct and private and there are no operator delays. Conferences among any number of executives are possible without anyone leaving his desk.

(c) *Staff location or paging systems*

(i) Loudspeakers; messages are relayed over all premises at once. This, though, may be distracting.

(ii) Bells and buzzers.

(iii) Radio call systems. The executive carries a small radio connected with the closed circuit of the firm. A call transmitted on an executive's wave-length is made and a buzzer indicates the call; the executive may then go to a telephone or may be able to reply direct into a two-way radio.

(d) *Closed circuit television*

Two-way sound can be added. This method is becoming cheaper; it eliminates the need to duplicate records and files, permits centralized record keeping, gives instantaneous transmission of recorded information, enabling it to be verified, identified or computed.

3. Other office services

(a) *Filing*

Careful thought is needed in determining a system of filing. In all cases local conditions and problems must be examined to decide on the most appropriate system.

Questions to be considered are:

How valuable is the record?
How long do records have to be kept?
How quickly must a record be produced when required?
Which departments may need to use the records?

The answers will help to determine the method of classifying files. Generally speaking, those with similar characteristics will be filed together.

The main methods of classification are alphabetical, numerical, geographical, subject, chronological, or combinations of these.

The essentials of a good filing system comprise:

(i) *Economy*—in money cost, labour and overhead cost.

(ii) *Simplicity and accessibility*—simple to understand and operate and sited so that records are easily inserted or extracted.

(iii) *Compactness and safety*—it should take up minimum space and important documents given special protection.

(iv) The system should be *capable of easy expansion* and records should be readily available.

(v) Filing should be kept *up to date*, cross-references being used where necessary, and the most appropriate system of classification used.

Filing equipment

Vertical filing is the most common method used. Documents are filed behind each other, on edge; also they may be in pockets individually suspended. A file drawer when extended uses valuable space; to overcome this there are variations on this theme:

(i) *Open-shelf filing*, in which the folders are on shelves, visibility is unlimited, filing is quicker and more compact.

(ii) *Roll-out filing*, in which drawers roll out sideways exposing all records in half the aisle space required by vertical drawer files.

Horizontal filing is used for storing papers such as maps or drawings in a flat position, on top of each other.

Lateral filing consists of suspended files with the *end* of each file in view, which bears the index strip.

Visible card filing equipment is available in the form of trays that lie flat horizontally in a cabinet, on revolving racks, or in loose-leaf binders. Signalling devices may be effectively used on the edges of the cards which are visible at all times. Cards can be located and entries made quickly.

Rotary card filing equipment is a variation of the visible card equipment. The cards are attached to a belt or series of rings which surround the centre of a rotating wheel. Desks may be specially constructed to keep wheels in a vertical or horizontal position. Other systems are available and are based upon the principle that it is more efficient to have the work brought to the worker, than to have the worker go to the work.

Records retention

There should be a definite policy regarding retention of filed material, destruction or microfilming. Some material must be kept for the legal period of six years for simple contracts, twelve for contracts under seal, etc. Whatever method is adopted, it should be made clear to all and efficiently carried out.

Microphotography

Photographs may be taken of records and they can be reduced in size and stored in a very small area. Microfilming records may save filing cabinet space of up to 90 per cent. They are usually stored in one of two main forms: in very small 100-foot reels containing 600 frames, or in *aperture cards*. Aperture cards are thin, flexible manilla cards similar to punched cards. The film is processed and fixed on the card, which has reference data punched on it, which can then be sorted and processed by automatic machines. About 75,000 of these can be stored in a normal four-drawer filing cabinet. With a reader-printer enlarged copies of any document can be quickly reproduced from the reel of film, or shown on a screen. Retrieval speeds and methods are being constantly improved. It has been estimated that sufficient economies can be achieved in one year to repay the cost of an installation. Some firms buy only the reproduction equipment, and have the photographing and processing done by a service company.

Whatever system of filming is adopted, the records must be protected. Methods include fire-resisting safes and vaults, dispersal of essential records and duplication of vital documents.

(b) Mailing

An important supplement to correspondence, transcription and records management is the efficient handling of mail, which comprises incoming, outgoing and inter-departmental mail. No matter what size of firm the job must be done efficiently and economically, making the best use of staff and space.

The *situation* of the post room is important. It should be as near as possible to the ground floor. The next item to consider is the number of temporary or permanent staff and the extent to which mechanization can be usefully employed. There are inevitably 'peaks and troughs' of work flow and this can be helped by mechanization. Procedures must be established for incoming and outgoing mail and full use should be made of available machines of which the following is a brief summary.

Before posting, letters must be folded, inserted in an envelope, sealed, and the postage charge accounted for in one way or another.

(i) Folding, inserting and sealing machines. These machines can produce a neat consistent fold or a number of folds. Some machines can fold the main enclosure, then insert a second enclosure inside the fold. The price of this model is of course rather high. Other machines slit, score or perforate if necessary. Inserting machines usually have attachments that seal also.

(ii) Franking machines make the laborious task of sticking stamps redundant. They operate quickly, obviate the need for storing and guarding stamps, tearing, moistening and sticking them. The machine is purchased from manufacturers who are licensed by the G.P.O. A lever on the machine can be set for the desired postage; before it can be used, payment for the required amount of stamps to be used must be made to the G.P.O. When this number is reached, the machine locks. Dials record postage used and sometimes unused postage.

The firm's trademark, or slogan or advertising message can also be imprinted beside the stamp impression. Franked mail now accounts for nearly one-third of the G.P.O.'s postal revenue. Machines range from a hand-operated table model under £100 to £500 for another table model which feeds, seals, franks, counts and stacks letters at a rate well over 5000 an hour. Machines exist which do everything, i.e. collate, insert, seal, print advertisements, etc., meter the postage, count and stack at a rate of over 7000 per hour, but the number of firms able and willing to pay nearly £6000 for this model is low.

(iii) Letter openers and scales are useful. Some openers are automatic, opening several hundred letters in a few minutes, they can also feed and stack. Scales for weighing letters are needed to assess correctly the postage for packets and parcels.

4. Reproduction

Reproduction services in offices are increasingly important as conventional clerical help is costly, information is needed more quickly and technical improvements in duplicating and copying machines have made it cheap to obtain almost perfect reproductions.

In selecting the proper equipment from a very wide range, the suitability of the type of copy must be considered, plus cost, speed, ease of operation, servicing facilities and durability. Proper supervision is essential and this may mean centralization. A study of costs within the department should be made as compared with the costs of using outside agencies.

In some firms a reproduction department is set up, use being made of outside printers or, in some cases, a firm will have its own printing department.

Reproduction services can be classed as duplicating, copying and imprinting.

Duplicating

This is used where there is a need to produce many copies of reports, letters, etc. Points to note are:

(i) Duplication is basically a substitute for printing, it may be cheaper to duplicate than to have items printed.

(ii) There is no delay as compared with an outside printer, and as the material is reproduced in the office it remains confidential.

There are three main duplicating processes.

(*a*) *Stencil duplicating*

A master copy is prepared on a typewriter (or by hand stylus). The coating on the stencil is pushed aside and, when placed on an inked cylinder of the duplicating machine, ink is forced through the openings on the stencil producing the image on absorbent paper which is fed into the machine. As many as 500 to 15,000 copies may be obtained from a good stencil. Duplicating machines can reproduce from 50 to 200 copies a minute. They are cheap and mistakes can be easily altered. *Electronic* stencils are automatically copied originals which have been photographically cut by an electric eye which scans the original and cuts a stencil at the same time.

(*b*) *Spirit duplicating*

A master copy is prepared on special paper by typing or writing, the special paper is backed by a carbon transfer sheet. A reverse image is formed on the back of the master. The master is placed on the cylinder of a machine. As the cylinder turns, the reproduction paper is fed between moistened rollers, which lay a thin coating of spirit on the paper; the paper is pressed against the master and the moisture dissolves a small portion of the carbon, transferring the image to the copy. About 100 to 250 copies may be obtained from each master copy. By using different coloured carbons, up to seven colours can be obtained on the master. It is a cheap method, easily prepared, and is the only method whereby many colours can be duplicated *simultaneously*. The master copy cannot easily be altered and the quality of reproduction is not as good as that from a stencil.

(*c*) *Offset duplicating*

The basic principle rests upon the antipathy of ink and water. The master can be prepared by typewriter, written or photographed on a metal plate. The master is placed on the duplicator and comes in contact with ink and water. The image on the master repels the water solution but attracts the ink; the inked image is transferred to, or 'offset' on, a rubber-covered roller, giving a negative image. When paper is fed through this roller and a pressure roller, the positive image is transferred. Colours can be used, but for each colour the ink must be changed.

Quality of reproduction is good, any paper can be used, it is cheap, and over 50,000 copies may be made from a metal master. It does, though, need a trained operator, and is more expensive initially, and needs space for storing chemicals, etc.

Typewriters are often used to prepare additional copies of an original. By using carbon paper about eight copies can be made on a manual or twenty copies on an electric typewriter. An *automatic* typewriter can be operated by input media of the following types—punched tape, punched cards, paper rolls. These media activate the electric typewriter, the perforated paper taking the place of the typist operating the keys. It is a fast, error-free method. Some automatic typewriters have over a hundred buttons, each button reproducing a standard paragraph. It is useful for reproducing recurring data, e.g. direct mail selling, communications to shareholders.

5. Copying

Typing is still the method used for copying in many offices, but will be used less and less, as methods of document duplication become faster and cheaper.

(a) Diffusion transfer

This is a popular type of copying and is very cheap. Briefly, the original is placed between negative and positive paper and exposed to light. The original is then moved and the negative and positive are fixed and developed, then peeled apart, when the image will have been transferred from the negative to the positive paper.

This method gives good quality of reproduction and it can copy all colours. It requires wet chemicals and a competent operator.

(b) Dyeline (Diazo)

Originals need to be translucent, and are placed in contact with special dyeline paper and exposed to ultra-violet light, the printed areas on the original block the light rays, while the unprinted areas allow rays to pass through and de-activate the coated copy sheet. The blocked areas of the coated sheet remain activated and when joined with another chemical form a dye.

This method has the lowest cost per copy. Great use is made of this method in systems application, e.g. accounting, invoicing and purchasing. A new development in this field is a heat-processing copier, which needs no chemicals, at present costs of material are high, but no developing is needed and about 1000 an hour can be produced.

(c) Thermal (Thermography)

This is a dry-copying process. The equipment contains an infra-red lamp which emits heat to form the image. The original document and a heat-sensitive copy sheet are placed together in the machine. Heat rays pass through the copy sheet, striking the original printed material, which absorbs the rays and retains the heat in the image area causing the corresponding area on the copy sheet to turn dark, thus forming the copy image. A few seconds is all the time needed to process; spirit duplicating masters can also be made and the system is easy to operate. It does not give good quality image and the equipment is relatively insensitive to some inks and colours; the ink on the original needs to have a carbon content.

(*d*) *Electrostatic*

This copying process is based upon the law that opposite charges attract. Light strikes the original document and the charge remains where the light strikes the printed area, while light striking the unprinted areas is dissipated. A black powder carrying an opposite charge is spread over the electrical photograph covering the plate. The powder adheres to the charged areas, producing a reverse, visible image. A sheet of paper is placed above this plate and both pass between charging wires; the paper receives a charge opposite to that of the plate, the powder image then leaves the plate and clings to the paper where it is permanently fixed by heat. No wet chemicals are used and the process gives good quality reproduction. It is feasible only for a large amount of work and requires a fair amount of maintenance. As cost is high, the equipment is often rented. The maximum number of copies that can be produced economically is between six and twenty; offset litho is justified if more copies are needed. The electrostatic copies may be used as masters on the offset litho unit.

(*e*) *Imprinting processes*

Devices which print or stamp the same information on a number of forms and papers are numbering, addressing and signature machines.

Numbering machines vary, some record date, time or numbers.

Cheque writing machines ensure control and prevent fraud.

Addressing machines are most useful in preparing duplicate standard information at regular intervals. The master may be:

(i) A *metal* plate embossed with details, e.g. name and address.
(ii) A *wax* stencil prepared on a typewriter.
(iii) A hectographic *paper* stencil, for spirit duplicating.

Machines may be hand operated or electrically driven, and in general may have some or all of these features:

(i) Automatic feed and ejection of plates.

(ii) A masking device, allowing only part of the information on the plate to be printed, e.g. names of company employees.

(iii) Automatic selection of those plates required; this is done by having signals on plates which actuate the selection device.

(iv) Repeat and omitting devices. Numbering and dating devices may be incorporated.

The printed information is always accurate, after the initial checking, and when used for printing dividend warrants, notices, etc., can be a great help to companies.

Choice of duplicating machine or method

This involves consideration of: frequency of use, capital outlay and running costs, simplicity in use, whether several colours are required, or photograph reproduction required, ease of preparing and correcting master copy, durability and consistency of image, number of copies required from each master and quality of reproduction.

6. Calculating machines

The current range of machines is:

(*a*) Rotary and electric, including comptometers.
(*b*) Printing calculators, producing a tally-roll record.
(*c*) Electronic models, which are very fast, but mainly non-printing.

A small office may use a hand-operated calculator. Comptometer training takes about three months and the work done can cover any type of calculation; models range from hand-operated to automatic. New developments in printing calculators have speeded up the printing and provide a carbon copy if required. Electronic calculators are fast and silent in operation. New models allow calculation direct into currency and then immediate decimal conversion. One model has remote keyboards that can be shared by as many as five operators. Other models have basic formulae 'programmed' into the machine, the user merely entering the variables.

Accountancy is aided by machines which have electronic calculators linked with book-keeping or typewriter machine carriages. Descriptive information is typed as usual and quantity and price inserted, the totals are electronically calculated and printed by the machine. It is widely used for invoicing.

A development of the ledger card is the *magnetic ledger card* which contains normal information, but has a magnetized strip fixed to it which carries coded information which can be transmitted electronically by a special reading unit into a computer. The magnetic ledger card approach makes end-of-month records and summaries easier to compile; headings and balances brought forward on new cards are typed automatically.

7. Tabulating

Most office work is composed of a pattern of office systems, procedures and methods. A *system* is a complete picture of personnel, forms, records, machines and equipment involved in particular phases of work. Each system is composed of a number of *procedures*, which are planned sequences of operations for handling recurring transactions consistently, e.g. procedure for claims. Major business systems involve purchasing, sales, finance, cost accounting and employee relationships, and with these systems and procedures are a large number of clerical practices; these may operate independently or be centralized and have just been described —e.g. dictation and transcription, filing, duplicating and reproducing, telephone services and mailing. The end product of any system is information for management to use in decision-making. Data processing systems are essential parts of any management system. As business grows, data must be processed more speedily, and more sophisticated systems are needed than have been discussed. These newer systems are the tabulating and electronic data processing systems.

Tabulating system

In this system numeric and alphabetic data are converted into code language so machines can understand. The *punched card* system can supply accurate information more completely than any other mechanical system.
   Basic equipment comprises:

(a) Key punch

Information from a source document is punched into a card by hand or automatic punch.

(b) Verifier

This machine is used by another operator, who re-punches the punched card, and if the depressed keys agree with the original punching the card is released; if a disagreement occurs the machine locks.

(c) Sorter

This arranges the cards in the desired sequence by sorting one column at a time at great speed.

(d) Tabulator

The punched and sorted data are passed to the tabulator which has a programme control board as its guide. Cards are fed to the machine which actuate adding counters and printing mechanisms; information is printed on continuous stationery, columns being automatically totalled.

Auxiliary equipment comprises:

(a) Reproducing punch

This punches, automatically, data from one set of cards to another set. One form of duplication involves the use of special cards which can be marked with a pencil, making a carbon deposit which, when placed in a reproducing punch, senses the marks and punches holes. These are known as *mark-sense* cards. *Gang* punching is another form of reproduction where information from a master card is automatically copied on to detail cards. An example of the use of this idea is found in retail stores, where goods have perforated tags indicating department, manufacturer, cost, etc. When goods are sold, the tag is removed and fed through a special machine which converts the data into standard punched cards for subsequent processing.

(b) Collator

This is like a sorter—it performs four functions, it merges cards, matches the series of cards, checks the sequence and makes special selections if required.

(c) Calculating punch

Calculations are made from two or more punched cards and the result is punched in one of the cards or on a summary card.

(d) Interpreter

This prints the punched information on the face of the card.

Integrated Data Processing (I.D.P.)

This is a comprehensive system of recording business information at the point of origin in a machine language, and later reproducing it to be used for *all* purposes by machines and equipment. An example is the coupling of a tape punch to an accounting machine—these data can be used for all subsequent operations on computer equipment.

Electronic Data Processing (E.D.P.)

An E.D.P. system involves the use of an electronic computer and related equipment for analysing and recording many facts. Data are obtained from numerous sources and are processed quickly by being converted into a code consisting of electrical impulses. The code is based upon binary language, that is, a number system using two as its base instead of ten, as in the decimal system.

Input media are read into the control processing unit, treated mathematically, classified, sorted and stored. Data may be read into the processing unit by magnetic tape, paper tape, punched cards or cathode scanners. Output may take the form of magnetic or paper tape, punched cards or automatic printing on business forms and reports.

The electronic computer is an integrated system of electronics which computes mathematical operations and retrieves information at speeds of around one millionth of a second or less.

Digital computers count numbers (e.g. trip mileage on a car).

Analogue computers are used mainly in scientific research and measure physical variables, e.g. voltage or speed (e.g. the speedometer of a car). Business processing involves the digital computer. To be called a computer, equipment should:

(i) Be automatic in action and have the power to obey stored instructions.

(ii) Be able to discriminate between different courses of action and operate at electronic speed.

Figure 35 shows the five components of a computer. These components are:

(a) Input

This consists of data to be processed and the instructions to process the data. *Programmers* plan the logical arrangement, sequence, and correlation of data from various sources. The sequence of instruction to the computer is called the program.

The following media may be used in preparing the input from the source of data: punched cards, punched tape, magnetic discs and drums, optical scanners, magnetic ink character readers, a console typewriter.

Some input media can be read directly into the control and the processing units, others may need to convert the data on punched cards or tape to magnetic tape; or, to adapt input media to the type of equipment used. If magnetic discs are used, *random access* is possible, i.e. the retrieval of data quickly from any portion of the disc. Punched cards and tapes are cheaper and adaptable, but are bulky, susceptible to damage and unable to hold large amounts of data, they are also slow in use.

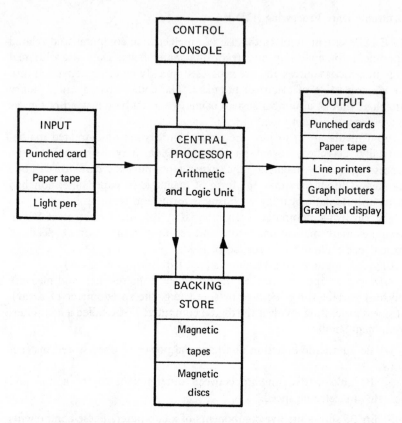

Fig. 35.   Data processing system. Computer installation.

(*b*) *Storage*

This unit is often called the memory and retains input in coded form until called forward for processing or to be 'read out.' Data are stored *internally* by magnetic cores, or *externally* in the form of punched cards, paper tape, magnetic drums or tape, discs, or cards, until ready to be read into the computer.

(*c*) *Arithmetic unit* (*or processing unit*)

Data are mathematically manipulated according to the program.

(*d*) *Output unit*

This unit deals with results of the computing operations. The manner and position of printing are determined by the instructions. The results may be on a formal report or document or statement, or in a form for subsequent processing, e.g. on magnetic tape or punched cards.

It may be useful to have results presented in the form of a graph or diagram. If the computer is connected to a *graphical display* unit, this unit then traces the image with a spot of light on the face of a cathode ray tube. It can also be used as a combined input system in conjunction with a device known as a *light pen*. An engineering drawing can be displayed on the television screen and by using the light pen the designer can make amendments or additions on the screen. The computer will then execute alterations. Another feature is a *graphical output* which can be obtained when pen and paper move to trace out a diagram or graph.

On-line output means that the printing devices are operated *directly* from the computer and results are immediately available.

Off-line output refers to the results punched into cards or paper or magnetic tape. These are then placed in printing machines which are *separate* from the computer.

As printing is usually done mechanically, speeds are far slower than the electronic speeds of the computer, so storage devices are needed to accumulate data until the output unit can deal with them.

(e) *Control unit*

This interprets instructions recorded on input media, directs the various processing operations and checks to see instructions are correctly carried out. This unit directs the receipt of information in the storage unit, stores the intermediate results, and releases the information when needed in the arithmetic operations.

Procedure to determine whether to install a machine

This may vary a little in detail depending upon the type of machine, but the main points are relevant to all machines.

(*a*) An *initial survey* can be carried out by the staff of the organization or by a machine company. Usually a special *Steering Committee* is formed and they are asked to make recommendations on the feasibility of using new equipment.

(*b*) Once a broad decision has been taken to proceed, a special *study group* can be formed, using existing personnel who may be relieved of normal duties, to make a full, detailed investigation of all sections of the firm and all types of available equipment.

(*c*) A *complete examination of existing systems* and methods is required and progress periodically reported to the steering committee. This report will include detailed costs of equipment, accommodation, staff required, operating and running, ease of operation and flexibility of equipment, and potential savings, e.g. where a computer replaces keyboard machines. Other items include experience of manufacturer and servicing arrangements.

The *final report* and recommendations will be made to the steering committee for consideration, which will have to bear in mind the future overall policy and objectives of the organization before recommending a course of action to the board. Such a report may include—advantages to be gained, the best type of equipment to be installed, whether to buy or rent, estimate of total cost, depreciation and rental charges, site of installation and staffing, and the position in the organization of the new section.

This section may be placed under the control of an existing department, e.g. accountancy, or it may act as an independent service bureau to the rest of the organization, under its own manager. The installation of a computer can have a major effect on the company using it. An integrated management information system is needed and organization structure must be re-appraised.

Visible record computers

These are small computers with a distinctive feature of a ledger card with a strip of magnetic tape attached to one side of the card. Both machine and operator can read the data which are automatically read and processed by the machine. In the past many errors occurred in mis-reading previous balances.

Data can be transmitted more quickly now by using a *computer terminal* at remote points, linked to a central computer; this is an *on-line* system, i.e. direct input to computer from the terminal user. Data may also be transmitted from a terminal to a processing point, for example, transmitted to a paper tape punch, which will punch a tape at the receiving end, which can then be processed by computer; this is an *off-line* system.

Newer methods of transmitting data by Post Office systems enable greater speed and accuracy of input. In addition, communication and control is improved, as data from and to remote points can be transmitted via a central processor. *Visual display* units at terminals can show data visually on a television screen, e.g. balance on a customer's account. New forms of terminals are really small computers which carry out simple processing as well, so the central machine is not called upon, e.g. invoices may be prepared at a district office by the mini-computer and then sent direct to the central processor for up-dating accounts.

Management and computers

Computers have been used in many ways for large amounts of repetitive processing and often the amount of assistance given to management has been small. Properly utilized, the computer can provide information rapidly and process quantitative data easily, so decision-making is aided. More use is being made now of the computer for making quantitative *models*.

In fast-response (real-time) systems, as soon as the input is entered the result is obtained immediately. An input to take away or add to a person's personal account would be made and the balance calculated instantaneously. If the program was arranged to indicate if the limit of credit had been reached, a note of this would also appear, thus enabling action to be taken quickly.

There is no doubt such systems are costly, especially where they have large memories and use complex soft-ware terminals and direct access storage devices are needed. It is almost essential for a duplicate computer to be available as breakdowns or delays would upset the system which is designed for immediate response and has a heavy program load.

E. MANAGEMENT SERVICES

A British Institute of Management study group in 1963 described management services as a 'generic term used to describe a number of specialist activities and services provided centrally especially in large companies or groups of companies. It is generally agreed that these centralized Management Services should be essentially of an advisory nature in effect, an internally consultancy service to general, divisional and departmental managers as well as to the board of directors.'

This definition can be amended with the experience obtained in the years since 1963. It should particularly emphasize its rôle in change. A variety of skills is needed which may need to alter as problems change. It is really a methodology for approaching management problems through analysis based upon modern management techniques.

The current changes in the external environment have been particularly great and this has been reflected in the internal results of companies. The rôle of management services is very important in seeking out new ideas and introducing relevant new techniques to implement changes smoothly within the company.

In his book *Future Shock* (1970, Random House), Alvin Toffler points out the great rates of change in the gross national product of countries. Countries that had high per capita growth rates, e.g. United Kingdom and United States of America, would find a marked fall in the future.

The directors should as we have seen try to foresee possible change and plan accordingly.

It is important that the board of directors use management services effectively. Whether this involves corporate financial models, design of management information systems, *information* is needed, not just *data* from the computer. Information must be related to a manager who is committed, e.g. to be responsible for a profit target. Computers issue vast amounts of *data*, but it is management's responsibility to check their relevance and arrange for the production of *useful information*.

The place of management services in a company

There will not be complete agreement with the following list of skills required in a management services team, but it is a guide:

(*a*) Management accounting—standards, investment appraisal, information systems, costing, pricing systems.

(*b*) Productivity services—value analysis, work study, job evaluation, engineering.

(*c*) Computer systems—analysis and design of commercial systems.

(*d*) Management science—operational research, financial modelling.

Other related skills may be considered as part of management services, and advice in these areas is obviously important, e.g. manpower planning, industrial relations, and market research.

The management services section may report to a related function, e.g. finance, or related operation, e.g. communications.

The section is usually centralized at first, responsible to a director, and it is advisable for it to be represented on the board of directors. The leader should have comparable status with senior executives, e.g. other functional heads.

The business of management is becoming more complex as there is an increasing rate of change in technological and social areas. Management services has emerged as an aid to management and has in the past been identified with the operation of computer systems, usually on a basis of centralization. Now that computers are more dispersed by terminal systems and management services staff have been decentralized, central management services groups can act more effectively and more objectively.

There is one problem where companies are formed into divisions, where line managers have a profit responsibility and where high costs of a centralized management service are charged to them. If overheads are to be kept low, then there is a direct incentive *not* to call in management services to assist. Thus short-term actions may be to the detriment of the future as valuable assistance is not available, and the trading divisions are encouraged to use their own less highly qualified staff.

Suggested responsibilities of a typical management services department

(1) To assist operating divisions through the development and application of management services skills.

(2) To give information and advice on relevance of management techniques and be involved with project work in divisions.

(3) To give proper training, to develop and to deploy effectively management services staff.

(4) To advise the board of directors on matters affecting company success.

(5) To introduce and develop group standards (e.g. in accounting, productivity services and computers).

(6) To develop contacts with educational organizations.

It is generally best for the computer department to be treated as a service to the organization as a whole and ideally it should form part of a management services department, which may comprise operational research, organization and methods and work study. The manager of this department should report direct to a director of the company.

Figure 36 shows a typical organization chart for a large establishment: in smaller concerns some functions will be combined.

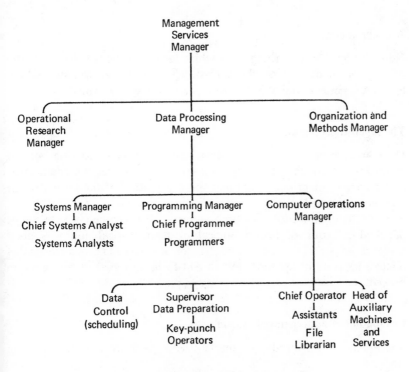

Fig. 36.   Management services section.

The Data Processing (D.P.) Manager

He is head of the computer department and requires a good technical knowledge as well as practical experience of data processing. He must have imagination and creative ability, clear and logical thought, ability to communicate with clarity and be diplomatic. He plans, co-ordinates and controls all activities relating to data processing and automation of office work, these activities comprise systems analysis, programming of computers and the operational control of the D.P. centre.

A Systems Analyst

He is responsible for detailed design of systems. He should possess a good balance of commercial and data processing knowledge and be fully aware of the company's organization and procedures. He must be able to understand complex and possibly ill-defined problems, and be able to devise and select the most practical solutions. Ability to mix, communicate and be tactful is essential.

A Programmer

He is responsible for writing, in machine language, the detailed programs of the system devised by the analyst. He must be logical, meticulous, tenacious, patient, and able to work as a member of a team.

The Operations Manager

He plans, co-ordinates and controls the operational activities of the computer, the auxiliary machines and services for the receipt, codification and punching of primary data and the distribution of the results to the sections concerned.

As far as qualifications for programmers are concerned a certain type of mind is required. Proven logical or mathematical ability is good evidence, so is skill at crosswords, chess or bridge. Tests give a reasonably reliable measure of aptitude, but should form only *part* of the selection procedure.

Installation of a mechanized system

The procedure for installing a mechanized system involves the following steps:

(*a*) *Plan the system*, defining machine specifications, forms design, write programs, etc.

(*b*) *Train staff*—special courses may be needed; this may in some cases precede the planning stage.

(*c*) *Physical take over* of machines, testing and parallel running to establish the reliability that may be needed.

(*d*) *Final transfer* to new system and *periodic review* of progress.

Organization of machine room

In this brief, final section, the organization of the machine room is considered. This includes physical conditions, flow of work, supervision and control and breakdown arrangements. The following points must be considered:

(*a*) There must be sufficient space to allow for expansion and access to the machines.

(*b*) Heating, ventilation and humidity are important, and air conditioning may be needed to ensure that a suitable atmosphere is maintained.

(*c*) Lighting must be adequate and sound-proofing essential.

(*d*) Power, of sufficient capacity, must be available and many power points are needed. There may need to be special alternative arrangements in the event of a power failure.

(*e*) Machines may be laid out on a 'product' or 'process' basis. (See chapter 7.)

(*f*) The flow of work must be regular to obviate peak periods. Shift-working may be necessary, especially where a computer is installed.

(*g*) Efficient records are needed for effective control, e.g. time sheets, progress charts, machine breakdown records.

(*h*) Breakdown arrangements may include plans to rearrange work flow and obtain use of equipment of another company, or make use of agency services.

Use of computer service bureau

When a company grows in size and the data processing side needs to be modernized, management can:

(*a*) employ more staff and use existing manual system;
(*b*) buy a visible record computer;
(*c*) buy a small computer;
(*d*) use a computer bureau.

One of the most common reasons for not using a bureau is lack of knowledge of their services.

A firm with a low work volume, which is not large enough to justify purchasing its own machine could use a bureau. Even if a company had its own computer, it may have periodic problems with large quantities of data at peak periods; again, a bureau could be useful at these times.

A bureau can offer:

(*a*) skill from specialization of staff in data processing;
(*b*) technical economies of scale;
(*c*) accountability; the true costs of data processing are known.

The first stage is to decide exactly what requires to be done at the bureau, whose services vary with size. These services may include the use of the bureau's own computer, systems analysis, writing programs, training company's staff, collecting, processing and distributing data.

Certain bureaux offer contract terms allowing computer time exclusively to a company each week.

When the company decides on the services it requires, the bureau conducts a survey to assess the situation and to enable a quotation to be given. Other bureaux offer package programs to companies with similar problems. Companies must adapt their own system to the prepared program, which is cheaper to use. Examples of these are programs for sales analysis, payroll and market research.

Good liaison is essential between bureau and client and this can be achieved by appointing a senior member of the company's staff to do the job.

REVIEW QUESTIONS

Office management

(1) Draw up a schedule of responsibility for an office manager.
(2) Discuss the centralization of distinct office services, such as (*a*) typing, (*b*) filing, (*c*) duplicating.
(3) What advantages are claimed for open offices?
(4) What do you understand by the organization and methods function? To whom should O. and M. be responsible?
(5) Mention the various means for controlling the quality and accuracy of office work.
(6) To what extent can work study be applied to the office, and with what objects?
(7) What points must be attended to in selecting the media for office communications?
(8) What forms of external communication are available?
(9) What are the types of machines used for internal communication in an office?
(10) What are the essentials of a good filing system?
(11) Describe the various types of filing equipment available.

(12) What machines may be used in the mailing section of an office to ensure speedy and efficient working?

(13) Describe the three main duplicating processes.

(14) List the salient features of each of the following methods of copying: diffusion transfer, dyeline, thermal, electrostatic.

(15) Explain the main features of an addressing machine and suggest a few of its applications.

(16) Comment upon any new development in ledger posting machines.

(17) What features must characterize office work if the use of tabulating machinery is to be justified?

(18) Describe the basic equipment of a punched-card system.

(19) Distinguish between integrated data processing and electronic data processing.

(20) Of what basic units is a digital computer composed? How can information be fed into a computer and in what forms may the results be provided?

(21) What do you understand by the term 'management services'?

(22) Draw an organization chart for a department concerned with management services.

(23) Consider the procedure necessary for the installation of a mechanized system.

(24) What points should be considered in the organization of a machine room?

(25) Outline the work of a computer service bureau.

REVIEW PROBLEMS

Office management

(1) Discuss the stages in an O. and M. assignment. Explain how the investigation is carried out and the methods used for analysis and presentation of information.

(2) The commercial director of your organization is attempting to make the paper work within the organization more efficient and effective. You are asked to advise on the re-designing of the forms used within the organization. Outline the points, in a report, to which you would give particular attention in form designing.

(3) 'As an office increases in size, it becomes more and more necessary to organize it according to some logical plan.' Comment on this statement and describe the steps you would take in re-planning an office organization.

(4) In an organization where the volume of work has increased considerably, it is intended to introduce dictating machines and establish a central typing bureau. Senior executives only will retain personal secretaries.

(a) Describe the organization required to make the system efficient, paying particular attention to matters such as:

(i) giving priority to urgent matters,
(ii) making additions or alterations to recordings.

(b) List briefly the advantages that should accrue and the problems which might arise.

(5) Outline the investigations which a company should require to be undertaken before a decision is made whether to purchase a computer for commercial work within the company.

(6) The average earnings of a skilled craftsman are today likely to be significantly higher than those of a clerk in the same organization.

What problems may this situation impose on the office manager?

What effect may it have on staff attitudes to union membership?

What action should management take?

(7) Your company has 500 employees, some of whom are paid by way of a bonus scheme. The present manual system used for payroll preparation runs late because of undue clerical work and the payroll analysis is inadequate.

What are the suitable alternatives to improve the situation and what factors would be taken into account in making your selection?

(8) As newly appointed office manager, you soon come to realize that (i) many of your older men clerks are working excessive overtime, and (ii) there is a high rate of turnover of more junior staff. Of what problems are these likely to be symptomatic? How may the situation be improved?

(9) The Fulton Committee recommended that management service units should have much wider functions than O. and M. in the Civil Service. Does this apply in other forms of organization?

BIBLIOGRAPHY

Office management

Burton, A. H. A. and Mills, R. G., *Electronic Computers and their Business Applications* (London, Benn, 1960).

Cemach, H. P., *Work Study in the Office* (Glasgow, MacLaren, 1965).

Denyer, J. C., *Office Management* (London, Macdonald & Evans, 1964).

Dyer, F. C., *Executive Guide to Effective Speaking and Writing* (London, Prentice-Hall, 1962).

Gregory, R. H. and Van Horn, R. L., *Business Data Processing and Programming* (London, Chatto & Windus, 1965).

H.M.S.O., *Computers in Offices*, Ministry of Labour, 1965.

H.M.S.O., *The Practice of Organization and Method*, 2nd edition, 1965.

Laver, F. J. M., 'Introducing Computers,' H.M.S.O., 1965.

McRae, T. W., *The Impact of Computers on Accounting* (London, Wiley, 1964).

Mills, G. and Standingford, O., *Office Organization and Method* (London, Pitman, 1968).

Milward, G. E. (ed.), *Applications of Organization and Method* (London, Macdonald & Evans, 1964).

Wallis, P. N., *Quality Control in the Office* (London, Current Affairs Ltd, 1961).

10 Developments

This short chapter attempts to set out some trends in the process of management which will have a marked effect upon business administration and management in the future.

A. GROWTH AND SCALE

There is a tendency for firms to grow in size, particularly by merger or take-over.

Growth may be generally desired because of these advantages:

(a) General economies of scale.
(b) Managerial ability can be used to the full.
(c) Staff may be easier to recruit as large firms can pay more.
(d) Risks may be spread over more products.

The main disadvantages include:

(a) A loss of co-ordination and control.
(b) Slower communication and divided authority.
(c) Remoteness of leadership and personal contact.
(d) Inflexibility and excess paperwork.
(e) As technology advances, more specialists are brought into the firm, e.g. computer and operations research personnel. Such specialists must be integrated in the organization and this may mean some staff may have their duties taken from them, or their 'status' may be affected.
(f) The addition of new products to the existing range may result in increased turnover, but there may later be a problem where the diversity of products may mean producing them in uneconomic batch quantities. Also increases in sales volume may impose unexpected costs of market development. Growth, therefore, may not always be desirable.

B. MULTI-NATIONAL COMPANIES

This is a comparatively recent development whereby a company has its headquarters in one country and exercises some or all of the functions of a company in other countries.

Foreign interests are not large for most British companies but 10 out of the top 40 companies (in size) *produce abroad* over 25 per cent as much

348

as they produce at home. The impetus for this development probably came from improved communication and transportation systems, the growth of larger regional markets through Common Market and freer trade agreements.

Some companies are bi-national, where their ownership and control are shared with another country, for example, British and Dutch companies share Shell and Unilever. It is worth noting that the European Economic Community's proposals for laws for a European Company will greatly encourage this type of development in the future.

Many foreign companies own subsidiaries in the home country. In Great Britain over 3000 companies are now owned and controlled from abroad. Over 10 per cent of the total United Kingdom output is in the hands of American companies. British subsidiaries of American companies employed over 700,000 British workers in 1976.

There are points for and against these companies from a national point of view. These usually agree that foreign investment can be helpful, especially in the creation of jobs. In many cases lack of capital would have meant the company would have to close down. The Trades Union Council (see p. 96) in their Economic Review of 1975 reinforced their uncertainty regarding the increase in multi-national corporations. They stressed that government and unions were liable to be threatened because:

(1) Manufacturing *operations could be transferred* out of the home country to foreign countries.

(2) Capital invested in the home country may lead to practices of blackmail. In order to avoid strikes it may be stated that capital and labour may be transferred elsewhere.

(3) Profits could be transferred out of this country, thus affecting the balance of payments.

(4) Lack of control by British planning authorities over key sectors of the economy.

(5) *Transfer pricing.* These are prices which are charged by one subsidiary to another subsidiary of the same company in a different country. The prices are decided by the head office of the multi-national company in accordance with *its* need. By raising or lowering prices charged, profits can be transferred out of countries with high taxes and moved to those with low taxes.

(6) The main company may not be so concerned to increase the export potential of subsidiary firms in a country and can switch markets and sources of supply to enable profits to be made more easily and products to be made more cheaply.

Decisions of the multi-national company are made with a view to maximizing profits of the company as a whole and not of its individual subsidiaries. There are, therefore, a number of important problems which may never be satisfactorily agreed. The recent trend towards giving more information to employees and unions may produce a situation where the figures for home subsidiaries may not be sufficient. Questions which will be asked are:

(1) To what extent should, or can, the company be asked for a global breakdown?

(2) Will trade union co-operation extend across frontiers, especially as union structures vary greatly between countries?

From the point of view of the home country where the parent company is registered, there are points for and against such an operation:

Advantages

(a) There is access to wider markets and the ability to deal in larger investments through organized capital market.

(b) Law of comparative advantage could be applied in allowing movement to low-cost areas of production.

(c) Ability to affect decisions or ideas of government because of their size and effect on the economy of countries.

Disadvantages

(a) Foreign policies of countries vary and *disputes* between countries who each have within them subsidiaries of the parent company can cause problems (e.g. possible nationalization).

(b) *Laws* of countries vary, especially taxation laws.

(c) Uncertainty of *loyalty* of citizens abroad to the parent company.

(d) Difficulty of *co-ordinating* policies over numerous countries.

(e) *Local management* may not be too proficient.

C. HUMAN ASSET ACCOUNTING

It has already been stated that accounting information is prepared and presented to interested persons with a view to influence their behaviour and decisions. A good system of providing information for management to control future activities of an organization should record *every* financial or economic fact in a manner which is understood by everyone; this information is usually presented in monetary terms.

Management must control and utilize resources effectively; this includes physical resources, e.g. patent rights and human resources.

One simple definition of management is 'getting things done through people,' and yet it is strange that the value of *human* resources does not appear in reports and statements of organizations. Some personnel are very valuable and they may leave or join a company. Normal accounting information does not give any indication of the value of personnel in the firm. Points which should be known are: has a change occurred in human assets during the year? Is the value of the company significantly affected? Decision-making may be said to be inaccurate if information on the effects on human assets of alternative courses of action are not made available to managers.

Accounting procedures usually treat expenditure on building up human assets as expenditure of a revenue nature. Expenditure on recruiting, induction, training and developing personnel is charged against the income of the period in which the expenditure was incurred. Other assets deemed 'capital' are shown in the accounts, some at a reduced value (because of depreciation), some perhaps at an increased value. The main point being that they are shown as being part of the company's present asset value. If human assets were treated in the same way, the statement of income of an organization, and also the *attitude* of management to such expenditure, would be greatly affected. That is, if the expenditure were not regarded as costs to be borne out of current income, but contributing to the building of assets which would bring benefits for future years. A number of writers have pointed out this need to evaluate human assets, but only recently has serious thought been given to this problem.

The need for such a measurement of human assets and the difficulties were mentioned by W. A. Paton in his book *Accounting Theory*, published in 1922. He referred to a well-organized and loyal personnel being of greater importance as an asset than a stock of merchandise: this of course leading to one of the limitations of the conventional balance sheet.

There are, of course, many difficulties in isolating and measuring the cost of human assets, for example:

(*a*) What period should be used to calculate the benefit to be received?

(*b*) Accounting conventions were influenced by social and economic influences which were quite different from those existing at the present time.

(*c*) Management do not think of people as assets, or owning people as other assets are considered to be owned, in a legal sense.

(*d*) People may feel degraded in being given a money value.

It is only when other assets are combined with human assets that the full potential of an organization can be realized, so it ideally should be possible and preferable to find a system which includes all assets. Any such information system would show the investments made in human assets and the financial effects of any changes.

Professor Rensis Likert of Michigan University has recommended that human assets should be accounted for in an accounting system. The system could isolate expenditure on recruitment and training of employees and the cost written off over the expected working lives of employees.

The R. G. Barry Corporation of Columbus, Ohio, U.S.A., on January 1, 1968, started the first human asset accounting system. The firm had over 2000 staff. It had low capital assets and the management recognized that success depended largely upon the organization's human assets, especially employee and customer loyalty. The corporation contacted Professor Likert and a team of Michigan University staff and they helped the corporation staff to develop a system. The system specified seven functional accounts: recruiting, acquisition, formal training and induction costs, also informal training, familiarization, investment building experience and development costs.

Investments in human resources are regarded as being of two types:

(*a*) Direct expenditures on, for example, recruiting and training people.

(*b*) Allocations of salary for periods of training and development when the firm is not fully benefiting from a person's efforts.

Managers receive quarterly reports showing how actual performance compared with the plan—'The Human Resource Capital Plan.' It is operated independently of the accounting system. A British working party was set up in 1973 by the Institute of Cost and Management Accountants and the Institute of Personnel Management. A system was advocated which differed from the American one. Briefly, this method produces human asset values by using multipliers. The staff is divided into four categories: senior and middle management, supervisors and clerical and operative grades. Multipliers are then applied to the salaries of each of these groups and an asset value obtained.

The behavioural impact of this method must be considered. Most accounting information reflects the results of the activity of successful and unsuccessful efforts of human beings, and influences their decisions in an attempt to control the future. Unless the system is carefully explained to staff and their participation encouraged adverse reactions could occur. All managers involved should examine carefully the behavioural problems and ensure that the systems of communication are working well in order that the system can be effected.

Benefits are numerous. Management will be stimulated to take appropriate action to reduce the cost, when they become aware of the true cost of labour turnover. Industrial relations may improve as conventional accounting tends to encourage management to underestimate the importance of employees. The fact that a company is making an effort to record and report investments in the human resources has developed an interest among managers in the economic importance of people. Managers are now provided with information regarding human assets which will help them to budget more effectively and ensure a more satisfactory allocation of human resources.

Finally, it is important to note that human asset accounting systems can be developed to become an important element in information systems. The main aim of the systems will not be to value the individual employee, but rather to evaluate the investment in the human assets of the organization. Can industry afford to ignore such valuable assets when making decisions affecting the future of the firm, its employees and society?

REVIEW QUESTIONS

Developments

(1) Are there any disadvantages associated with the increasing size of businesses?

(2) What is meant by the term 'multi-national company'?

(3) What is meant by 'human asset accounting'?

REVIEW PROBLEMS

Developments

(1) How can the disadvantages associated with the increasing size of businesses be overcome?

(2) List the factors which may limit the expansion of a business.

Discuss the various ways in which a limiting factor in any industry of your choice might be overcome.

(3) Discuss Drucker's suggestion that 'concentration is the key to economic results, but no other principle of effectiveness is violated as constantly.'

What does this mean to the general manager in:

(*a*) a manufacturing company? and

(*b*) a service concern?

BIBLIOGRAPHY

Developments

Acton Society Trust, *Size and Morale* (London, 1953 and 1957).

Drucker, P., *The Practice of Management* (London, Heinemann, 1961). Chapters 18–19.

Edwards, R. S. and Townsend, H., *Business Enterprise* (London, Macmillan, 1958). Chapters 7 and 8.

Gower Press, *Directors' Guide to Europe* (1974).

De Hanika, F. P., *New Thinking in Management* (London, Hutchinson, 1965).

Penrose, E. T., *Theory of the Growth of the Firm* (Oxford, Blackwell, 1960).

Taylor, Bernard and Wills, G. (eds.), *Long-Range Planning for Marketing and Diversification* (Crosby Lockwood, 1971).

Further Review Problems Relating To Chapters 1-10

(1) 'Every managerial act rests on assumptions, generalizations, and hypotheses—that is to say on theory' (Douglas McGregor). Examine this statement in relation to:

    (*a*) The exercise of authority.

    (*b*) Effective leadership of staff.

    (*c*) Team work in management groups.

(2) 'Every manager is concerned with the quality of discipline and morale that characterizes his subordinates, for these factors have an important bearing upon the productivity of his department.' Discuss this statement showing any evidence you have of the relationship between discipline and morale on the one hand and productivity on the other.

(3) In considering a large company in the consumer durable product field with highly developed modern marketing techniques, give your understanding of product planning, describing the various phases involved. Write a position description for a product planning and development manager in this company. What errors would you seek to avoid in test-marketing your new products?

(4) Illustrate with a diagram your concept of the planning-control feedback cycle in business from policy planning to performance and results. What do you understand by control? Give examples of the forms of control operating in various parts of a business.

(5) Many businesses are now engaging in long-range planning of their production and marketing effort. Why have they become conscious of the need for long-range planning? What benefits can be anticipated for such planning? In the planning process definite goals must be set in five fields. What are these fields?

(6) Show why *innovation*—the creation and application of new ideas—is fundamental to the progress of a business in all its activities. What are the blocks to effective innovation? In what ways would you set out to remove these blocks and to induce an atmosphere favourable to new ideas? Outline a method of training management in creative thinking in relation to the business.

(7) Packaging is an important factor in business, especially where the product is distributed through retailers to the public. What purposes are

served by packaging a product? What factors should be considered in designing the container? What organization procedure would you advocate to ensure that all aspects of the packaging problem are considered and co-ordinated?

(8) As secretary of an engineering company employing 9000 people, outline the mandate, or schedule of responsibilities for the manager, responsible to you, of a proposed electronic data processing department.

(9) Outline a comprehensive training scheme to produce skilled employees in a large factory. The scheme should also provide for further training for senior technical posts, supervision and management.

(10) What is a learning curve?

How can the benefits obtainable from the learning process be hastened?

Consider how management would use learning curves when fixing selling prices.

(11) The works manager wants to engage a young, technically competent, skilled craftsman whom he believes to be a potential supervisor but is concerned about two much older men who have been in the section for many years and are reasonably able but appear to have reached the limit of their development.

Describe the problems that could arise and the solutions thereto.

(12) Indicate the benefits likely to arise from the operation of a company suggestion scheme. What features would you build into a suggestion scheme to avoid problems and ensure the success of the scheme? How would you organize the evaluation of suggestions?

(13) What are the factors which cause clerical work to be more difficult to measure precisely than production work?

What are the short-term and long-term objectives which should be determined by management regarding the purpose of clerical work measurement before its introduction in an organization?

(14) The XYZ Co. has used the services of a computer bureau for the past two years, but as its requirements for computer usage are increasing, a feasibility study is to be carried out to determine whether or not a small 'in-house' computer should be purchased. Before the study is undertaken, you are required as chief accountant to prepare a report for the company chairman, comparing the advantages and disadvantages of using a bureau with those of owning a small computer. In your comparison you should refer to developments in the computer field expected within the next five years. A comparison of running costs will be considered by the feasibility study and should not be included in the report to the chairman.

Note: You are not required to report on how to conduct the feasibility study.

Index

Tabulator, 323
Taylor, F. W., 12, 89
Team spirit, 107
Telephone, 323
Teleprinter, 323
Television advertising, 168
Telex, 323
Termination of work, 285
Terminology, 5
Test marketing, 171
Test room studies, 14
Tests, recruitment, 250
Theoretical requirements forecasting, 240
Theory X and Y, 98
Thermal copying, 330
Thom, R., 45
Time-span of discretion, 55
Tofler, A., 82, 339
Top executive, 5
Top management, 5
Trade associations, 199
Trade Unions, 291–2, 301
Trades Union Congress, 96, 349
Trading stamps, 156
  Act, 1964, 157
Training—
  apprentice, 256
  management, 257–60
  needs, 253, 265
  operative, 256
  programme, 252
  simulation, 133
  supervisory, 257
Training Opportunities Scheme, 256
Training Services Agency, 256
Training within Industry, 256
Transfers of staff, 277
Transport, 162 *et seq.*
Trist, E., 82, 86, 295
Typewriters, 330
  automatic, 330

Typing section, 328
Unfair dismissal, 287–8, 302
Unit production, 194 (*see* job production)
Unity of command, 89
Unity of objective, 89

Value analysis, (*see* value engineering), 211
  method, 212
  place in organization, 212
Variable budgets, 121 (*see* flexible budgets) 121
Variable factor programming, 320
  method, 320
Venture groups, 275
Verifying punch, 334
Vertical filing, 326
Vertical organization charts, 77
Visible card filing, 326
Voluntary groups, 156

Wage administration, 277
Wages councils, 301
Warehouse—
  design, 159
  function, 159
Warehousing, 159
  automated, 228
Weber, M., 51
Weiner, N., 19
Wholesale trade organization, 156
Wholesaler—
  cash and carry, 156
Woodward, J., 84, 272
Worker participation, 94
Working groups 64
Work measurement, 214, 319
Work study, 212
  need for, 213
Works order, 216
Works Safety Committee, 290
Written communications, 322